Disembedded

Disembedded

Regulation, Crisis, and Democracy in the Age of Finance

BASAK KUS

OXFORD
UNIVERSITY PRESS

Oxford University Press is a department of the University of Oxford. It furthers
the University's objective of excellence in research, scholarship, and education
by publishing worldwide. Oxford is a registered trade mark of Oxford University
Press in the UK and certain other countries.

Published in the United States of America by Oxford University Press
198 Madison Avenue, New York, NY 10016, United States of America.

© Oxford University Press 2024

All rights reserved. No part of this publication may be reproduced, stored in
a retrieval system, or transmitted, in any form or by any means, without the
prior permission in writing of Oxford University Press, or as expressly permitted
by law, by license, or under terms agreed with the appropriate reproduction
rights organization. Inquiries concerning reproduction outside the scope of the
above should be sent to the Rights Department, Oxford University Press, at the
address above.

You must not circulate this work in any other form
and you must impose this same condition on any acquirer.

CIP data is on file at the Library of Congress
ISBN 978–0–19–776487–9 (pbk.)
ISBN 978–0–19–776486–2 (hbk.)

DOI: 10.1093/oso/9780197764862.001.0001

Paperback printed by Marquis Book Printing, Canada
Hardback printed by Bridgeport National Bindery, Inc., United States of America

To Lila, my little baklava.

Contents

Preface	ix
Acknowledgments	xiii
Note on Sources	xv

1. Polanyi on Wall Street — 1

Ten Years, Two Presidents	1
Reading Polanyi in the Aftermath of the Financial Crisis	3
The Crisis of the Early Twentieth Century and the Postwar Expansion of the Protective State	6
Late Twentieth-Century Economic Transformations and Political Shifts	8
The Financial Turn in the Economy	9
The Neoliberal Turn in Government	16
Disembedded Financialization: American Economy and the Deficit in Risk Protection	19
American Government and the Great Recession	22
Outline of the Book	24

2. A New Creed on Regulation — 26

The Rise of the Economic Theories of Regulation in the 1970s and 1980s	27
Regulatory Capture	28
Regulation as a Source of Rent-Seeking	31
Limitations of Bureaucracy as a Technique of Government	31
Regulatory Perspectives in the 1990s	32
Conclusion	37

3. The Political Ascent of the New Creed — 39

Substantive Regulation Comes Under Scrutiny: Ford and Carter Administrations	40
From a Pragmatic Critique to a Systematic Rejection: Reagan Administration	45
Reinventing the Government as a Private Entity: Clinton Administration	51
Conclusion	54

4. From Politics to Policy: Regulation and Finance — 56

Deregulation and Finance	58
Regulatory Drift and Finance	65

viii CONTENTS

Micro-Orientations in Risk Regulation 70
Information Provision as Risk Regulation 72
    Caveat Emptor: Risk Regulation by Disclosure 73
    Rating Agencies 75
    Financial Literacy 77
Conclusion 78

5. Disembeddedness in Financial Times 80
The Regulatory Underpinnings of Disembedded Finance 81
    The Limitations of a Micro-Oriented Approach 81
    The Limitations of an Information-Based Approach 83
The Fragmented Regulatory Structure of US Finance 85
Disembeddedness as Deficit in Risk Protection 86
    Deficit in Systemic Risk Protection 86
    Deficit in Consumer Financial Protection 89
    Deficit in Social Protection in the Time of Financialization 95
Conclusion 96

6. The Crisis 98
Relief and Recovery: Technocratic Realism, Cautious Keynesianism 98
    Relief 100
    Recovery 104
Regulatory Reform 106
    Dodd–Frank 112
Conclusion 117

7. In Search of Protection: From Disembeddedness to Populist
Persuasions 122
Takeaways 122
    A New Regulatory Creed 123
    The Political Reception of the New Creed 123
    The Translation of the New Creed into Policy 124
    American Financialization: The Regulatory Dimension 125
    Disembeddedness and "Risk Society" in Financial Times 125
    The Crisis and the Limitations of Reform 127
From Regulation of Finance to the Crisis of Democracy 131

Notes 135
Index 171

Preface

They called it the "roaring 1990s." It was a period of growth, low unemployment, and a budget surplus. I still recall President Clinton, in 1998, announcing an anticipated budget surplus of approximately $70 billion. At the time, I was an undergraduate in Istanbul, making an effort to read American newspapers in an attempt to improve my English. This particular news made a strong impression on me. Turkey's entire GDP was only $270 billion at that time. The country grappled with economic instability, mounting public debt, and recurrent currency crises. Despite studying at the nation's top university, my job prospects did not seem promising. Hearing about the American surplus, I couldn't help but think of what that kind of money could achieve.

I would later learn, of course, after moving to the US, that the 1990s had not roared for everyone, that President Clinton had signed several significant pieces of legislation that unraveled some of the central tenets of postwar liberalism, and that beneath the veneer of prosperity, both inequality and socioeconomic insecurity had intensified in many ways. Yet, this realization came slowly. For quite a while, I remained awestruck with America in a way only perhaps new immigrants are capable of.

Fast forward to 2007. I was thirty, living in the US, pursuing my PhD, and expecting a child. My partner and I had a small apartment in Queens, NY. In the third trimester of my pregnancy, thinking we would want to take our soon-to-be born to places outside of town, we decided to get a car. We looked on Craigslist for a used vehicle. We saw a promising listing for a second-hand Nissan in our neighborhood and went to check it out. The sellers, an immigrant family like my own, seemed to be living their American dream. They were also expecting a child, which was why they were selling their old car and getting a new one. They had just bought a new house, and when we went inside to handle the paperwork, they excitedly gave us a tour. While chatting with them, we learned that they both worked in the lower-paying end of the service economy. Yet, there we were, sitting in their lovely home—which was much larger and nicer than our apartment—buying their old car.

X PREFACE

Driving home on our way back, I went on and on about how this country seemed to have solved the problem of inequality, how income didn't matter, how people's access to credit was essentially a redistributive tool. Markets do the job here, I said to my partner; the state doesn't have to. In my native Turkey, the reality of underdeveloped credit markets meant families like my own had to save for years, sometimes decades, to purchase essential assets like homes or cars. But here in America, I was seeing a different picture. Credit was much more widely accessible, making it possible to own houses and cars, and to live a comfortable life, even for those with modest jobs and incomes. Wasn't the immigrant family we had just met a prime example of this? The notion of credit as a redistributive tool of sorts was new and fascinating to me! As our conversation continued, however, we couldn't help but acknowledge the other side of the coin. How leveraged was this family? Were their jobs secure? What were the terms of their mortgage? If they lost their jobs tomorrow, could they still make their payments? How much risk were they taking on to achieve their version of the American dream? These questions swiftly brought our conversation to the less glamourous realities of American capitalism. We talked about how many people in the US still didn't have access to government-sponsored health care, how they had to pay crazy sums to put their kids through college, and how so many people had to work well into old age. In contrast, our parents back in Turkey had it pretty good, didn't they? My parents, both public high school teachers, had retired by the time they were fifty years of age. My dad continued giving private lessons to boost his income, while my mom, having some health problems, did not work and could afford not to work. Did they lead a luxury life? No, they didn't. But not once did they have to worry about financing my education or about not being able to get the medical care they needed.

About a year after that car ride, the American economy found itself in troubled waters. Even the nation's political leaders appeared to be caught off guard by the downturn. On September 15, 2008, the day Lehman Brothers went bankrupt, Senator John McCain, the Republican nominee for the presidency, asserted that the American economy was "fundamentally sound." For students of American political economy, McCain's words echoed a similar assertion by President Herbert Hoover on the eve of Black Tuesday's market crash, on October 25, 1929. Hoover had confidently asserted that the fundamentals of American economy were "sound and prosperous." In the months following those short-sighted remarks, production plummeted, and unemployment soared. By October 1931, nine million Americans were without work, the fabric of life in neighborhoods and communities in industrial cities across the country had been laid waste, and farm and home foreclosures had spiked sharply. The booming economy of the previous decade had spiraled into the abyss of the Great Depression. The recent financial crisis, often referred to as the Great Recession, was not as catastrophic as the Great Depression but it was undoubtedly the most extended and severe economic downturn since then. The buoyant optimism of the Clinton years was gone. America no longer felt like the land of opportunity. In fact, when I graduated from my doctoral program in December 2008, the academic job market appeared so grim that I began to contemplate returning to Turkey.

In the following academic year, I was fortunate enough to secure a postdoctoral fellowship. Subsequently, I took a faculty position overseas, in Dublin. During this time, I began to delve deeper more systematically into the complex interplay between credit, consumption, class, and inequality, and a grant from the Irish Research Council for Humanities and Social Sciences gave the research program a much-needed boost. I still recognized the potential of credit markets to bridge economic divides and enhance welfare—many scholars, including myself, have written extensively about this in the past decade. But I also gained a better understanding of the reasons for credit reliance in the first place, and the implications of the indebtedness that accompanied it. In the subsequent years, I published several articles addressing these questions. I wrote about the impact of financialization on inequality, how access to credit impacted people's understanding of inequality and the government's commitment to redistribution and welfare. These inquiries piqued my curiosity about the broader political economic context underpinning these relationships. I sought to better understand the evolution of the relationship between the state and the financial sector, and what the American government had done—or left undone—to shield the broader economy and the public from the risks stemming from the financial sector. The prevalent view—that the crisis occurred because the US government, guided by neoliberal ideas, pursued deregulatory policies, creating an environment in which financial institutions were able to act recklessly until their inevitable downfall—seemed incomplete. I wanted to unpack said ideas, find out about the array of policies adopted rather than tucking them all under the banner "deregulation," and learn how the government had understood and mitigated risk. While there remains much more that I wish I could explore and understand, this book, not exhaustive and decidedly imperfect, is my attempt to provide insights into these compelling questions.

Acknowledgments

I have had the privilege of presenting various segments of this book at numerous academic forums, such as the ASA pre-conference in Seattle, the MaxPo seminar in Paris, the UCSD Sociology department colloquium, the ECPR and Law & Society Association conferences, Wesleyan Division II luncheon, and most recently, the Science and Technology Studies summer school at Harvard. I deeply appreciate the valuable questions and feedback I received from my esteemed colleagues in these forums.

I owe thanks to Lila, my one and only daughter, and Oz, my dear friend and former partner, for their support, and for ensuring that I had the time and space I needed to work on this book. I would also like to extend heartfelt gratitude to my dear friends, colleagues, and mentors who kept me company and offered thoughtful advice when I needed: *Neil Fligstein, Gregory Jackson, David Levi- Faur, Chris Hogendorn, Onur Ozgode, Niamh Hardiman, Don Moon, Peter Gottschalk, Sonali Chakravarti, Joel Pfister, Daniel Steinmetz-Jenkins, Michael Reisch, Evren Savci, Catherine Egan, and Hirsh Sawhney. Chris, David, Onur, and Don* read various parts of the manuscript, and their critical feedback was invaluable.

I am fortunate to teach such bright students at Wesleyan, and sometimes they are kind enough to agree to be my research assistants. Ariel Deutsch and Sofia Aslan were superbly helpful in that capacity. I am grateful to them both.

During the final stages of this book's editing, I became associated with the SASE Woman and Gender (WAG) forum. It's heartening to know that such forums exist, and I sincerely hope to see more women making their mark in this field. To the women whose scholarship has inspired me throughout my academic journey, my deepest gratitude.

Many thanks, also, to Carol Ross and Laura Long, whose meticulous proofreading significantly enhanced the manuscript's clarity and flow.

Lastly, my appreciation goes to David McBride, my editor, the anonymous reviewers who have offered their insights and expertise, and the other members of the dedicated team at OUP.

Note on Sources

The epigraphs included in this book are from "The Great Transformation" by Karl Polanyi. Copyright © 1944, 1957, 2001 by Karl Polanyi. Reprinted by permission of Beacon Press, Boston.

Parts of the analysis included in Chapter 6 have previously been published in Basak Kus, "Relief, Recovery, Reform: A Retrospective on the US Policy Responses to the Great Recession," *Intereconomics* 54, no. 4 (2020): 257–265.

1

Polanyi on Wall Street

Ten Years, Two Presidents

On September 30, 1998, Erskine Bowles, the White House Chief of Staff, greeted the press gathered in the Old Executive Office Building, declaring the day to be historic. Shortly afterward, President Bill Clinton took the podium amid a standing ovation to announce that the US government had posted a record-breaking budget surplus of $70 billion, the largest since the 1950s. The American economy, the President remarked, was the "strongest in a generation."[1] This was during Clinton's second term. When he left office a little over two years later, major stock market indices had increased several-fold from their levels at the start of the decade; corporate profits had doubled; the homeownership rate had reached nearly 68 percent; more than twenty million jobs had been created; and unemployment had dropped to 4 percent— its lowest level since the early 1970s.[2]

On September 30, 2008, precisely ten years after Clinton's remarks, another President spoke about the state of the economy at another White House press conference. The atmosphere was markedly different. The silence in the room mirrored the grave reality of the moment, as President George W. Bush urged Congress to act. Just the day before, the House of Representatives had voted down a financial rescue plan, leading to the Dow Jones Industrial Average recording its largest daily drop in history—roughly 7 percent. The weeks leading up to this event had been tumultuous: the Treasury had taken over Fannie Mae and Freddie Mac—government-sponsored enterprises (GSEs) operating in the mortgage market; the Federal Reserve had bailed out American International Group (AIG); the Federal Deposit Insurance Corporation (FDIC) had arranged the sale of Wachovia's assets to Citigroup. Amid these events, Lehman Brothers had filed for bankruptcy, Merrill Lynch had been bought by Bank of America, and, most notably, the country's largest savings and loan institution—Washington Mutual—had failed. The country was spiraling into a recession that would see over three hundred banks failing, ten million houses entering foreclosure, and 8.5 million jobs

Disembedded. Basak Kus, Oxford University Press. © Oxford University Press 2024.
DOI: 10.1093/oso/9780197764862.003.0001

2 DISEMBEDDED

disappearing.[3] Ultimately, 22.5 percent of Americans would find themselves with a negative net worth, with millions more postponing retirement or losing hope of ever being able to retire.[4]

Major economic crises bring forth questions that periods of prosperity often bracket away. The 2007–2010 financial crisis was no exception. It posed new questions and necessitated new thinking about old questions. The most pressing question in the aftermath of the crisis was: what is the role of government in a market economy? The three decades preceding the crisis had seen significant structural shifts. On one hand, the economy had become considerably financialized; on the other, its relationship with the state had been fundamentally redefined as a result of a neoliberal turn in politics and policymaking. The crisis starkly exposed the underlying fault lines of these two structural transformations. Discussions abounded. Could the crisis have been averted, depending on the policies the government could or should have pursued? Why hadn't the government done more to oversee the financial sector and mitigate the risks it imposed on the entire economy? Why hadn't there been better consumer protection for the millions of people whose lives were increasingly intertwined with financial markets, whether as borrowers, savers, or investors? And looking forward, what could be done to prevent such massive crises in the future?

This book stemmed from a desire to delve deeper into these questions, centering primarily on the state's role in regulating the economy and protecting against the inherent risks and uncertainties it produces. I examine how the US government navigated this role in an economy that was increasingly driven by financialization, and where and how it fell short with regard to risk protection and mitigation. My hope is that this investigation will enrich our understanding of the American political economy, particularly the regulatory environment that shaped financialization, while also providing historical insights into the financial crisis that spanned from 2007 to 2010, and its subsequent impact on American politics.

The prevalent view seems to suggest that the crisis occurred because the US government, guided by neoliberal ideas, pursued deregulatory policies, creating an environment in which financial institutions were able to run amok and take excessive risks until they inevitably crashed and burned. This narrative is not flat out wrong, especially from a bird's eye view, but it is incomplete in some ways, and misleading in others. First, rather than referring to neoliberalism loosely, we need to specify which ideas, precisely, shaped the state's regulatory relationship with the economy during the last quarter of the twentieth century as financialization was under way, and how these ideas gained political traction under successive administrations. Second, we need a more comprehensive view of the policy tools that these ideas inspired. Regrettably, the narrow focus on deregulation resulted in overlooking some very critical institutional and policy transformations that fundamentally reshaped the state's regulatory relationship with the economy, particularly with the expanding and evolving financial sector.[5] Finally, the narrative of "finance running amok" also requires reconsideration. Many practices today labeled as "running amok" were viewed differently in their time. Policymakers and financial actors alike regarded them as rational, even prudential, strategies for boosting institutional profitability through risk diversification and distribution. Moreover, the "running amok" narrative spotlights the activities of individual firms, essentially characterizing "risk taking" as something firms do or refrain from doing, both obscuring and concealing the systemic nature of risk. What we should focus on, instead, is the deficit in risk protection as a structural feature of the American political economy, irrespective of any particular firm's actions or decisions. I describe this lack of risk protection as "disembeddedness," a concept inspired by Karl Polanyi's work.[6]

Reading Polanyi in the Aftermath of the Financial Crisis

"Nineteenth-century civilization has collapsed," Polanyi wrote on the first page of his book, *The Great Transformation*, as he reflected on the economic and political crises that shook both sides of the Atlantic in the first half of the twentieth century.[7] He saw the roots of this collapse residing in "a market society that refused to function."[8] The march of industrial capitalism had produced significant social dislocations, and yet the governing paradigm— the liberal creed—had failed to respond because it had "misread the history of the Industrial Revolution by insisting on judging social events from the economic viewpoint."[9] This assumption that life and human beings could be viewed through an economic lens constituted an "economistic fallacy," according to Polanyi.[10] Although the economy was supposed to be embedded in the social, the social had been subjugated to the economic.[11]

Polanyi's analysis of the downfall of nineteenth-century civilization, which he identifies as both an economic and a political collapse, focuses on several intertwined elements. First, he emphasizes the structural changes in the

4 DISEMBEDDED

economy, drawing parallels between England's Tudor-era enclosure movement and the Industrial Revolution, in terms of the social and economic upheavals they brought about.[12] Then he turns to the governing ideas that have informed political responses to these economic dislocations, aiming to "clarify the alternatives facing a community which is in the throes of unregulated economic improvement."[13] He praises the Tudor statesmen for understanding that the power of the Crown had to be harnessed to lessen risks and safeguard the public during a time of major economic disruption, while he criticizes modern economists for viewing the Industrial Revolution through the narrow lens of economic liberalism and inaccurately applying modern free-market theories to historical situations where these concepts did not apply.[14] In doing so, he also highlights the political responsibility that the state must shoulder as a protective entity in these circumstances.

As Christopher Ansell notes, the provision of protection against risks constitutes "an implicit social contract between state and society."[15] Certainly, as with other aspects of government, what is done in the name of risk protection and mitigation can ignite intense ideological debates regarding whether the actions are desirable, fiscally feasible, or simply inevitable. These debates tend to be particularly contentious in the US. The actions that the government takes to safeguard its citizens from risks and volatilities often face criticism for fostering a culture of over-caution, and "turning America into a nation of ninnies," as David A. Moss points out, while budget hawks never let anyone forget the price tag of the government's protective endeavors.[16] Nevertheless, history shows that systematic effort on the part of the state is necessary to monitor and mitigate risks, especially to maintain the stability and legitimacy of democracy. And this remains another aspect of Polanyi's analysis: his apprehension regarding democratic futures—or more specifically, the challenge to democracy brought about by the political backlash against disembedded structures.

Despite their distinct ideological foundations, Polanyi contends, fascism, socialism, and the New Deal share a common thread: they all represent society's response to the economistic fallacies of the nineteenth century that sought to disembed the economy from its broader social context. Each acted as a protectionist countermovement against the growing influence and reach of markets.[17]

Reading Polanyi in the aftermath of the financial crisis, one cannot help remembering the dictum, "history repeats itself."[18] The economic and political circumstances that are central to this book mirror those Polanyi analyzed

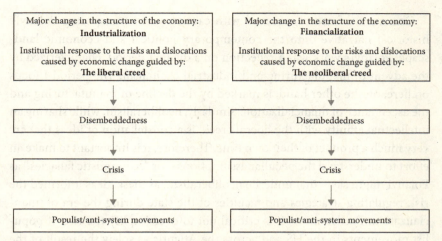

Figure 1.1 Disembeddedness, Crises, and Counter-movements: A Polanyian Lens

(see Figure 1.1). Both periods were marked by structural changes in the economy subsequently leading to major crises. In both cases, a creed that sought to organize economic, political, and social life in the image of markets had been espoused in the decades leading up to the crisis. Both historical periods laid bare the liabilities of advanced nations in mitigating the risks of capitalism. And on the political front, populist and protectionist movements of different varieties ascended in conjunction with dislocations that economic changes inflicted on large segments of the populace.[19]

Given these similarities, it seems fitting to follow the breadcrumbs Polanyi left behind to explore the relationship between the neoliberal creed, the state, and the financializing economy in the years leading to the 2007–2010 crisis. The book, in that sense, can be construed as an endeavor to think about disembeddedness during the era of financialization—how it has come about, what constituted it, and what political ramifications it engendered. Drawing from Polanyi's seminal insight that the free-market economy was "opened and kept open" through the sustained and deliberate actions of the state, my analysis predominantly focuses on the government's role in the development of disembedded financialization. I posit that to truly comprehend the financial crisis of 2007–2010, and the consequential political shifts that arose in its aftermath, such as the surge of populist politics, we must transcend the common perception of it as merely a severe economic recession, and rather acknowledge it as a crisis of disembeddedness.

6 DISEMBEDDED

One must, of course, proceed with caution when transposing Polanyi's historical narrative onto the contemporary political and economic landscape. Polanyi's work was a reflection on a distinct period, characterized by the advent of manufacturing and industrial capitalism. The period I focus on here, on the other hand, is marked by the decline of manufacturing and the ascendance of financialization. Similarly, neoliberalism, while sharing an intellectual affinity with the liberal creed, is a constellation of ideas that are very much a product of their own time. Therefore, it is important to make an effort to understand the peculiar assumptions—or "economistic fallacies," as Polanyi might say—that underlie neoliberalism, as these ideas informed the risk-regulating strategies and faculties of the state during the era of financialization. Furthermore, it is critical not to oversimplify the rise of populist movements in the US and across the Atlantic as solely the result of the disembeddedness resulting from the neoliberal state's failure in mitigating the risks and vulnerabilities of a financialized economy. As I discuss later, those risks and vulnerabilities that emerged in the absence of adequate state mitigation form just one part of an otherwise complex historical equation fraught with ethnic and racial prejudices. Nevertheless, their role warrants scrutiny, especially given the historical precedent that Polanyi astutely analyzed.

The Crisis of the Early Twentieth Century and the Postwar Expansion of the Protective State

Economic crises are known to be catalysts for change. The Great Depression mobilized Americans to demand more protection from the state and created a conducive ideological and political space to develop policies and institutions to make that possible.[20] The first and second New Deal gave way to a form of "embedded liberalism"[21] as the state expanded its protective reach, both by granting more social security to the public, and by regulating economic activity in line with "the public interest rhetoric that leading progressive economists had been shaping since the 1880s."[22] As Marc Eisner notes, in this period "new policy initiatives extended the national government's authority to problems that had formerly been the province of states, communities, or private organizations."[23] Signing the Social Security Act in 1935, a significant step in the development of the risk protection faculties of the state, Franklin D. Roosevelt noted: "The civilization of the past hundred years, with its startling industrial changes, has tended more and more to make life insecure."[24] With the new act, he remarked, US citizens would be able to "reap direct benefits through unemployment compensation, through old-age pensions and through increased services for the protection of children and the prevention of ill health."[25] Government's commitment to socio-economic risk protection expanded in the immediate decades that followed. The 1950s saw the extension of disability benefits, and during the Great Society years in the following two decades Medicare and Medicaid were established, expanding health insurance to the poor and elderly.[26]

The state's commitment to consumer protection also expanded during this time, culminating in the creation of new consumer offices within New Deal agencies. As Lizabeth Cohen explains, "Roosevelt justified the new consumer offices in his New Deal agencies as representing 'a new principle in government'—that consumers have the right 'to have their interests represented in the formulation of government policy . . . . Never before had the particular problems of consumers been so thoroughly and unequivocally accepted as the direct responsibility of government.' "[27] This policy outlook embracing consumer protection as the responsibility of the government also continued in the following decades. The US remained a global leader in identifying and regulating the risks markets embodied and imposed on consumers in an advanced industrialized economy. As David Vogel notes, for instance, the regulations concerning additives used in food, chemicals used in agriculture, and parts used in manufacturing products were all a lot more stringent in the US than in Europe until the mid-1980s.[28]

The postwar period also saw a significant expansion of regulatory supervision over economic activities, especially in finance, as elucidated by Rahman.[29] Foremost among the pivotal laws that formed the backbone of the American financial regulatory framework was the Banking Act of 1933. This Act barred commercial banks from participating in investment banking and established the FDIC to insure bank deposits. In 1934, the Securities Exchange Commission (SEC) was established, and in 1940 the Investment Company Act was enacted to regulate firms involved in securities investment and trading, including mutual funds. This regulatory orientation persisted in the following decades. In 1956, the Bank Holding Act Company Act clarified the status of bank holding companies and expanded the power of the Federal Reserve over the banking industry. The Truth in Lending Act of 1968 mandated accurate disclosure of loan terms and costs to borrowers. In 1970, the Fair Credit Reporting Act aimed to enhance the accuracy and fairness of

8   DISEMBEDDED

consumer reporting agencies, and protected consumers' right to know of the information being reported about them. Because of these efforts on the part of American government, the US financial system remained more heavily regulated than its European counterparts for most of the postwar period, all the way up until the 1980s.[30]

Essentially, the roughly four decades following the Great Depression saw a steady expansion in the protective role of the government, its risk regulation commitments, and its capacities. However, before proceeding further, it is crucial to note certain caveats to avoid presenting an oversimplified and linear narrative of the postwar relationship between the state and the economy. After all, the history of postwar embedded liberalism in the US, like all histories, is complex. It blends the radical with the pragmatic, the progressive with the conservative, and the continuous with the discontinuous. Therefore, it's not surprising to find various, somewhat contradictory, narratives coexist side by side, each equally valid, depending on which facets of the historical landscape one chooses to focus on. For instance, the widely accepted narrative of the New Deal and the ensuing decades as a period when the US government implemented policies to curb the worst tendencies of capitalism has been challenged by some scholars, on the grounds that those policies in question were, in many ways, compatible with and served business interests.[31] It is also crucial to acknowledge that the protective hands of the state did not reach out to every segment of the society equally.[32] However, at the end, as Mary O. Furner notes, "for all their shortcomings, and they were many, postwar American local, state, and national governments generally moved, in Polanyi's terms, to 're-embed' the market in society."[33]

Late Twentieth-Century Economic Transformations and Political Shifts

Beginning in the last quarter of the twentieth century the structural underpinnings of the state–economy relationship began to shift. By the second half of the 1970s, economic indicators signaled trouble for the US economy. Increasing unemployment, high inflation, and lower economic growth coupled with an energy crisis challenged the postwar stability that the embedded liberalism compromise had kept in balance. The postwar state had been assuming responsibility for the risks that the growing capitalist economy imposed on the social body, and yet, as Greta Krippner notes, this task was "increasingly challenging as economic conditions deteriorated in the 1970s, marking a turning point from the broadly shared prosperity of the early postwar decades to a period of slower growth and higher employment."[34] This was not, as Krippner argued, simply an economic and social crisis. Rather, the state's failure to make good on its social commitments meant that it was also a "legitimation crisis."[35]

This impasse led to two consequential developments. First, it opened political space conducive to challenging the ideas that had underpinned the state-economy relationship since the New Deal era (including Keynesian demand management theories and public interest theories of regulation) and provided more credibility to policy discourses that envisioned a limited role for government in the economy.[36] Second, as policymakers endeavored to tackle economic stability and the distribution of prosperity, their initiatives, in both domestic and international capital markets, ultimately created a macroeconomic environment that fostered the ascendance of the financial sector.[37] It is at the intersection of these two developments—that is, the financial turn in the economy on the one hand, and the neoliberal turn in government on the other—that there emerged a disembedded political-economic landscape over four decades. The government, guided by the neoliberal creed, failed to respond to the risks that the expanding and rapidly changing financial sector embodied and imposed on the overall economy, its workers, and its consumers, savers, and investors.

The Financial Turn in the Economy

The financialization of the American economy in the final quarter of the twentieth century was evident at the macro, the organizational, and the household/individual levels.[38] At the macro level, the financial sector's share of total corporate profits increased substantially, as did its relative value added to GDP.[39] On the organizational front, financialization altered corporations' objectives and activities. By the 1990s, American corporations were predominantly led by finance-oriented executives whose primary focus was boosting stock prices.[40] These executives divested from their core businesses to invest heavily in financial instruments, a move the markets rewarded. As manufacturing profits had declined, the turn to finance to generate income and profits seemed a sound decision. One glaring example was General Electric (GE) under CEO Jack Welch, who drastically downsized

10 DISEMBEDDED

the company's traditional units. According to a 1996 *Business Week* article, "Welch barnstormed through GE, shutting factories, paring payrolls and hacking mercilessly at its lackluster old-line units."[41] By the time he stepped down in 2001, more than one-half of GE's revenue and over one-third of its profits stemmed from its financial division, and its stock prices had grown immensely.[42] GE was not an outlier; by the dawn of the new millennium, revenues from financial sources were nearly on par with those from non-financial sources for many manufacturing companies.[43]

Households and individuals as consumers, investors, and borrowers also became more enmeshed with financial institutions and instruments. Prior to 1980, household debt in the US accounted for about 65 percent of disposable income, as Ken-Hou Lin and Megan Tobias Neely noted; however, by the onset of the financial crisis in 2007, debt had surged to 132 percent of income.[44] On the asset side, financial assets grew substantially relative to total household assets.[45] Notably, the US stood out among all OECD nations for the size of financial assets, including deposit accounts, bonds, stock shares, mutual funds, and life insurance, as part of household wealth.[46]

These broad figures certainly reflect the rising size and prominence of finance in the American economy. For a more complete understanding of America's financial turn, however, we also need to understand how the financial sector was transformed *within*. This was after all, not merely a quantitative change in the size, revenue, or profit share of finance. Over the three decades from the early 1980s, what constituted the financial sector itself had changed.

First, non-bank financial institutions (NBFIs) became key actors in the US financial system. In just the two decades before the financial crisis started, the assets of these institutions had increased drastically (see Figure 1.2 and Figure 1.3). At the start of the financial crisis, they held more than 60 percent of the outstanding credit market debt in the US (see Figure 1.4).

Secondly, there was a notable rise in both concentration and interconnectedness within the financial sector. Concentration had not been an historical feature of American finance. In fact, for most of its institutional history, the banking sector had been quite fragmented.[47] However, by the early 2000s, a handful of banks controlled a substantial portion of commercial banking assets. As of the onset of the crisis, the number of banks in the US had halved compared to two decades earlier, and the five largest banks held 45 percent of all commercial banking assets (see Figure 1.5 and Figure 1.6). To be clear, not all these large financial institutions in the US were, or are, traditional banks. As the financial system has evolved, the

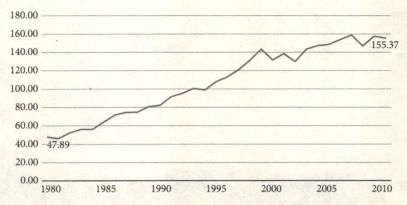

Figure 1.2 The Rise of Non-Bank Financial Institutions: NBFI Assets to GDP, United States, Percent

Federal Reserve Bank of St. Louis, "Non-Bank Financial Institutions' Assets to GDP for United States, Annual, Not Seasonally Adjusted," https://fred.stlouisfed.org/graph/?g=lGeY.

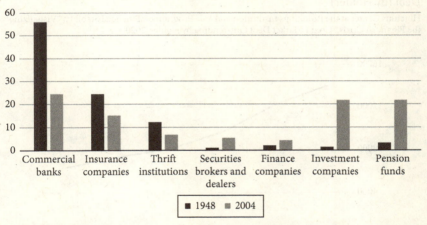

Figure 1.3 The Rise of Non-Bank Financial Institutions: Shares of Assets of Financial Institutions in the United States (Percentage)

Source: Data is from "Percentage Shares of Assets of Financial Institutions in the United States, 1860–2004" presented in Randall S. Kroszner and P. E. Strahan, "Regulation and Deregulation of the U.S. Banking Industry: Causes, Consequences, and Implications for the Future," in *Economic Regulation and Its Reform: What Have We Learned?*, ed. Nancy L. Rose (Chicago: University of Chicago Press, 2014), 501.

so-called too-big-to-fail financial institutions—those with assets exceeding $100 billion—came to include NBFIs (see Figure 1.7). In fact, in 2007, of the thirty-three US companies on *Forbes*' list of the world's largest public companies, eleven were NBFIs.[48]

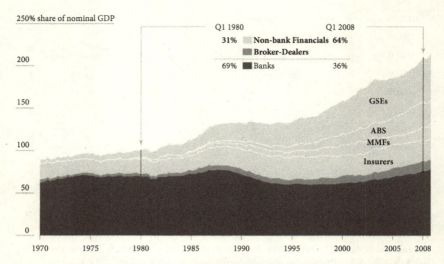

Figure 1.4 The Rise of Non-Bank Financial Institutions: Share of Credit Market Debt (by Holder)
Hutchins Center at the Brookings Institution and Yale Program on Financial Stability, "Visualizing the Financial Crisis," Credit Market Debt Outstanding by Holder, 2020.

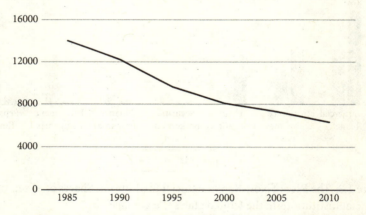

Figure 1.5 Concentration in Finance: Number of Commercial Banks in the US
Reserve Bank of St. Louis, "Commercial Banks in the U.S. (Discontinued)," https://fred.stlouisfed.org/series/USNUM.

The financial sector also grew increasingly interconnected. Banks' cross-border exposure and their presence in foreign markets saw a substantial increase, with consolidated international claims of banks doubling from the end of the 1990s to the beginning of the financial crisis.[49] Once again, this

Figure 1.6 Concentration in Finance: Assets of Five Largest Banks
Federal Reserve Bank of St. Louis, "5 Bank Asset Concentration for United States," https://fred.stlouisfed.org/series/DDOI06USA156NWDB.

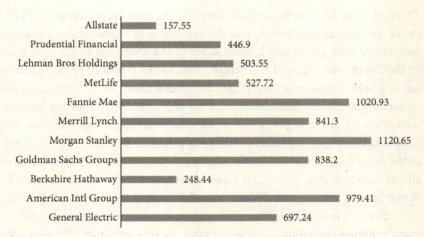

Figure 1.7 Concentration in Finance: NBFIs with Assets Exceeding $100 Billion, circa 2007
Forbes, *The Global 2000*, 2007.

trend was not confined to banks alone but also included NBFIs, such as insurance companies, hedge funds, and brokers.[50]

A third crucial aspect of the changing financial environment was the emergence of new and complex financial instruments and products.

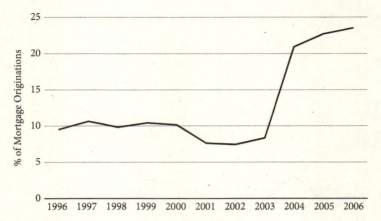

Figure 1.8 Subprime Share of Entire Mortgage Market
Source: Data is from US Financial Crisis Inquiry Commission, The Financial Crisis Inquiry Report: Final Report of the National Commission on the Causes of the Financial and Economic Crisis in the United States, January 2011, https://www.govinfo.gov/content/pkg/GPO-FCIC/pdf/GPO-FCIC.pdf.

Three of these had particularly noteworthy impacts on the economy: subprime lending, securitization, and the expansion of the derivatives market. Subprime loans, previously a small share of the mortgage market, took off in the 2000s (see Figure 1.8). Before then, banks typically refrained from lending to borrowers without "established credit histories" or with "troubled financial histories."[51] Such borrowers instead turned to subprime lenders, who offered loans at higher interest rates. Subprime lending, back then, did not invite the negative, predatory images it would acquire a few decades later. In the decade leading to the financial crisis, the market more than doubled in size as rising housing prices and financial innovations "suddenly made subprime borrowers—previously shut out of the mortgage markets—attractive customers for mortgage lenders."[52] Lending standards declined, and riskier loans at higher and adjustable interest rates became prominent.[53] Many subprime loans were originated by NBFIs. In fact, as Senator Elizabeth Warren noted, as of 2006, "More than half—52 percent, to be exact—of all subprime mortgages originated with companies with no federal supervision at all, primarily stand-alone mortgage brokers and finance companies."[54]

Meanwhile, securitization changed mortgage lending from an "originate to hold" model to an "originate to distribute" model. As loans evolved into marketable securities, banks transitioned from being merely lending institutions into originators and distributors of loans.[55] In the 1980s and early 1990s, the securitization market was primarily dominated by government-sponsored enterprises (GSEs). However, private institutions eventually entered the market, and as securitization "became an affair of the private financial sector, it spurred further innovation in products."[56] By the onset of the financial crisis, over 80 percent of all loan originations were securitized.[57] Without the expansion in securitization, the subprime market would not have grown to the extent that it did. By the mid-1990s, less than 30 percent of subprime loans were securitized; a decade later, this figure had risen to almost 60 percent.[58] As was true for subprime lending, the financial crisis cast securitization in an exceedingly negative light; however, in its early development, securitization had been viewed as a tool that helped to allocate resources effectively, ensure liquidity, and disperse risk. As Pernell argues, banking regulators in the US "embraced and actively encouraged bank participation in the securitization process, consistently fighting against initiatives that threatened to constrain the operation of securitization markets largely because they understood securitization to be a prudential practice (a practice that increased the safety and stability of the banking system)."[59]

Finally, the growth of derivatives, specifically credit default swaps (CDS), played a significant role in the proliferation of securitization, particularly with regard to subprime loans. CDS is widely seen as a form of insurance designed to protect buyers who trade in mortgage loans from defaults in the underlying assets. Should a default occur, the CDS seller compensates the buyer for the loss. When, in 2006, Alan Greenspan argued, "The credit default swap is probably the most important instrument in finance" because what it did was "lay-off all the risk of highly leveraged institutions . . . on stable American and international institutions,"[60] he could not have been more precise in his articulation that from the perspective of the government and regulatory authorities, CDS were a risk-managing, insurance-like tool. The CDS market saw remarkable growth in the 2000s. By the end of 2007, it had ballooned into a massive sixty-one trillion dollar market.[61]

In short, and to reiterate, over the course of three decades the landscape of the financial sector—the market participants, scale of operations, products, and services—had all changed substantially. In the period when the financial sector was expanding and transforming, the state was also changing. New ideas were in circulation about how the economy operates and what should be the state's relationship to it.

16 DISEMBEDDED

The Neoliberal Turn in Government

A great deal has been written about neoliberalism as a political project, a policy paradigm, and more broadly, "a peculiar form of reason that configures all aspects of existence in economic terms."[62] Neoliberalism seems ubiquitous in its various manifestations, "in statecraft and the workplace, in jurisprudence, education, culture, and a vast range of quotidian activity," wrote Wendy Brown, and yet it bears "no fixed or settled coordinates" and is characterized by "temporal and geographical variety in its discursive formulations, policy entailments, and material practices."[63] Perhaps it is this ubiquitous nature, combined with substantive variations, which makes neoliberalism difficult to pin down, and for that matter, to determine what is "neo" or "liberal" about it. And this is why in recent years we have seen an intellectual movement to discard the concept neoliberalism. However, as Quinn Slobodan argues, it is not dispensing the concept that needs to happen, but clarifying it, historicizing it, and specifying its ideational and institutional coordinates better.[64] In this respect, it is critical to clarify a few points.

To begin with, I disagree with views that portray neoliberalism as the "second coming" of the liberal creed. Nancy Fraser made that argument, for instance, when she said that "neoliberalism today is nothing but the second-coming of the very same nineteenth-century faith in the 'self-regulating market' that unleashed the capitalist crisis Polanyi chronicled."[65] To be sure, the ideas we associate with neoliberalism today are similar and related to the nineteenth-century liberal creed. However, they are shaped by the political, social, and economic currents of their own time. After all, ideas do not develop in a vacuum. The new creed may have preserved faith in the "self-regulating market," but the "market" in question is not the same, and the meaning and policy manifestations of "self-regulation" have surely not remained frozen in time. Adopting a Polanyian perspective to examine the interaction between the state and economy under the spell of neoliberalism necessitates unearthing the underlying assumptions, styles of reasoning, and "economistic fallacies" that constitute neoliberalism and its imprint on the state's regulatory principles and mechanisms during the period of financialization, instead of merely labeling it as a repetition.

From the vantage point of this study—focused on the formation of the regulatory state, more specifically, the risk-managing state—the new creed originated in a set of economic theories in the 1970s. These theories, whether they problematized regulatory capture, rent-seeking, or bureaucracy as an administrative technique—joined in their understanding of the shortcomings of direct and substantive government regulation. Over time, the objectives and policies of the US regulatory framework began to take shape in their image, as economists who embraced these theories ascended to positions of influence within the government. While direct and substantive government regulation came under attack, private regulation—the idea that the self-interests of actors and market discipline would ensure safety and soundness—began to gain acceptance. This transition—namely, the delegitimization of direct and substantial government regulation, coupled with the endorsement of private regulation rooted in market discipline and individual rationality—was further fortified in the 1990s by breakthroughs in financial economics and the growing allure of the New Public Management approach to governance (see Figure 1.9). It materialized in four primary ways within the policy domain:

- *Deregulation.* On the one hand, the dismantling of various regulations established post-Great Depression became possible. Indeed, this wave of deregulation, coupled with technological change, paved the way for the emergence of new actors, products, and financial instruments, as discussed earlier.
- *Regulatory drift.* Despite substantial changes in the financial markets, the US did not update or develop new risk regulation tools to correspond with these new market realities. Instead, the country largely embraced deliberate inaction. This was the second manifestation of neoliberal regulation: regulatory drift. As Elizabeth Warren remarked, markets changed, but statutes remained "frozen in time."[66] Although

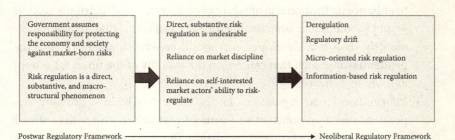

Figure 1.9 The Neoliberal State and the Financializing Economy: A New Regulatory Framework

18 DISEMBEDDED

the prominence of NBFIs had increased tremendously, the regulatory system remained bank centered. Although the financial assets had become significantly concentrated and financial institutions immensely interconnected, the government did not monitor or mitigate the risk this expansion in size and interconnectivity posed—a phenomenon later referred to as the "too big to fail" problem. As securitization, subprime lending, and derivatives markets expanded, US government chose to maintain a hands-off approach. In a nutshell, while the economy, and particularly the finance sector, grew larger and more complex, the formal policies and institutions tasked with risk regulation failed to keep up. Instead, the government shifted toward a micro-oriented and information-based approach to risk regulation.

- *Micro-oriented risk regulation.* As substantive regulation and risk protection was increasingly seen as something that the government is neither good at nor should be responsible for, the regulatory framework began to favor an increasingly micro perspective. Economic processes and associated risks were seen as best managed by self-interested, rational, and responsible actors (whether firms, investors, borrowers, or savers) themselves on an individual level. The focus was inherently on the safety and soundness of individual financial institutions (micro-prudential regulation), rather than a systemic perspective concerned with the stability of the whole financial system with its correlatively moving parts. In this context, the government's role was redefined from prescribing and enforcing detailed rules to setting broad guidelines and principles (principles-based regulation). Circling back to a previous point, many financial practices later labeled as excessively risky were, in fact, perceived as acceptable and even advantageous during the 1990s and 2000s. Seen through the prevailing micro lens, these practices appeared to enhance institutional profitability and diversify and distribute risks. It would become clear later, during the financial crisis, that to "adequately identify risks that developed *across* and *between* markets," a "macro-prudential approach that centers on the stability of the financial system as a whole" is necessary.[67]

- *Information-based regulation.* Lastly, there has been a growing dependence on non-substantive forms of regulation, rather than direct and substantive government regulation, to mitigate and accommodate market-borne risks. The most significant manifestation of this trend was the emergence of information provision and access as a crucial tool for risk regulation. Although they might look rather unrelated at first glance, part and parcel of this were the increasing prevalence of disclosure regulations, initiatives at both the national and state level to enhance financial literacy, and the growing importance of credit rating agencies.

Disembedded Financialization: American Economy and the Deficit in Risk Protection

Against this background, let me reiterate the primary thesis of this book: as the American economy became increasingly financialized over three decades commencing in the 1980s, it also became increasingly disembedded. The state—reimagined and retooled by a new set of ideas about how governments, markets, and individual actors operate—fell short of monitoring and mitigating the risks posed by a financializing economy. The deficit in risk protection, which I conceptualize as disembeddedness, could be observed in relation to systemic risk protection, in relation to consumer financial protection, and in relation to socio-economic protection. While my focus primarily rests on the first two, it is crucial to acknowledge all three aspects as integral to the disembeddedness of the financialized American economy.

Systemic risk—"the risk that financial instability becomes so widespread that it impairs the functioning of a financial system to the point where economic growth and welfare suffer materially"[68]—was hardly on regulators' radar before the financial crisis, despite becoming a key focus of subsequent regulatory reforms (see Table 1.1). When discussing the "safety-and-soundness" of financial institutions, federal financial regulators primarily focused on the

Table 1.1 The Salience of Systemic Risk as a Policy Concern

"Systemic Risk" Mentions	Before 2007	2007–2017
In congressional hearings and congressional bills *Initial mention in 1993	130	882
In *The New York Times* *Initial mention in 1988	45	350

Source: Govinfo.gov and LexisNexis. The count of occurrences of "systemic risk" in the news was retrieved from LexisNexis by specifically selecting The New York Times as a source.

20 DISEMBEDDED

profitability of individual institutions, with little consideration for the wider systemic impact or costs associated with achieving such profitability. The US government deliberately refrained from imposing direct, substantive tools to mitigate systemic risk. In fact, Onur Ozgode argues, "Elite policymakers at the Fed refused to elevate systemic risk to the status of an official macroeconomic policy objective and thereby refrained from publicly communicating the role systemic risk played in their overall emergency mitigation strategy."[69] This disregard seems particularly stark in retrospect given that systemic risk—regardless of how it's operationalized or measured—was notably escalating during the 2000s.

Similar trends characterized consumer financial protection. Millions of Americans had become intertwined with financial markets through mortgages and consumer credit, stock market participation, and retirement planning. Many of the financial institutions and instruments they were interacting with were novel, such as subprime loans and non-bank mortgage originators. Nevertheless, consumer protection regulation drifted in the face of such changes because the government did not consider it as an issue that required a direct, substantive regulatory approach.

Linking back to the previous point on systemic risk, federal financial regulators' focus on the safety-and-soundness of individual financial institutions, which prioritized institutional profitability of said institutions, had little regard for whether their practices were exploitative or harmful to consumers; therefore, the regulatory framework not only fell short in protecting consumers, but in effect made their participation in financial markets particularly risky.[70] The prevailing idea was that consumer protection could be tackled at the individual level and through non-substantive means—namely, it was assumed that if individuals had access to product and service information through disclosures and credit ratings, and the financial literacy to interpret that information, they would be able to protect themselves, all without substantive government regulation of the financial marketplace. This presumption was underpinned by the idea of consumers as rational and responsible actors. As Brown elaborates, "Neoliberalism normatively constructs and interpellates individuals as entrepreneurial actors in every sphere of life . . . as rational, calculating creatures whose moral autonomy is measured by their capacity for 'self-care'—the ability to provide for their own needs and service their own ambitions . . . . But in so doing, it carries responsibility for the self to new heights: the rationally calculating individual bears full responsibility for the consequences of his or her action no matter how severe the constraints on this action."[71] This was certainly the case when it came to consumer financial protection.[72] The micro approach to risk-regulation meant, with respect to consumer protection, "responsibilization"—a "technique of governance" that places the burden of risk protection on citizens, rather than the institutions of the state.[73] Citizens, as Norah MacKendrick argues, were "expected to draw on their capacities as self-governing subjects."[74] The 1999 Clinton–Gore Plan for Financial Privacy and Consumer Financial Protection in the 21st Century is a case in point. The plan largely focused on "expanding the consumer's right to know" and repeatedly declared support for legislation requiring clear disclosure of various aspects of financial transactions.[75] It also emphasized the importance of financial literacy. While the need to take action against abuses concerning high interest loans, including subprime loans, was briefly mentioned, the recommendations mostly focused on requirements that lenders disclose the exact terms of their loans. As with systemic risk protection, while consumer financial protection was a central concern of the reform agenda after the financial crisis, before the crisis, it was not a politically salient issue (see Table 1.2).

Table 1.2 Consumer Financial Protection as a Policy Concern

"Consumer Financial Protection" Mentions	Before 2007	2007–2017
In congressional hearings and congressional bills	0	988
In The New York Times	0	1,070

Source: Govinfo.gov and LexisNexis. The count of occurrences of "consumer financial protection" in the news was retrieved from LexisNexis by specifically selecting The New York Times as a source.

Lastly, a few words about the government's approach to socio-economic risk, although it falls outside the scope of this book. It is noteworthy that socio-economic risk regulation exhibited a similar logic and shared comparable characteristics. A vast amount of research has shown that, since the 1980s, structural changes in the economy, particularly financialization, have exacerbated socio-economic risks and inequalities.[76] The proportion of workers with precarious and non-standard jobs has climbed along with Americans who describe themselves as "insecure."[77] Income and wealth inequality have increased, and retirement security has declined.[78] Despite the growing socio-economic insecurity stemming from stagnant wages, inequality, employment volatility, and retirement instability in a globally

22   DISEMBEDDED

financialized economy, the state has not effectively intervened with the necessary social insurance and redistribution measures.

As the government has retreated and drifted away from tackling socio-economic risks directly, socio-economic risk management has increasingly been framed as an endeavor that responsible, rational individuals address with market-based tools. The state's responsibility to shield the populace from the unequal outcomes and volatile forces of the market has been reframed as the responsibility of individuals to be managed through education (financial literacy) and financial instruments. Both the Personal Responsibility and Work Opportunity Reconciliation Act of 1996 and the Savings Are Vital to Everyone's Retirement Act of 1997, for example, were efforts in this direction. To put it in sociologist C. W. Mills' terms, these policies endeavored to characterize public issues as private troubles, and promoted individual, privatized solutions to structural challenges. Millions of Americans sought these individual privatized remedies in financial markets. Since the late 1980s, consumers have turned to credit markets at unprecedented rates to boost their consumption and meet their needs, from groceries and housing, to education and medical care.[79] For families at the lower end of wealth and income distribution, credit served to bridge the gap between their actual economic means and their consumption needs and aspirations.[80] In essence, the state failed to deliver social citizenship, "the right to a modicum of economic welfare and security . . . to live the life of a civilized being according to the standards prevailing in the society,"[81] and instead, a form of "financial citizenship" emerged whereby individuals manage themselves within the market place.[82] In the absence of adequate social welfare mechanisms, individuals are left to rely on financial markets to address the precarity of life in a financialized economy. In Polanyian terms, then, rather than embedding financialization into the social order, the neoliberal era has enveloped the social within the financial. This model, of course, has its limits. The mitigation the credit market may provide is not the same as embeddedness.[83] There is a world of difference between using credit to access products and services in exchange for future indebtedness and having higher wages and a secure job to actually afford those things.[84]

American Government and the Great Recession

By the time President Obama was inaugurated in 2009, the American economy had been engulfed by a crisis. Growth rates were plummeting, unemployment and home foreclosures were skyrocketing, and major financial institutions were seeking bailouts. As previously mentioned, crises can create a political space conducive to policy changes. "You never want a serious crisis to go to waste,"[85] Obama's Chief of Staff Rahm Emanuel observed in 2008, echoing Winston Churchill. For policy change to happen, however, those who sit at the helm of policymaking first need to agree on what the problems are, why they arose, and what must be done about them. An important point of contention in these political deliberations concerned the role of the government—the size, substance, and tools of government intervention in the crisis. In the US, following initial emergency measures, the government's response had three components: relief, recovery, and reform. While relief and recovery measures were swiftly implemented, regulatory reform took almost two years of debate and negotiation.

The crisis revealed not only the risks the financial sector imposed on the overall economy and the social body, and the ways in which the state had failed in mitigating those risks, but also the political limits of the government's response to it. It served to amplify public discontent with the existing political and economic structures. The decade following the crisis saw the rise of both left- and right-wing populist politicians. The resentment toward and distrust in the political and economic elites was palpable (see Figure 1.10). This was not a phenomenon unique to the US.[86] While we

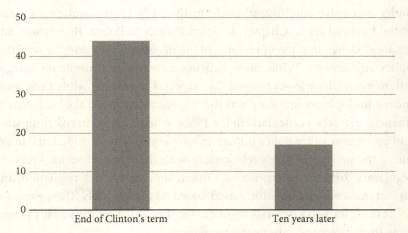

Figure 1.10 Percentage of Population Who Trust Washington Always or Most of the Time

PEW Research Center, "Public Trust in Government: 1958–2021," https://www.pewresearch.org/politics/2019/04/11/public-trust-in-government-1958-2019/.

24   DISEMBEDDED

cannot attribute rising populism solely to economic structures, we would not be entirely remiss to suggest that the disembeddedness of the financialized American economy played an important role.[87]

Outline of the Book

The primary goal of this book is to contribute to ongoing discussions surrounding the relationship between neoliberalism, the state, and financialization in the US. The present chapter introduces the book's key questions and concepts. Chapter 2, "A New Creed on Regulation," examines the ideas and assumptions that shaped the state's regulatory involvement in the economy during the last quarter of the twentieth century. I explore the rise of an intellectual movement skeptical of direct and substantive government regulation in the works of economists like George Stigler, Sam Peltzman, Gary Becker, James M. Buchanan, Gordon Tullock, Anne Krueger, William A. Niskanen, and others in the 1970s and 1980s. Furthermore, I discuss how this anti-statist approach to regulation gained further momentum in the 1990s bolstered by insights from the increasingly influential field of financial economics, as well as the rising popularity of New Public Management theory of government. In Chapter 3, "The Political Ascent of the New Creed," the focus shifts to politics. I explore how economic theories of regulation gained political traction under successive administrations from the early 1970s through the onset of the financial crisis. Chapter 4, "From Politics to Policy: Regulation, and Finance," delves into the operations of the neoliberal state and the resulting policy adjustments. While many existing accounts concentrate on deregulation, my analysis looks beyond this aspect. I argue that while there were indeed multiple deregulatory acts that significantly altered the landscape of financial markets, particularly in the 1980s, when it comes to risk mitigation and protection, other policy initiatives were arguably more influential in defining the neoliberal state's relationship with the financial sector—namely, regulatory drift, the emergence of a micro approach to risk regulation, and an increased reliance on information-based regulatory tools. These elements collectively formed a new risk regulation regime as the state gradually moved away from direct and substantive regulation.

Chapter 5, "Disembeddedness in Financial Times," explores the disembedded nature of American financialization in terms of three major manifestations: a deficit in systemic risk protection, consumer financial protection, and social protection. Although the chapter primarily focuses on the first two, I argue that each of these dimensions is interconnected, and only by considering them in relation can we comprehend the full scope of financial disembeddedness in the US. In Chapter 6, "The Crisis," I turn to the crisis of disembedded financialization and discuss how policymakers understood and responded to it, and the extent to which those post-crisis policy responses constituted a form of re-embedding. Finally, Chapter 7, "In Search of Protection: From Disembedded Financialization to Populist Persuasions,"[88] considers the relationship between the rising wave of populism in the US and disembedded financialization. I also contend that insofar as the state's regulatory shortcomings in terms of risk protection are linked to public discontent with the government and the surge of populist politics, questions of regulation inherently pertain to the future of democratic governance and should be addressed as such.

2

A New Creed on Regulation

> Before we can proceed to the discussion of the laws governing a
> market economy, such as the nineteenth century was trying to estab-
> lish, we must first have a firm grip on the extraordinary assumptions
> underlying such a system.
>
> —Karl Polanyi, *The Great Transformation*

It is broadly recognized that the ideas guiding economic policy in the final
quarter of the twentieth century departed significantly from those that
prevailed in the postwar years. Although variations exist due to the unique
historical and institutional contexts of individual countries, this paradig-
matic shift—commonly known as the "neoliberal turn"—has been felt globally. This chapter seeks to unpack the ideas that constituted the neoliberal
creed as it pertains to regulation of the economy in the US.[1] After all, to understand how the US government tackled the complexities and challenges of
a rapidly financializing economy, we must first have a "firm grip," as Polanyi
emphasized, on the foundational ideas and assumptions driving policy
decisions.

When the neoliberal turn is discussed in terms of its ideational content—
what Stephanie Mudge[2] calls its "intellectual face"—it is often Friedrich
Hayek, Milton Friedman, the Mont Pelerin Society, and its fraternal think
tanks that get mentioned as the intellectual forces propelling the shift toward
"the market." While it is not inaccurate to speak of neoliberalism broadly
as a Hayekian or Friedmanite intellectual movement, focusing singularly
on these figures as the prophet and the high priest of neoliberalism can ob-
scure the specific programmatic ideas that shaped policy on the ground and
the intellectual agents behind them, who as Quinn Slobodian argues, got
their hands dirty "advising business, pressuring governments, drawing up
charts, and gathering statistics."[3] Furthermore, such an approach depicts "the
market" being turned to as a conveniently abstract concept, disconnected

Disembedded. Basak Kus, Oxford University Press. © Oxford University Press 2024.
DOI: 10.1093/oso/9780197764862.003.0002

from time or place, rather than a living and breathing structure that has material, political, and cultural coordinates.[4]

What constituted, then, the neoliberal perspective with regard to regulation, and who were the actors behind these ideas? I maintain that the neoliberal creed involved, on the one hand, a multifaceted critique of direct and substantive government regulation, and on the other hand, an endorsement of private regulation based on the principles of market discipline and actor rationality. The former gained momentum in the 1970s, when a new set of economic theories scrutinized the shortcomings of government regulation, raising concerns about regulatory capture, rent-seeking, and the limitations of bureaucracy as a government technique. Collectively, these theories—whose proponents often occupied the highest echelons of government during the 1970s and 1980s—eroded the legitimacy of the idea that the state is responsible for and good at regulation. In the 1990s, two further intellectual currents significantly influenced the government's regulatory approach vis-à-vis the economy. First, financial economics, an increasingly powerful subfield in an already prominent field, provided a further intellectual arsenal that undermined the rationale for government regulation. Secondly, the New Public Management (NPM) approach to governance started to shape how leading policymakers perceived government functions. NPM proposed a transformative vision for government where bureaucrats were seen as service providers, citizens took on the role of consumers, and the public sector sought improvement by mirroring the practices of the private sector. In an evolving economic landscape, as the economy was rapidly financializing, the state's regulatory role was shaped at the intersection of these ideational forces.

The Rise of the Economic Theories of Regulation in the 1970s and 1980s

While American political discourse has long been characterized by an anxiety over excessive state power, the extent and nature of this concern have fluctuated depending on both domestic and international circumstances. As Jodi Short notes, the 1970s marked a period of notable intensification of these concerns, after several decades of New Deal administrative state expansion on the one hand, and the Cold War-fueled fear of communism, on the other.[5] It was within this context that critiques of direct and substantive

28 DISEMBEDDED

government regulation—what would come to form the "intellectual basis for late-twentieth-century regulatory reform"[6]—began to flourish, primarily within the field of economics. Economics was not just any discipline, of course, in terms of its relation to the corridors of political power.[7] Although economists always had a seat at the table dating back to early twentieth century, in terms of policymaking, both the degree and the breadth of their influence had gradually expanded over time.[8] By the time the "suspicion of government action grew markedly" in economics in the 1970s, as Marion Fourcade et al. put it, the field had already garnered a level of legitimacy and power that was quite unmatched.[9] Economists were considered experts par excellence on questions of policy, and were increasingly recruited for the country's top policymaking jobs, thus gaining the ability to shape the contours of state–economy relationship.

In the interplay between economics and policymaking—or state-making more broadly—the issue was not just the increasing sway of economics, but also about the nature of that influence—the type of economic ideas rising to the fore, their influence on policies, and the potential impact of this influence on state functions. As Elizabeth Berman explains, the economists who shaped policy debates in the final quarter of the twentieth century, including those of regulatory policy, were trained in a "microeconomic style of reasoning" and understood economics "as the science of rational decision-making."[10] They applied microeconomic theories and tools to a broad set of policy questions, including that of regulation, and in doing so, played an important role in terms of expanding the reach and influence of the field.[11] It is in their hands, as Berman articulates, that "efficiency, incentives, choice, and competition" supplanted or even marginalized other goals based on values such as "rights, universalism, equity, and limiting corporate power."[12] The rise of what is broadly referred to as "economic theories of regulation," which significantly shaped the institutional terrain of financialization in the US, was part and parcel of this transformation.

Regulatory Capture

One of the key economic theories of government regulation that became prominent in the 1970s was regulatory capture, most notably associated with George Stigler: the idea that "as a rule, regulation is acquired by the industry, and is designed and operated primarily for its benefit."[13] Stigler posited that this phenomenon was influenced by a few key factors. First, industries capitalized on information asymmetry, leveraging their in-depth understanding of their own operations compared to that of regulators. Second, their financial motivations drove them to shape regulations to their advantage. Later, Sam Peltzman, another Chicago School economist who had previously served as the senior staff economist on the President Nixon's Council of Economic Advisors, expanded on and refined Stigler's analysis in his 1976 paper, "Toward a More General Theory of Regulation."[14] Peltzman, like Stigler, challenged the notion that regulatory measures primarily served to protect consumers. He argued that regulators, in seeking to maximize political support from both producers and consumers, formulated policies that balanced these interests, resulting in partial protection for both groups. Gary Becker, another Chicago economist, also made significant contributions to the development of capture theory. He argued that when groups compete for political influence, the balance of political power is determined by factors such as their efficiency in exerting pressure, the size of the group, and the societal costs of the policies they advocate for.[15] In other words, what shaped regulatory policies, according to Becker, was the competition among interest groups in the political arena rather than considerations of consumer or public welfare. Friedman, perhaps the most renowned of all Chicago School economists and later a member of Ronald Reagan's Economic Policy Advisory Board, also echoed the central tenet of capture theory in various public appearances.[16] This idea also came up in *Free to Choose*, a popular book he co-authored with Rose Friedman, arguing that regulatory agencies "will almost always be overpowered by the groups that have already demonstrated a greater capacity to take advantage of available opportunities."[17]

It is worth noting that, although Stigler's 1971 paper "The Theory of Economic Regulation" is often credited as the most influential articulation of regulatory capture, the concept predated Stigler's work. Before achieving broad recognition within the economic discourse during the 1970s, the idea that regulation could be subverted to favor the entities it was supposed to oversee, rather than the public interest, had been proposed by political scientists in the early postwar period.[18] For example, in a 1952 article, Samuel Huntington posited that the Interstate Commerce Commission (ICC), established in 1887 to supervise railroads, gradually became reliant upon, and subsequently overly accommodating to, the railroad industry's interests.[19] Similarly, in 1955, Marver Bernstein offered an even more extensive analysis

30 DISEMBEDDED

of capture in his book on independent regulatory commissions where he argued that in the later years of a regulatory agency's life, administrators tend to rely on the industry under regulation itself to understand what needs to be regulated and how.[20] According to Bernstein, independence was not a solution to this issue; in fact, he warned that a lack of involvement from the executive branch could make the agency even more susceptible to industry influence.[21] In the 1960s, the argument about industry dependence was taken up also by left-wing historians, most notably Gabriel Golko, who argued that regulatory reform initiatives of the Progressive era, often portrayed as manifestations of public interest, were actually orchestrated by the very industries they were meant to regulate and were "directed towards ends they deemed acceptable or desirable."[22] Another historian, James Weinstein, similarly argued in his 1968 book that the Progressive era regulatory reforms were primarily "the product, consciously created, of the leaders of the giant corporations and financial institutions, and American liberalism should not be portrayed as a progressive attempt to restrain business power."[23]

Even within the field of economics, the thesis of regulatory capture was not entirely brand new when Stigler published his renowned paper. For instance, in 1965, Paul W. MacAvoy, an economist who would later contribute to both the Council of Economic Advisors and the President's Task Force on Regulatory Reform during the Ford administration, authored a book on the ICC, in which he argued that regulations were antithetical to public benefit, and actually served the interests of the cartel.[24] What is it, then, that led to Stigler's 1971 analysis gaining such immense traction? I contend that this was mainly for two reasons. One, the paper succeeded at expertly interweaving "political behavior with the larger body of economic analysis" at a time when economics as a discipline became the major influencer of policy ideas.[25] And two, during the 1970s, after years of state expansion and in the face of various economic challenges, both academic and policy circles were increasingly receptive to theories critical of government. The Center for the Study of the Economy and the State at the University of Chicago, founded by Stigler himself in 1977, was in fact at the forefront of this intellectual shift.[26] In the decade succeeding Stigler's initial formulation, the regulatory capture thesis effectively promoted the idea, both within economics and beyond, that direct and comprehensive government regulation would ultimately fail to safeguard public interest and protect consumers from the myriad risks inherent in market processes.

Regulation as a Source of Rent-Seeking

The late 1970s and 1980s witnessed the rise of another critique against direct and comprehensive government regulation—the idea of regulation as a source of rent-seeking, within the work of economists like James Buchanan, Gordon Tullock, and Anne Krueger. Buchanan, initially at the University of Virginia and later at George Mason University pioneered, together with Tullock, the development of what is known today as "public choice theory."[27] They described this theory as "the extension and application of the tools and methods of economics to the subject matter of political science."[28] In other words, they set out to explain how individuals, acting as voters, representatives, legislators, bureaucrats, or political agents behave within the institutions where they undertake these roles.[29]

Rent-seeking theorists essentially embraced the main premise of the regulatory capture thesis, that business groups would succeed at getting regulatory agencies to do their bidding given that political agents working in these regulatory agencies act to maximize their own self-interests, like everyone else, rather than working toward public interest. However, for these theorists, the problem with regulation was not just confined to this. They argued that the resources businesses invest to secure favorable regulatory outcomes represented "a diversion of value from consumers generally to the favored rent-seeker, with a net loss of value in the process."[30] More explicitly, resources devoted to rent-seeking—that is, for advocating in favor of regulations favorable to a particular business or industry—could be better spent on more productive activities. In Tullock's articulation, the issue wasn't with the notion of "rent" itself, which he considered "a perfectly good economic category," but about "bad rent-seeking," which was a waste of resources.[31] Buchanan, in a similar vein, drew a parallel between the rents secured and the "royal monopoly privilege" of bygone eras.[32] This very concern was also at the heart of Krueger's analysis. By studying data from India and Turkey, she demonstrated that government regulation could create rents that constituted a significant percentage of national income in both countries.[33]

Limitations of Bureaucracy as a Technique of Government

A third critique of direct and substantive regulation emerging from the field of economics dealt with the inherent limitations of regulatory bureaucracies,

32 DISEMBEDDED

and more broadly, the bureaucracy as a technique of government. William Niskanen, a Chicago-educated economist and a protégé of Friedman who later served as acting chairman on President Reagan's Council of Economic Advisors, proposed a critique reminiscent of the argument Ludwig von Mises put forward in the 1940s—namely that, while in the capitalist system, "consumers are the sovereign people," and "profit and loss are the instruments by means of which the consumers keep a tight rein on all business activities," and that bureaucracy "destroys initiative and the incentive to do more than the minimum required."[34] In this vein, Niskanen argued that regulatory agencies lacked the incentive to excel at their assigned tasks, which included mitigating risks to consumers, the broader public, or other producers. His reasoning was that "the bureau 'sells' its service only to the government, and the government 'buys' the service only from the bureau."[35] This relationship, according to Niskanen, diminished the motivation for regulatory bodies to strive for optimal performance.

In short, throughout the 1970s and 1980s economists produced a set of regulatory theories that consistently chipped at the legitimacy of government regulation. While these perspectives varied in their specific arguments—be it the danger of regulatory capture, the phenomenon of rent-seeking, or the inherent limitations of bureaucratic governance—all shared a common theme: they portrayed direct and substantial government regulation as problematic. Over time, the influence of their ideas rose substantially (see Figure 2.1).

Regulatory Perspectives in the 1990s

The 1990s saw the ascending influence of NPM theory and financial economics. Drawing heavily from public choice theory[36] for its disapproval of bureaucracy, NPM advocated for making government "less bureaucratic and more entrepreneurial."[37] The prevailing organizational structure characterized by large, centralized bureaucracies with "elaborate rules and regulations and hierarchical chains of command" was seen as a relic of the industrial era, unsuitable for the contemporary world.[38] As Mark Bevir elucidates, NPM reimagined government agencies as private businesses, public officials as "managers or service providers," and citizens as "consumers or service-users."[39] Under this model, governments had to focus on making money just as much as spending money; they had to be mission-driven rather

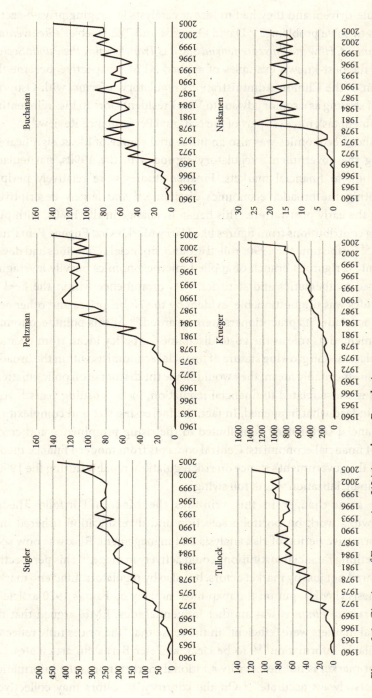

Figure 2.1 Citations of Economists Writing about Regulation

34   DISEMBEDDED

than rule-driven, and they had to "act as catalysts leveraging private-sector actions to solve problems."[40] David Osborne and Ted Gaebler's *Reinventing Government: How the Entrepreneurial Spirit is Transforming the Public Sector*, one of the best-known examples of applied NPM perspective, became the eponym of the Clinton Administration's regulatory reforms, with Osborne himself serving as a senior advisor to Vice President Gore in his "reinventing government task force" as part of the National Performance Review.[41]

Financial economics was also an influential source of ideas, significantly shaping the government's regulatory approach in the 1990s, particularly in relation to financial markets. Finance studies were relatively peripheral within the broader economics discipline,[42] and largely descriptive[43] during the early postwar era. This began to change in the 1960s, with pioneering contributions from figures like Harry Markowitz, Eugene Fama, and others.[44] By the time the 1990s rolled around, financial economics had developed into a rigorous branch of applied microeconomics heavily leveraging advanced mathematics and statistics.[45] Its prominence within the field of economics was unquestionable, evident by the Nobel prizes and other academic accolades its practitioners were awarded.[46] At this point, economics had cemented its role as the go-to discipline for policy ideas, from taxation to regulation. The growing stature of financial economists within the broader discipline inevitably meant they would shape the discourse on policy matters, including those related to financial regulation, in the ensuing years.[47] And that is indeed what happened. In fact, the increasing size and complexity of the financial sector itself contributed to the rising prominence and credibility of financial economists. Central concepts from modern finance theory shaped the government's stance on risk regulation, notably during the 1990s, when financialization was in full swing.

One game-changer in this vein was the Modern Portfolio Theory. Markowitz's work on portfolio selection and diversification ushered in a transformative period of risk analysis and management. Risk was now seen as something financial institutions could actively manage.[48] This perspective was shared not just by market actors, but also by regulators. Efficient-market hypothesis (EMH), put on the map most notably by Fama's 1970 article in the *Journal of Finance*, was another influential idea. EMH argued that the financial markets were "efficient" in the sense that "the prices fully reflected all available information."[49] To be clear, as Peter Bernstein articulates, "an efficient market is not necessarily a rational market, nor is the information it reflects always accurate."[50] On the contrary, investors may collectively overvalue or undervalue prices. In circumstances like this, sooner or later, the theory holds, the market adjusts the prices; however, it remains in an efficient market that "no single investor has much chance, beyond luck, of consistently outguessing all the other participants."[51] As Binyamin Appelbaum articulates, what this meant in practice was that "markets were stable and self-correcting, and that substantive and direct regulation served little purpose."[52] By the time the financial crisis started, Fama already had over thirty thousand citations (see Figure 2.2).

As pointed out by Ronald Gilson and Reinier Kraakman, when an academic theory transitions into the domain of policymaking, it inevitably finds itself within the political sphere, and is reworked to support certain political arguments.[53] Modern finance theory was no exception. EMH "expanded from a narrow but important academic theory about the informational underpinnings of market prices to a broad ideological preference for market outcomes over even measured regulation."[54] It provided the scientific justification for the idea that private investors could effectively oversee and sway corporate conduct, that "governments did not need to write new rules for emerging areas of financial activity."[55] In fact, financial regulators being "openly contemptuous of financial regulation" in the period leading to the financial crisis and believing that market participants would "police misconduct and maintain financial stability"—the essence of market discipline (MD) as a risk regulation framework—was in great part the impact

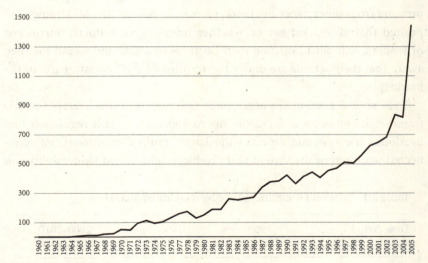

Figure 2.2 Citations of Eugene Fama

36 DISEMBEDDED

of modern finance theory.[56] The increasing size and complexity of financial institutions made these institutions challenging to supervise and regulate using conventional tools, as Robert Bliss and Mark Flannery explain, and amid an atmosphere of optimism fueled by robust growth and profitability, the idea of market discipline as a mode of risk regulation seemed especially enticing to regulators (see Table 2.1 for evidence of the increasing appearance of "market discipline" in news coverage).[57]

To elucidate further, MD, as a regulatory framework, held that market participants, being rational, would monitor one another's conduct, and adjust their expectations and conduct based on the information available to them, and rein in excessive risk-taking behavior. Private investors' assessments of the information they obtain, for instance, would be incorporated in the firm's security prices, or in the case of deposit-taking institutions, investors would be "withdrawing funds and/or demanding higher rates of return" upon finding out that their bank has taken on higher levels of risk.[58] When these things happen, not only would firms themselves see how the market reacts to their behavior, but also regulators would be alerted to such elevated risk, and would take regulatory action "before that risk manifested itself into insolvency."[59] These mechanisms are known as "market monitoring" and "market influence." Market monitoring refers to the idea that "investors accurately evaluate changes in a firm's condition and incorporate those assessments promptly into the firm's security prices."[60] The latter mechanism, "market influence," refers to the process by which the firm changes its actions due to pressure from supervisors and market forces. In essence, the MD framework posited that all market actors, whether investors, consumers, borrowers, or lenders, will opt to operate their business in a safe and sound manner, aware that their actions are under the scrutiny of their counterparts in the marketplace.[61]

To be sure, the rationality assumption that remains at the heart of the MD framework embodies a decidedly micro approach to risk regulation that overlooks the systemic aspects—the larger, multi-dimensional, interconnected workings of the system that produces failures and vulnerabilities. It

Table 2.1 "Market Discipline" in the News (United States)

Time Period	1980–1990	1990–2000	2000–2010
Number of Mentions	427	1449	4698

Source: LexisNexis search for "market discipline" in English-language news in the US.

implies that government involvement is unnecessary. If firms can be trusted to protect "their own shareholders and their equity in the firm," as Alan Greenspan once noted,[62] and if consumers/investors are capable of shielding themselves from predatory transactions and junk/toxic products, whether they be mortgages or cosmetics, then with the exception of providing "some measure of paternalism" reserved for the members of society who are incapable of protecting themselves,[63] the government is not required to assume the responsibility of mitigating and protecting against risks.

It is vital to understand that in the realm of consumer protection, relying on market discipline and the foundational assumption of actors' rationality as a regulatory mechanism also carries an inherent moral stance on personal responsibility. The premise is not only that consumers *can* take care of their own affairs without meddling Washington bureaucrats, but also that they *should*. Conceptualizing risk at the individual level reallocates the responsibility of risk regulation from government to self-regulating individuals.[64] Self-auditing, risk-managing rational entities, whether handling risks associated with purchasing a beauty product or a mortgage, are disciplined actors in "the age of responsibility."[65] For this mechanism to function properly, market participants need access to timely and precise information. And that is precisely what made disclosures and other forms of information provision in the marketplace important, as I will discuss in detail in later chapters.

Conclusion

To comprehend how and why the state regulated finance in a particular manner, it is imperative to first recognize the ideas that have influenced government policy since the early 1970s and the individuals who advocated for them. This chapter underscored the pivotal role economists have assumed in shaping the trajectory of the American regulatory state. Pushing back against broad generalizations about the neoliberal pivot in regulation, it identified distinct ideas emerging from diverse schools of thought in economics, ranging from regulatory capture and rent-seeking to criticisms of bureaucracy and the influence of financial economics.

In the next two chapters I will discuss the political ascent of these ideas under successive administrations, and the specific policies and institutional changes they have inspired. To reiterate what I have said early on, my goal here is to destabilize the now-established narrative that neoliberalism,

38   DISEMBEDDED

broadly depicted as a Hayekian turn to the market, led the American government to deregulate the economy beginning with the Reagan administration, as a result of which financial institutions were able to run amok for several decades until the economy crashed. As I will argue in the next chapter, the shift in the state's thinking about regulation preceded Reagan, and the policy tools and institutional changes that this shift inspired was by no means limited to deregulation. It is only by looking at the neoliberalism–state–finance relationship through a more far-reaching lens that we can begin to understand what was disembedded about finance, in a Polanyian sense, in the decades leading to the crisis.

3

The Political Ascent of the New Creed

Although it is commonly believed that it is with the Reagan administration that the neoliberal creed began to find reception in the corridors of government, these ideas had already started their political journey before Reagan assumed office. In fact, it was during the early 1970s when economic pressures and inflation were escalating that a new political willingness emerged across the political spectrum, from both Republicans and Democrats, to reconsider the objectives, tools, and reach—that is, the *what*, *how*, and *why* of regulation. Ideas critical of direct and substantive risk regulation, which I discussed in the previous chapter, started gaining political ground in this context. This culminated in a regulatory reform movement that brought together "historically pro-regulation congressional liberals, free-market economists, various corporate lobbies and individual businesses, and public interest groups."[1] This was a coalition of strange bedfellows largely concerned with cost-saving and inflation reduction, and its fundamental premise was that regulation was only beneficial if the prospective benefits outweighed the potential costs.

In 1971, President Richard Nixon set up the Quality-of-Life Review Program under the Office of Management and Budget (OMB). This was to centralize and streamline the review of regulatory agencies and to make them cognizant of the burden their regulations placed on the industry. A significant driving force behind it was the new Environmental Protection Agency (EPA), whose establishment had already sparked industry-wide concerns about the cost of regulations.[2]

This pragmatically critical approach to government regulation continued under the Ford administration. As part of its strategy to combat inflation, the administration consciously employed a cost–benefit approach requiring regulatory agencies to prepare reports weighing the benefits of regulations against their inflationary impact. By the time Carter assumed office, economic theories of regulation, and more broadly, what Elizabeth Berman describes as the "microeconomic style of reasoning," had already penetrated the political realm, offering policymakers a new lexicon and rationale regarding a wide range of government affairs.

Disembedded. Basak Kus, Oxford University Press. © Oxford University Press 2024.
DOI: 10.1093/oso/9780197764862.003.0003

40   DISEMBEDDED

Under the Reagan administration a full-on critique of government regulation as interference in markets and private decision-making began to take hold. While Ronald Reagan's term wasn't the first to scrutinize government regulation or to acknowledge economic theories of regulation politically, it was during his presidency that these notions were integrated more systematically into a philosophy of government. While during the Ford and Carter administrations, government regulation was met with pragmatic skepticism, at the end of the day, it was still largely seen as a solution, as something in the public's interest, only to be trimmed or modified as necessary when its cost to the economy outweighed its benefit to the public. The Reagan administration, on the other hand, saw government regulation not as a solution but as an inherent problem, and as something that would best be largely dismantled. Dismantling the regulatory state would prove to be a formidable challenge, however, as Reagan soon found, especially during a period when the financial system was in tatters with a significant number of bank failures. Nonetheless, his administration effectively shifted the conversation and perception around government regulation, going beyond just cost-cutting.

In the 1990s, the Clinton administration adopted the tenets of New Public Management (NPM) to reshape government in the image of a private enterprise. This led to a rather more skeptical stance toward regulatory agencies. Concurrently, the discipline of financial economics, which had attained considerable prominence by this time, as discussed earlier, found political resonance within the administration, lending credence to the viability of private regulation in financial markets. The American economy's rapid financialization in the 1980s, and especially in the 1990s, which saw the proliferation of new financial products and services, unfolded against this backdrop.

Substantive Regulation Comes Under Scrutiny: Ford and Carter Administrations

Shortly after President Gerald Ford assumed office in 1974, he convened a summit with industry leaders and economists. The main objective was to address the nation's pressing economic issues, most notably inflation, which was hovering around 11 percent at the time. Following this summit, a new government agency, the Council on Wage and Price Stability (CWPS), was created.[3] Ford's aspiration to tackle inflation resonated with prevalent economic criticisms of government regulation. The CWPS, predominantly staffed by economists, was tasked with reviewing the rulemaking of regulatory agencies for potential contributions to inflation. In an address to a joint session of Congress a few months later, Ford stated that his administration would require all major legislative proposals, rules, and regulations to be assessed for their inflationary impact. He asked Congress to establish a national commission to undertake a long-overdue total re-examination of independent regulatory agencies, with the goal of eliminating "federal rules and regulations that increase costs to the consumer without any good reason."[4] The year next, in 1975, Ford held a meeting with the members of ten independent regulatory commissions, and asked them to focus on: "(1) measuring and considering the costs and benefits of proposed regulations; (2) reducing the backlog and delays in regulatory proceedings; (3) suggesting changes in the legislation under which each regulatory commission operates, including deregulation where appropriate; and (4) assuring that the consumers' interests prevail in regulatory proceedings."[5] The Executive Order 11821 was issued subsequently, formally requiring government agencies to prepare inflation impact statements before they issued costly new regulations. In the same year, yet another advisory group—the Domestic Council Review Group on Regulatory Reform (DCRG)—was created, also heavily staffed by economists. The DCRG, chaired by Paul McAvoy, known for writing extensively on regulatory capture, met weekly at the White House to assess the impact of regulations on the economy, consumer prices, and inflation. In addition, another economist well-known for his staunch criticism of government regulation, Alan Greenspan, led Ford's Council of Economic Advisors.[6]

According to President Ford, a healthy economy meant "freedom from the petty tyranny of massive government regulation."[7] In his remarks to the National Federation of Independent Business, Ford argued that "Although most of today's regulations affecting business are well-intentioned, their effect—whether designed to protect the environment or the consumer—often does more harm than good. They can stifle the growth in our standard of living and contribute to inflation."[8] Explicitly embracing a cost–benefit approach to regulation, he continued:

> Obviously, we cannot eliminate all regulations. Some are costly but essential to public health and public safety. But let us evaluate the costs as well as the benefits. The issue is not whether we want to control pollution. We all do. The question is whether added costs to the public make sense

42 DISEMBEDDED

when measured against actual benefits. As a consumer, I want to know how much the tab at the front-door checkout counter is raised through the back door of regulatory inflation. As President, I want to eliminate unnecessary regulations which impose a hidden tax on the consumer.[9]

The financial sector was not immune to this increasingly critical perspective on regulation. The House Committee on Banking, Currency, and Housing commissioned an investigation called the Financial Institutions in the Nation's Economy Study (FINE), led by Congressman Fernand J. St Germain, to examine the ways in which the regulation of depository and non-bank institutions, and the operations of the Federal Reserve, could be reformed. The hearings lasted weeks. As pointed out by economist James Pierce, who served as a consultant to the study, the committee received testimonies from a diverse array of ninety-six witnesses, which included consumers, scholars, business representatives, government agency officials, and financial firm representatives.[10] In light of the findings, the Financial Reform Act of 1976 (FRA) was drafted. Early in the FINE hearings, Chairman St Germain noted that "artificial and outmoded constraints which have served to inhibit capital formation required of a flourishing economy must be dealt with comprehensively if the credit needs of this nation—private individuals, governments, and businesses—are to be met."[11] A common theme of the hearings was the necessity to break away from restrictive financial regulations stemming from the Great Depression. "Blind allegiance to the concepts and maxims of times past should not be permitted to stand in the way of today's needs," argued Thomas Kauper, assistant attorney general for the Department of Justice Antitrust Division, adding that "many of the existing limitations on financial institutions should be altered or eliminated" in order to increase reliance "on competition in a free marketplace, and less on direct government regulation."[12] Pierce echoed these statements. Although financial markets have changed substantially since the 1930s, and "we now live in a world of highly integrated money and capital markets that bring ultimate borrowers and lenders together in many efficient and elegant ways," he argued, "the federal statutes and regulations that specify the rules of the game for the participants in financial markets have not kept pace with the financial revolution" and "are still grounded in the New Deal legislation of the 1930s."[13] Milton Friedman testified specifically about Regulation Q, a 1930s regulation that restricted how banks could pay interest on deposit accounts, arguing that the measure was "traumatic in terms of the composition of the deposits of commercial banks" and that previously there had "never been any legal prohibition on the payment of interest on demand deposits."[14] Ultimately, FRA did not pass. However, by the end of Ford's term, the idea that regulations concerning the financial sector had to be rolled back had achieved bipartisan traction.[15]

Jimmy Carter's presidency continued the anti-statist sentiment that had begun to take root in the preceding term. On the economic front, the challenges had aggravated. The oil shock of 1978–1979 on the one hand, and stagnant economic growth accompanied by high inflation on the other, compelled the Carter administration to rethink the role of government in the economy. The influence of economists and the micro-economic approach to policymaking began to expand in this context. As Binyamin Appelbaum points out, by the mid-1970s, over half the seats on every federal regulatory commission were filled by lawyers, while economists held almost no positions.[16] As economists took on more of the positions, cost and efficiency became the guidelines for policy.[17]

The Carter administration's regulatory reform program had three major elements: "deregulation legislation, regulatory procedural reform legislation, and improved presidential supervision and control of the regulatory agencies."[18] The president appointed former economics professor and Brookings Fellow Charles Schultze to chair the Council of Economic Advisors. Before his appointment as Chairman of the Council of Economic Advisers (CEA), Schultze had authored a book, *The Public Use of Private Interest*, in which he made a case against the command-and-control approach. Instead, he contended that regulations should work through incentives for the private market "so that public goals become private interests."[19] Under Schultze's leadership, the CEA set out to undertake a broad review of regulatory agencies. Another economist who had a key role in the Carter administration and who remained critical of direct and substantive regulation was the President's advisor on inflation—"inflation czar," he was called—Alfred Kahn, the author of *The Economics of Regulation: Principles and Institutions*. Khan, like Schultze, believed the government's regulatory reach needed to be curbed. When asked about his opinions about regulation, whom they served and benefited, Kahn responded, "if you look back historically you see that the prime proponents were the industries themselves and their unions . . . . it's the people who got the monopoly privilege and protections."[20] At this point in time, the costs of regulation to the economy were being widely and explicitly discussed. Regulation and inflation were linked in policy discourse, almost as if there

44 DISEMBEDDED

was an indisputable cause-and-effect relationship between them. Pursuing deregulatory policies, for Kahn, was an anti-inflationary strategy.

In 1978, Carter announced "a new top-level review process" to reduce "government regulation that drives up costs and drives up prices."[21] Later that year, he reiterated that controlling government deficits and spending would not suffice; instead, "we must also control the costs of government regulations," and cut "the regulatory thicket that has grown up around us" to give "our competitive free enterprise system a chance to grow up in its place."[22] With this goal, he established the Regulatory Analysis Review Group (RARG) and issued the Executive Order 12044, titled "Improving Government Regulations," requiring agencies to analyze the economic impact of government regulations and identify alternatives.

Carter's final two years in office were infused with mounting pressure from the business community to cut regulation. As inflation persisted, the cost–benefit perspective had become the center of the administration's thinking about regulation. However, it should be noted that the cost of regulation to business was conceived in broader terms than just its inflationary pressures on the economy. In 1979, Arthur Andersen published the "Cost of Government Regulation Study," a report commissioned by the Business Roundtable using data from forty-eight of the Roundtable's member companies.[23] The report argued that the participating companies "incurred $2.6 billion in regulation-induced incremental costs in 1977."[24] The same year, Chase Manhattan took out a full-page advertisement in *The Washington Post* informing the public that regulations cost businesses more than $100 billion per year.[25] The American Enterprise Institute's Governmental Regulation Program, directed by economists James C. Miller and Murray Weidenbaum, who later served as President Reagan's director of the OMB and chair of the CEA, respectively, also joined the chorus. They argued that federal regulations not only increased inflation but also reduced economic growth.

The business sector was not alone in pushing for regulatory reform. Intellectuals and politicians on both the left and right sides of the ideological spectrum also voiced critical views regarding direct and substantive government regulation.[26] Consumer advocate Ralph Nader spoke out for deregulation, and Senator Ted Kennedy, a powerful Democrat, called for "a new pragmatism in regulation."[27] It is important to note, however, that these calls for deregulation from the left side of the political aisle targeted regulations that appeared to favor established corporate interests over those of consumers and the broader public. In other words, as Monica Prasad puts it, it was "a populist issue rather than a pro-market one."[28]

What did all this mean for financial regulations? By the end of the 1970s, the idea that Great Depression regulations, which had been put in place to curb the risks in financial markets, no longer served the American people's interests had gained steam. For instance, in May 1979, when Carter urged Congress to reform the financial system to reduce regulations that were hurting ordinary Americans, his target was the rate ceilings, in particular, which he believed were "increasingly unfair to the small saver":[29]

> I am asking that the Congress permit an orderly transition to a system where the average depositor can receive market-level interest rates on his or her savings. I am also proposing measures to protect the long-term viability of savings institutions so that they can pay fair and competitive rates to depositors and continue their traditional role in meeting our nation's housing needs.[30]

His administration successfully eliminated rate ceilings and, like the Ford administration before it, laid the groundwork for a broader transformation of the state's role in regulating and managing economic risks. However, it's important to note that at this time, although the costs of regulatory actions were openly questioned and theories about regulatory capture gained traction in government circles, the political tide against regulation had not yet gone fully critical. Both the Ford and Carter administrations, like the Nixon administration before them, approached regulatory reform in a pragmatic way, as a matter of a sensible government strategy to deal with the economic challenges they were facing at the time. It wasn't until the Reagan administration that a more comprehensive critique of government regulation emerged, based on a fundamentally different view of the government's role and purpose. Reagan unapologetically embraced the idea that "most economic and social regulation was an unwarranted intrusion of the federal government into private decision-making."[31]

From a Pragmatic Critique to a Systematic Rejection: Reagan Administration

Regulatory reform was one of the four pillars for Reagan's economic growth program, along with reducing overnment spending, tax cuts, and steady monetary growth.[32] It involved increasing presidential oversight of regulatory matters, decreasing the power and discretion of federal regulators and

46 DISEMBEDDED

transferring some of their authority to the states, freezing or rescinding pending regulations, and overall, making "the regulatory process more cooperative and less combative."[33]

On his first day in office, President Reagan created a Task Force on Regulatory Relief with Vice President George Bush as chair, remarking that "government regulations impose an enormous burden on large and small businesses in America, discourage productivity, and contribute substantially to our current economic woes."[34] Shortly after, he issued Executive Order 12291 to ensure that no regulatory action would be undertaken "unless the potential benefits to society from the regulation outweigh the potential costs to society."[35] The 1982 Economic Report of the President similarly argued that the "the government [had] spun a vast web of regulations that intrude into almost every aspect of every American's working day," and that these regulations "adversely affect[ed] the productivity of our nation's businesses, farms, educational institutions, state and local governments, and the operations of the federal government itself."[36] The result, the report maintained, is a lessened productivity growth that "increases the costs of the goods and services we buy from each other," ultimately raising "the cost of government at all levels and the taxes we pay to support it."[37] In the report, the Reagan administration continued endorsing a cost–benefit approach and advocated for curbs on regulation, with the understanding that such analysis "is only the second-best solution," and "that the best solution is to respect the judgment of the private market whenever it is available."[38] The idea that risk regulation can be tackled by and is the responsibility of individuals, whether they are firms or households, was also in the report. In fact, a notable emphasis on "personal responsibility" was evident in the section outlining the principles guiding the president's economic program. According to the report, programs like safety regulations stemmed from the government's reluctance "to let individuals make decisions for themselves" and were "paternalistic."[39] The report contended that such paternalism was unwarranted—not only does the government not necessarily do "a better job of increasing an individual's economic welfare than the individual can by making choices himself," it argued, but also "the long-term costs of paternalism may be to destroy an individual's ability to make decisions for himself."[40]

The Reagan administration's aspiration to loosen the regulatory grip of the government extended to the financial sector. In 1982, as he signed the St Germain Depository Institutions Act, Reagan noted that the legislation "represents the first step in our administration's comprehensive program of

THE POLITICAL ASCENT OF THE NEW CREED   47

financial deregulation."[41] It is during this time that the idea of market discipline began to gain political currency as a mode of risk regulation in financial markets. In 1981, Reagan named William M. Isaac the Chairman of FDIC. Isaac was a firm believer in the power of market discipline as a risk regulation mechanism in financial markets. In an article he wrote in 1983, Isaac had argued:

> Inexorably, the statutory and regulatory fetters are being loosened, and banks and other depository institutions are taking on new roles and providing new services. The day of the "financial supermarket" is approaching . . . But such drastic changes in our financial system result in a critically important set of considerations: Without government-imposed restrictions on competition, how do we control excessive risk-taking and destructive competitive behavior by financial institutions? . . . . There are two options. We can adopt countless new laws and regulations to govern every aspect of bank and savings-and-loan operations and hire thousands of additional examiners to monitor and enforce compliance. Or, we can substitute increased marketplace discipline.[42]

Industry publications began to tackle the issue at this time, as well. In an article he published in *The American Banker* in 1983, James Treadway Jr.—a commissioner of the SEC—remarked on "an apparently emerging preference, at least on the part of some banking regulators, for more regulation by 'market discipline.'"[43] Another article published in *United States Banker* by a former Senate staffer and banking attorney called market discipline "the new buzzword in the world of banking regulation," and noted that "market discipline and increased disclosure, its cornerstone, [were] threatening to become a regulatory theology."[44]

It is important to understand that at this point market discipline as a mode of risk regulation was not exactly embraced by all corners of the financial sector. In fact, many proposals associated with it—such as decreasing the level of deposit insurance coverage and the potential liability of the FDIC—faced opposition from significant segments of the financial industry. For small and independent banks especially, the reduction of deposit insurance looked like the disappearance of a safety net, a much-needed risk insurance. In any case, winds turned against market discipline rather quickly, partly due to the thrift and bank failures that became paramount (see Figure 3.1).[45]

48 DISEMBEDDED

Figure 3.1 Bank and Thrift Failures

Federal Deposit Insurance Corporation. "Failures of all Institutions for the United States and Other Areas," FRED, Federal Reserve Bank of St. Louis. https://fred.stlouisfed.org/series/BKFTTLA641N.

In his testimony to the US Senate Committee on Banking, Housing and Urban Affairs, in 1985, Federal Reserve Chairman Paul Volcker remarked, rather dismissively:

> Our financial history demonstrates unambiguously the dangers of relying on market discipline alone. Before the 1930s, market discipline did not prevent bank failures or systematically discourage excessive risk-taking—until after periodic crises had occurred, at great expense to the economy generally.[46]

An article published in *The American Banker* at the end of 1985 noted that market discipline was "no longer fashionable argot in bank regulation," and that instead "Washington [was] buzzing with talk of how government intervention can keep more banks alive."[47] Another article, also published in *The American Banker*, spoke of the return of "increased supervision, examination, and regulation," evident "in higher capital requirements, increased frequency of examinations, and the reluctance of the agencies to grant new powers."[48] In this context, the Reagan administration, despite all its anti-statist posturing, had to curb its enthusiasm for market discipline for a while. Thousands of financial institutions had failed and were still failing, Democrats had gained the majority in both Chambers of Congress in the 1986 elections; it was simply not the time for it.

In 1987, Greenspan was named chairman of the Federal Reserve Board, and Wendy Gramm, Reagan's "favorite economist,"[49] was nominated to lead the Commodity Futures Trading Commission (CFTC). Both economists were known for their views against substantive government regulation in the economy. Gramm, holding the view that "regulations stifle growth," attempted to limit the CFTC's regulation of the growing derivatives market.[50]

In 1988, Reagan established the President's Working Group on Financial Markets, which was composed of the secretary of the Treasury and the chairs of the Federal Reserve, the SEC, and the CFTC. Although the group's immediate objective was to consider "the major issues raised by the numerous studies on the events in the financial markets surrounding October 19, 1987"—the "Black Monday" stock market crash—the broader mission was to "consult, as appropriate, with representatives of the various exchanges, clearinghouses, self-regulatory bodies, and with major market participants to determine private sector solutions wherever possible."[51]

The President's Working Group on Financial Markets attempted to resuscitate the idea of market discipline as a form of risk regulation. The cost to the Federal Savings and Loan Insurance Corporation and to the FDIC of bailing out depository institutions had shown, according to the members of the group, the failure of instituting and relying on government-based risk mitigation tools. At this point in time, the turn to market discipline meant two things with respect to regulation. One, it meant that there would be more reliance on disclosures, rather than direct and substantive government rules. Disclosures would assure the provision of information necessary for market participants to make informed decisions. And two, the savers and investors would have to be responsible and conscientious about their actions. Rather than the government shielding them from the risk of failing financial institutions, the responsibility would fall on the savers and investors themselves to gather and evaluate the necessary information about the health of financial institutions, or the risk involved in particular financial transactions or instruments. As the White House Council of Economic Advisers put it, reducing protection for depositors would cause them to more closely "monitor the financial health" of the institutions holding their money.[52]

The reaction to the idea of market discipline as a form of regulation was divided this time around as well. Small banks continued to oppose the idea, which they believed would diminish their safety net and competitiveness in the marketplace. On the consumer side, the idea of market discipline was seen as the state retreating from its protective role in the financial marketplace. In the final analysis, the regulatory reform movement in the Reagan era did not live up to the passionate rhetoric that had been embraced in the beginning. Reagan himself lamented at the end of his first term that "regulatory reform has been painfully slow."[53] An administration keen on liberating finance from government interference had found itself bailing out depository institutions using massive government resources. That being said, as

50 DISEMBEDDED

Weidenbaum—economist and chairman of President Ronald Reagan's first CEA—noted, there had been a clear "avoidance of new regulation."[54] While the actual regulatory dismantling itself may have been limited, the government had managed to refrain from adding new regulations, which, considering the massive changes that had taken place in the market place, was no small feat.[55] Moreover, although immediate policy changes did not materialize as a result of it, it was during the Reagan era that the idea of private regulation as a substitute for government regulation in financial markets gained legitimacy. The idea that disclosures are necessary and important, and could substitute for substantive and direct regulation, gained a larger platform, as did the idea that investors and savers should act responsibly, do their due diligence, and choose safe and sound options for themselves in the financial marketplace.

President George Bush deviated little from Reagan's regulatory process reform program. The Council on Competitiveness, established in March 1989, replaced the Task Force on Regulatory Relief, and, like its predecessor, was headed by the vice president. The task force was authorized to review all federal regulations and to eliminate those that inhibited US competitiveness. By this time, the theory of market discipline was well established in the literature on banking. Bush directed the Treasury to do a study of "the incentives for market discipline . . . [and] methods to reduce the scope of deposit insurance coverage and the resulting liability of the FDIC."[56] Decreasing the scope of deposit insurance coverage, although it was brought up in the 1990 budget that the Bush administration disclosed, was, once again, not embraced by the small and independent bankers in the financial industry. The Independent Bankers Association argued that it would "oppose any lowering of deposit insurance."[57]

Instead, in 1991, the US Congress passed the Federal Deposit Insurance Corporation Improvement Act (FDICIA). The Act was a direct response to the losses Federal S&L insurance fund and FDIC had incurred during the widespread failure of thrifts and banks. As George Benston and George Kaufman explain, more than one thousand "commercial and savings banks had failed since 1983, almost double the total number of failures that had occurred from the introduction of the Federal Deposit Insurance Corporation (FDIC) in 1934 up through 1983, and equal to 8 percent of the industry in 1980."[58] Things did not look any better on the side of the thrifts: "900 savings and loan associations (S&Ls) were resolved—that is, closed or merged with the assistance of the Federal Savings and Loan

THE POLITICAL ASCENT OF THE NEW CREED   51

Insurance Corporation (FSLIC)—or placed in conservatorship from 1983 to 1990."[59] The Act did embrace some of the tenets of market discipline by mandating extensive disclosure requirements in the form of truth-in-savings rules. At the same time, in essence, it was a major direct and substantive regulation incorporating measures related to capital levels, loan concentrations, and underwriting standards, the kinds of which were becoming increasingly rare.[60]

Looking back at Reagan and Bush era regulatory thinking on financial markets, it can be said that while there was a big ideological push to elevate private regulation, and embracing the ideas of market discipline, the banking and thrift crises had clearly set back that agenda. When George Bush called FDICIA a "narrow legislation," that is what he was referring to: narrow in its embrace of market discipline. It would happen to be in the hands of a Democratic president that the private regulation logic and the tools of market discipline would be more decisively embraced.

Reinventing the Government as a Private Entity: Clinton Administration

From the perspective of this analysis, it was with the Clinton administration that the neoliberal creed would find its most mature articulation and application in regulation, particularly in relation to finance. In 1993, Clinton launched the National Partnership for Reinventing Government (RG) under the leadership of Vice President Al Gore. At the heart of this effort were key critiques of bureaucracy found in the analyses of economists like William Niskanen, and the NPM scholarship. In the Clinton administration's view, reinventing government meant that public agencies needed to be lean, entrepreneurial, customer-driven, and cost-minded, just like a private company; and thus, the initiative set out to cut government regulations and replace them with private incentives. Reinventing regulation became the focus of the second phase of the RG initiative. The administration lauded successes in replacing "the strictly command-and-control approach with available tools to encourage compliance," including "regulatory partnerships with the private sector," and the way in which regulatory agencies were "measuring customer satisfaction."[61] Federal regulatory agencies were directed to "cut obsolete regulations; reward results, not red tape; get out of Washington and create grass roots partnerships; and negotiate rather than dictate."[62] In his

52 DISEMBEDDED

January 23, 1996 State of the Union Address, Clinton noted: "To businesses this administration is saying: If you can find a cheaper, more efficient way than government regulations require to meet tough pollution standards, do it, as long as you do it right."[63]

This perspective, critical of government regulations, extended to the state's role in financial markets. The notion that the American financial system was heavily regulated and needed more freedom to be competitive on a global scale became especially prominent during the Clinton years.[64] The administration sought to limit direct and substantive regulation of finance and, where possible, replace it with private regulation reliant on market discipline and rationality of self-interested market actors. Modern finance theory substantially influenced the way the leading figures in the administration viewed financial markets in this juncture.[65] The President's Working Group on Financial Markets was comprised of individuals—Greenspan, Arthur Levitt, Robert Rubin, William Rainer—all of whom believed in the virtues of private regulation and had direct ties to the financial sector.[66] In 1997, at the Financial Markets Conference of the Federal Reserve Bank of Atlanta, then Federal Reserve Chairman Greenspan argued:

> it is critically important to recognize that no market is ever truly unregulated. The self-interest of market participants generates private market regulation. Thus, the real question is not whether a market should be regulated. Rather, the real question is whether government intervention strengthens or weakens private regulation.[67]

In practice, this meant that self-interested, rational agents and financial institutions could do their own risk assessments and discern what was best for them, and that market mechanisms would ensure risk regulation in the financial field. Regulators were expected to provide only general guidelines and principles, or "constructive feedback."[68]

The US government was not alone in moving in this direction. In 1999, the international Basel Committee on Banking Supervision announced that it would incorporate market discipline "as a fundamental element of the New Basel Capital Accord" and "encourage market discipline by developing a set of disclosure recommendations (and requirements) which will allow market participants to assess key pieces of information on the scope of application, capital, risk exposures, risk assessment and management processes, and hence the capital adequacy of the institution."[69]

THE POLITICAL ASCENT OF THE NEW CREED 53

By the time George W. Bush was inaugurated, the faith in self-correcting markets, and its corollary, the faith in the capacity of financial institutions for self-discipline, was well established. Policymakers and the public broadly assumed that these mechanisms would ensure the safety and soundness of financial markets. Speaking in 2003, Federal Reserve Chairman Greenspan said, "Except where market discipline is undermined by moral hazard—owing, for example, to federal guarantees of private debt—private regulation generally is far better at constraining excessive risk-taking than is government regulation."[70] In 2004, market discipline was formalized into the Basel II Accord, as a regulatory tool with "the potential to reinforce capital regulation and other supervisory efforts to promote safety and soundness in banks and financial systems."[71] In 2006, Greenspan passed the baton to Ben Bernanke, who continued on the same track. In a speech he gave on hedge funds shortly after assuming the chairmanship of the Federal Reserve, Bernanke said direct regulation may be justified "when market discipline is ineffective at constraining excessive leverage and risk-taking"; however, the better route is for regulators and supervisors to foster an environment in which market discipline "constrains excessive leverage and risk-taking."[72] Giving market participants the responsibility for discipline "makes good economic sense," he said, because they have the incentive and the information to be effective.[73]

In essence, the anti-statist turn was complete; the government's own regulators believed that their understanding and tools were no better than those of the market participants. Years later, Secretary Henry Paulson would remark at a meeting at the Brookings Institute in Washington, DC, that upon his arrival in Washington in the mid-2000s, he was astonished to discover the extent to which regulators believed that financial institutions would behave rationally and that their self-interest would prevent them from engaging in excessive risk-taking.[74] Tim Clarke, former Deputy Director of the Division for Supervision and Regulation for the Federal Reserve Board, who served during the Bush administration, similarly noted:

I would say that during my time as a supervisor leading up to the crisis there was a strong belief that if the banks thought they were adequately capitalized, they were adequately capitalized. Banks should know best. They had a self-interest in holding the capital that would make them safe. That was very much behind the whole supervisory framework we had. There was a strong belief that we should not push too hard against these

54   DISEMBEDDED

people who are clearly smarter than us. We thought it was their job to ensure that their firm is adequately capitalized.[75]

Of course, the 2007–2010 financial crisis would reveal the shortcomings of
market discipline and individual rationality as a regulatory framework, as
I will discuss later. Only three years after his 2006 remarks lauding market
discipline, Chairman Bernanke would come to note the necessity for the
Federal Reserve to augment "our traditional micro-prudential, or firm-
specific, methods of oversight with a more macro-prudential, or systemwide,
approach that should help us better anticipate and mitigate broader threats to
financial stability."[76]

Conclusion

In conclusion, since the early 1970s, economists took the lead in shaping the
government's regulatory relationship with the economy, and said relationship was seen in an increasingly critical light. Early on, this critique was of a
revisionist and pragmatic bent. Regulation was still largely seen as a solution,
as something that is in the interest of the public, which needed modifying
or curbing when the costs to the economy outweighed the benefits to the
public. Regulatory reform, likewise, was seen as something in service of
controlling inflation and boosting growth, and meant cutting regulations
and incorporating market incentives, when necessary, in line with the underlying cost–benefit calculation. Later, in the 1980s, the critique took on a
more systematic approach. Rather than a solution, government regulation
was construed as *the* problem itself. While the Reagan administration failed
to realize many aspects of its anti-regulation agenda in the face of economic
challenges—particularly in the context of a turbulent banking sector—it
succeeded at avoiding new regulation despite rapidly changing financial
markets, marking the arrival of drift as a distinct feature of American regulatory politics, as I will discuss in more detail in the next chapter. During
the Clinton and Bush administrations, a period when financial markets grew
rapidly, regulation was increasingly seen as belonging in the territory of private decision making, rational individuals, and market discipline.

In the next chapter I turn to policy and explore how new economic
ideas on risk regulation have translated into specific policy tools governing
a financialized economy. As the discussion will show, these policies are as

THE POLITICAL ASCENT OF THE NEW CREED   55

varied and multifaceted as the theories that informed them. Although the widespread understanding is that it was through deregulation primarily that American neoliberalism shaped financialization, when it comes to regulatory policy, particularly risk regulation, the policy menu was broader. By looking at deregulation only—or by mislabeling regulatory developments that were not about removing rules and regulation as "deregulation"—we both miss an important part of the story and mischaracterize aspects of it.

4

From Politics to Policy

Regulation and Finance

The liberal state was itself a creation of the self-regulating market.
—Karl Polanyi, *The Great Transformation*

The governing ideas on regulation in the decades leading to the financial crisis promoted less reliance on direct, substantive government regulation and more reliance on market discipline and individuals' rational, self-regulating conduct. As Scott Alvarez, former General Counsel for the Federal Reserve Board, described it: "The mindset was that there should be no regulation; the market should take care of policing, unless there already is an identified problem."[1] What exactly does it mean, from a policy perspective, for there to be "no regulation," and for the market to "take care of policing"? How did this view, the intellectual origins, and the political landscape of which I discussed earlier, translate into specific policy tools in relation to the financial sector of the economy? The mainstream answer to this question is deregulation—namely, the US government, influenced by neoliberal principles, implemented deregulatory policies, fostering a climate where financial institutions could operate without restraint, and this led to them taking extreme risks, ultimately resulting in their inevitable failure and collapse. In this chapter, I argue that the policy implications of the ideas outlined in previous chapters go beyond mere deregulation. The state's regulatory repertoire, after all, is multifaceted,[2] and the changes neoliberal regulatory creed induced have been equally complex. The regulatory transformation commencing in the 1970s was not simply a move from *more* rules to *fewer* or *no* rules. It was a profound redefinition of the roles and responsibilities of both the government and market actors in mitigating risk, and it involved a reconfiguration of the variety of tools and methods of intervention available for that purpose (see Figure 4.1). *Deregulation*, certainly, was one facet of this multifaceted

---

Disembedded. Basak Kus, Oxford University Press. © Oxford University Press 2024.
DOI: 10.1093/oso/9780197764862.003.0004

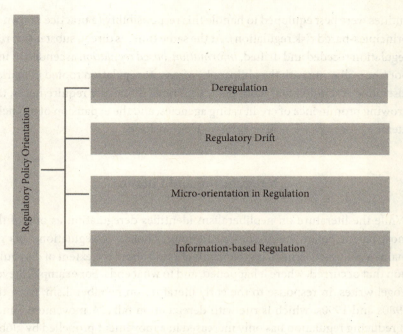

Figure 4.1 Regulatory Policy and Finance

transformation. Policymakers rolled back numerous financial regulations established in the wake of the Great Depression. In fact, it was those deregulatory initiatives, in conjunction with technological advancements, which led to the emergence of new market players, products, and instruments. As financial markets expanded and metamorphosed at a rapid pace, new risks and uncertainties emerged. However, the government did not adopt necessary measures to develop substantive risk regulation tools to respond to these evolving realities, giving rise to a second facet of neoliberal risk regulation: *regulatory drift*. In Warren's words, once again, as markets changed, statutes remained "frozen in time."[3]

When and where the government did regulate, it did so increasingly in line with the premises of market discipline and individual rationality. On the one hand, the government markedly pivoted toward a *micro-orientation in regulation*. This involved focusing prudential regulation on the stability and security of individual entities rather than the entire system (micro-prudential regulation) while at the same time entrusting financial institutions with defining the terms of risk management, premised on the belief that these

58   DISEMBEDDED

entities were best equipped to handle this responsibility (a practice known as principles-based risk regulation). At the same time, as direct, substantive risk regulation receded and drifted, *information-based regulation* ascended in importance, aligning with the philosophy of private regulation rooted in market discipline and individual rationality. The rise of disclosure requirements, the growing prominence of credit rating agencies, and the expansion of financial literacy programs were all integral to this transition.

Deregulation and Finance

While the literature on neoliberalism identifies deregulation as one of the most patent policy manifestations, among scholars of regulation, this remains a contested issue. Disagreements abound about the extent of deregulation that occurred, where it happened, and to what ends. For example, Steven Vogel writes, in response to the early literature on neoliberalism, from the 1980s and 1990s, which is rife with deregulation talk, "A movement aimed at reducing regulation has only increased it; a movement propelled by global forces has reinforced national differences; and a movement purported to push back the state has been led by the state itself."[4] Jacint Jordana and David Levi-Faur echo this sentiment, asserting that "In an era in which regulation has become synonymous with red tape, and deregulation has become a major electoral platform of the New Right, regulatory authorities have been created in unprecedented numbers and with unprecedented autonomy."[5] John Braithwaite, likewise, notes that deregulation is a "description of what the Chicago boys and the IMF [International Monetary Fund] thought should be happening," rather than what actually happened.[6] Although the "Reagan era was romanticized as one of deregulation,"[7] Braithwaite contends that, "genuine deregulatory zealotry" prevailed only in the early years of Reagan's term, and by the end of it, "business regulatory agencies had resumed the long-run growth in the size of their budgets, the numbers of their staff, the toughness of their enforcement."[8] More recently Martijn Konings has joined this critique, dismissing it as a "myth" that the neoliberal era was about deregulation.[9] "Neoliberal *practices* have never been about institutional retreat or diminishing political capacities," he counters, "but, instead, about the construction of new institutional mechanisms of control."[10]

Jacob Hacker, Paul Pierson, and Kathleen Thelen also challenge the deregulation narrative, although rather than attempt to refute the notion

FROM POLITICS TO POLICY 59

that significant deregulation occurred, they seek to describe the regulatory changes of the past few decades more completely. They acknowledge deregulation as a critical element of the neoliberal institutional shift, but they emphasize drift—"the failure of policymakers to respond to new market behaviors and technologies in part because of intense lobbying by the financial industry to head off such responses."[11] Marc Eisner is in the same camp. While not denying the occurrence of deregulatory changes in some areas, he argues that their significance is overstated, both in terms of inflation-adjusted spending and in terms of rulemaking activity (rules and proposed rules recorded in the Federal Register).[12] The most remarkable regulatory characteristic of recent decades, according to Eisner, has been the absence of new statues, which is akin to what Hacker et al. called "policy drift," and "the devol[ution] of authority on to regulated parties."[13]

By reframing the political narrative around deregulation, scholars such as Robert Horwitz and Charles Halvorson add yet another layer of complexity to the deregulation debate.[14] Although deregulation became a key political component of Reagan's small government initiative, they point out, the issue had been on the policy agenda throughout the 1970s and had gained support from Republicans and Democrats alike by the time Reagan took office. Monica Prasad also acknowledges the political convergence around deregulation, noting that both sides of the political spectrum advocated for deregulation in the 1980s, although the left and right ascribed different meanings to it, and saw it as a means to different ends.[15]

Concerning finance specifically, the views of deregulation are similarly variegated (see Figure 4.2). Economists Thomas Pillippon and Ariel Reshef argue that "1960 marks the beginning of the most regulated period in finance, while 1980 marks the beginning of the least regulated one."[16] Prasad agrees about the deregulatory trend in finance, but identifies the 1990s as the starting point of significant deregulation in finance: "The US financial system has traditionally been regulated more heavily than the financial systems of Europe," she notes, and "this tradition of heavier regulations compared to Europe was often given as a reason for the deregulation of the 1990s."[17]

For policy specialists associated with the Mercatus Center, on the other hand, the trend has not been one of deregulation, but "four decades of steadily increasing regulation" (see Figure 4.2).[18] Similarly, the Heritage Foundation argues that "most financial market activity has taken place under the careful supervision of the federal government since at least the 1930s,

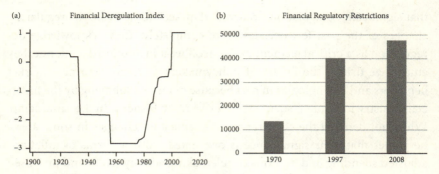

Figure 4.2 Regulation and Finance in the US: Deregulation or Regulatory Expansion?
a) Financial Deregulation Index
b) Financial Regulatory Restrictions

Source: The first figure is from Thomas Phillippon and Ariell Reshef, "Wages and Human Capital in the U.S. Financial Industry," *Quarterly Journal of Economics* 127, no. 4 (November 2012): 1551–1609, https://doi.org/10.1093/qje/qjs030; data for second figure is from McLaughlin and Sherouse, "Did Deregulation Cause the Financial Crisis?"

and Congress has continually expanded the number and nature of financial sector regulations."[19]

And yet another group of scholars argue that to the extent that deregulation occurred, its impact on the later developments—particularly on excessive risk-taking behavior and the financial crisis—remains exaggerated. According to Paul Mahoney, for instance, although it is often argued that the New Deal financial regulation "produced a quiet period in which there were no systemic banking crises, but subsequent deregulation led to crisis-prone banking," the deregulatory acts that are the subject of many of these analysis, such as the Gramm–Leach–Bliley Act (GLBA) of 1999 and the Commodity Futures Modernization Act of 2000 "did not remove existing restrictions that would have prevented the principal practices implicated in the subprime crisis, but instead codified the status quo."[20]

How to make sense of these varying views? To begin with, it is difficult to gauge *how* or *how much* an economy is regulated by looking at spending figures or the number of rules recorded in the Code of Federal Regulations.[21] Leaving aside the issue that scholars reach different conclusions based on such quantifications, these measures provide a limited window into what institutions do and how they do it. In his discussion on welfare states, Gosta Esping-Andersen had pointed out that to focus on spending figures would be misleading: "Expenditures are epiphenomenal to the theoretical substance of

FROM POLITICS TO POLICY 61

welfare states" and cannot "capture the ideals or designs that historical actors sought to realize in the struggles over the welfare state," he wrote.[22] This argument holds true for the regulatory state and its endeavors to mitigate risk. Spending figures or the number of rules in the Code of Federal Regulations can provide only so much insight. After all, budgets can be squandered on matters irrelevant to the principal risks; rules that seem to be ever expanding might not be pertinent to new market realities or might not be effectively enforced at all. All rules are not made equal, either. What meaning do these aggregate figures hold if, from a risk regulation standpoint, one significant rule is discarded for every ten insignificant rules introduced? The key issue here, therefore, is not how many rules have been removed or added, but how and to what extent the state exercised its protective functions through regulatory actions during the financialization of the economy. Although the deregulation argument has its limitations in conceptualization, evidentiary basis, and the surrounding political narrative, it is not without a basis. Finance was in fact freed from a series of regulatory restrictions beginning in the early 1980s, and we cannot make sense of financialization in the US without acknowledging that. Therefore, rather than referring to deregulation in the abstract, it would be more insightful to examine the actual changes, what they effectively repealed, and their subsequent impact on the markets (see Table 4.1 for a list of major deregulatory steps).

In 1997, before some of the most important deregulatory changes occurred, Alan Greenspan encouraged the American Bankers Association "not to lose sight of the remarkable changes that occurred in recent years," despite the frustratingly slow "pace of legislative reform and revision to statutorily mandated regulations."[23] He noted, specifically:

Deposit and other interest rate ceilings have been eliminated, geographical restrictions have been virtually removed, many banking organizations

Table 4.1 Major Deregulatory Steps

1978	*Marquette vs. First of Omaha* decision by the US Supreme Court
1980	Depository Institutions Deregulation and Monetary Control Act (DIDMCA)
1982	Garn–St Germain Depository Institutions Act (AMPTA)
1984	Secondary Mortgage Market Enhancement Act (SMMEA)
1994	Riegle–Neal Interstate Banking and Branching Efficiency Act
1999	Gramm–Leach–Bliley Act (GLBA)

62 DISEMBEDDED

can do a fairly broadly based securities underwriting and dealing business, many can do insurance sales, and those with the resources and skill are authorized to virtually match foreign bank competition abroad. Moreover, it seems clear that there is recognition by the Congress that the basic financial framework has to be adjusted further.[24]

Greenspan was right on that last point. Congress would indeed proceed to eliminate even some of the most deeply entrenched regulatory statues that had been active since the 1930s. The political narrative around reforming the state's regulatory relationship with finance, which had already begun to gain traction in the early 1970s, would begin to yield tangible outcomes by the end of the decade.

The first notable step toward deregulation came in 1978 via a decision of the highest court in the nation. In *Marquette vs. First of Omaha*, the US Supreme Court ruled that the law "authorizes a national banking association to charge on any loan interest at the rate allowed by the laws of the State where the bank is located."[25] With this decision, banks recognized the advantage of moving their headquarters to states with the most permissive usury laws. As a result, a "wave of deregulation" ensued as states competed for banks' headquarters, eventually leading to elimination of usury ceilings in some states.[26]

Then, during the Carter administration, in 1980, Congress passed the Depository Institutions Deregulation and Monetary Control Act (DIDMCA). The importance of this act cannot be overstated. Two of DIDMCA's noteworthy deregulatory features included repeal of the interest rate restriction on depository institutions (Regulation Q) and of usury caps on residential mortgages. Part of the 1933 Banking Act, Regulation Q had been put in place to prevent interest rate wars among depository institutions. However, with the inflation surge of the 1970s, maintaining interest rate ceilings proved challenging, as savers and investors sought instruments offering higher returns than bank deposits. Policymakers believed that repealing Regulation Q would not only help depository institutions remain competitive in the marketplace but would also benefit small savers who typically kept their funds at local banks rather than investing in more sophisticated instruments. Similarly, the repeal of usury caps on residential mortgages was viewed as a pro-consumer measure that would open homeownership to a greater number of people who could qualify for loans by agreeing to higher rates.

The deregulatory movement in finance continued during the Reagan administration. In 1982, Congress passed the Garn–St Germain Depository

Institutions Act, also known as the Alternative Mortgage Transaction Parity Act (AMTPA).[27] With this measure, thrift institutions could expand their businesses beyond mortgage lending into credit cards and commercial lending (up to 10 percent of their assets), thus being able to act "more like a bank and less like a specialized mortgage lending institution."[28] Furthermore, AMTPA allowed lenders to market new, more complex mortgage products, including adjustable-rate mortgages, loans with balloon payments, and negative amortization. As Patricia McCoy et al. observe, the rhetoric surrounding AMTPA echoed that of the 2003–2006 housing boom.[29] This deregulatory shift was praised not only for widening the pool of eligible borrowers but also for "making homeownership affordable."[30] However, over time, due to AMTPA's influence, the mortgage holdings of financial institutions, including savings and loan associations, began to gravitate from traditional home mortgage loans to higher-risk loans.[31]

The legislative efforts of Congress did not end there. Two years after AMTPA was passed, in 1984, lawmakers passed the Secondary Mortgage Market Enhancement Act (SMMEA), which removed "the regulatory barriers that previously inhibited the development of a private market for mortgage-backed securities."[32] SMMEA also "preempted a variety of state laws that inhibited private home mortgage securitization, including state retirement fund laws which prevented public pension funds from investing in private home mortgage securities."[33] Overall, the act facilitated the growth of the securitized residential mortgage market.

By the late 1980s, these successive deregulatory policies had transformed financial markets affecting *who* the market participants were, *what* they did, and *how* they did it. New products and services had emerged, new actors had joined the field, and the established ones had transformed their operations. This transformation was particularly salient in the mortgage market. The market offered new products—less traditional loans—to a more diverse profile of borrowers. The mortgage-backed security market had been privatized, and pension funds joined the ranks of its institutional investors. All this is to say, already by the end of the decade, the financial field had drastically changed and was teeming with a new set of risks and vulnerabilities. Few policymakers recognized the new set of risks and vulnerabilities, however, and significant deregulatory changes to contemporary finance carried on into the Clinton era.

In 1994, Congress passed the Riegle–Neal Interstate Banking and Branching Efficiency Act, which eliminated restrictions on interstate bank

64 DISEMBEDDED

acquisitions, mergers, and branching. The Economic Growth and Regulatory Paperwork Reduction Act followed in 1996. Although not as significant as some other deregulatory acts before or later, this law eliminated various application and recordkeeping requirements to ease the burden on lenders and decrease the cost of credit to borrowers. Then in 1999, the GLBA formally established that banks could expand beyond banking activities into securities and insurance operations, which had been prohibited under the Bank Holding Company Act of 1933 (the Glass–Steagall Act).[34] The first concerted effort to repeal the Glass–Steagall Act had emerged in the 1970s when, amid an inflationary climate, investors sought higher returns on their savings through securities and money market funds. As commercial banks' profitability declined, bankers began to advocate for the elimination of restrictions on their participation in the securities business. Their efforts intensified in the 1980s. Banks claimed "they were at a disadvantage vis-à-vis other financial institutions, because securities firms could innovate in ways that banks couldn't, such as packaging and reselling car loans and mortgages."[35] Early in the Reagan administration, the prospects for removing the Glass–Steagall Act looked promising to the American Bankers Association, according to Arthur Wilmarth, given the prevailing "political drift toward deregulation."[36] Greenspan, newly appointed as the Federal Reserve Chairman, voiced his support for the repeal of the Glass–Steagall Act in 1987, and in the same year Reagan's Treasury Department announced that "American banks should be allowed to merge with other financial institutions if they were going to be able to compete in the international arena."[37] US banks were not as large as some of their European and Asian counterparts, which was a cause for concern. Among the world's twenty-five largest banks, Japan had fourteen— including the four largest—Germany two, Britain three, and France four; the US had only two (Citicorp and Bank of America).[38] Bigger banks were believed to deliver higher rates of innovation, economic growth, and international competitiveness. Specifically, as Wilmarth notes, "universal banking" was thought to yield three specific benefits: "(i) increased efficiency and profitability for financial firms, due to larger economies of scale and scope; (ii) increased safety and soundness for financial firms through a greater diversification of their business lines; and (iii) lower-cost services and improved convenience for consumers based on the concept of 'one-stop shopping.'"[39] Yet, not all in the financial sector favored repeal; both the securities industry and independent community banks were opposed, and as on many other occasions, divisions among the financial sector would stand in the way of deregulatory moves. However, by the time President Clinton took office in 1993, repeal had gained sufficient momentum, and under Greenspan's leadership in 1996, the Federal Reserve began to allow bank holding companies "to own investment banking operations that accounted for as much as 25 percent of their revenues."[40] Thus, the Glass–Steagall Act had already been substantially weakened several years before the GLBA finished the job. By the time GLBA was passed in 1999, so much de facto deregulation had occurred already that some observers thought the repeal of the Glass–Steagall Act was not all that consequential. Speaking at the signing of the bill, Senator Paul Sarbanes (D-MD) noted:

> Well, one hardly need point out that the financial services industry has been undergoing rapid change. We've had these affiliations between banks, securities firms and insurance companies already occurring in the marketplace. This legislation seeks to provide a statutory framework. It wasn't a question whether these affiliations were going to happen; they were taking place. But we needed to have an overarching framework, a responsible statutory.[41]

GLBA's main outcome made it possible for a bank holding company to become a financial holding company (FHC), "an umbrella organization that could own subsidiaries involved in different financial activities" such as securities, insurance, and banking.[42] For two decades, the US banking industry had been consolidating. The number of commercial banks had declined by a third from the mid-1980s to the late 1990s, even as their average size grew.[43] By 2004, five years after GLBA passed, FHCs numbered 466 (compared to eighty-six in 2000) and accounted for 86 percent of industry assets.[44] As an example of this growth, Wilmarth noted that, by 2001, "Citigroup was four times the size of Citicorp, its banking predecessor, during the early 1990s."[45]

Regulatory Drift and Finance

Just as important as deregulation—if not more so—was regulatory drift, the adjustments that didn't happen despite significant changes in the markets. Drift is "when institutions or policies are deliberately held in place while their context shifts, changing their effects."[46] As Hacker et al. note, political environments with a high "status quo bias" and divided structure tend to be particularly conducive to drift.[47] The policy context of the US, "featuring

66 DISEMBEDDED

bicameralism and frequent divided government, as well as such supermajority hurdles as the Senate filibuster and presidential veto, create a high barrier to the enactment of new legislation."[48] In this case, regulatory drift occurred as the US government took no direct, substantive action against the risks entailed in major transformations in the financial markets: the proliferation and expansion of non-bank financial institutions, increased connection and concentration in the financial sector, and the emergence of new instruments and products such as securitization, derivatives, and subprime lending. "Openly contemptuous of financial regulation," as Appelbaum noted, "policy makers made little effort to write new rules for the rapidly changing industry" and instead "insisted that market participants would police misconduct and maintain financial stability."[49]

The drift was not merely happenstance. Greenspan, who was the chairman of the Federal Reserve (an institution with regulatory responsibilities) during this time, openly acknowledged the government's deliberate inaction in a 1997 speech in which he applauded the growing mismatch between a changing economy and the existing policies:

> With technological change clearly accelerating, existing regulatory structures are being bypassed, freeing market forces to enhance wealth creation and economic growth . . . As we move into a new century, the market-stabilizing private regulatory forces should gradually displace many cumbersome, increasingly ineffective government structures. This is a likely outcome since governments, by their nature, cannot adjust sufficiently quickly to a changing environment, which too often veers in unforeseen directions.[50]

Illustrating what did not happen is more challenging than showcasing what did happen. However, by focusing on specific cases where both scholarly consensus and post-crisis hindsight indicate that new risk regulations should have been established, we may be able to capture the phenomenon of regulatory drift in the financializing economy.

First, let's examine the absence of risk regulations in response to market changes spurred by the three deregulatory bills of the early 1980s—DIDMCA, which repealed interest rate restrictions on depository accounts and usury caps on home mortgages; AMTPA, which allowed thrift institutions to expand services; and the SMMEA, which privatized the mortgage-backed securities market. Together, these bills altered the structure of the residential mortgage market—the actors, the environment, and the activities and instruments available. As McCoy et al. explain, they caused an expansion in the private label residential mortgage-based securities market, which then facilitated the rise of subprime mortgages, and blurred the boundaries between financial institutions.[51] It is also a result of these acts that thrifts moved into a whole new terrain with new risks as their portfolios moved "away from traditional home mortgage loans into higher-risk loans."[52] To these changes, the US government's mere response was not new legislation to ensure systemic and consumer protection, but inaction. In fact, as McCoy et al. noted, "After 1982, Congress turned its back on any further regulation of residential mortgages, except for the Home Ownership and Equity Protection Act of 1994."[53] Instead, it largely relied on disclosure. The securitization process and subprime lending expanded with little to no governmental oversight, and the Federal Reserve did not even exert the authority it had. Here is how former Chair of the US Federal Deposit Insurance Corporation, Sheila Bair, described the regulatory drift in the subprime mortgage market that was taking place when she served at the Treasury in 2001–2002:

> Consumer groups were reporting increasing instances of unregulated nonbank mortgage brokers entering lower-income neighborhoods and "push marketing" mortgages with steep payments resets, negative amortization, and exorbitant prepayment penalties. The brokers were not banks, and thus fell outside the lending standards applicable to insured institutions. Some were affiliated with banks, but the Fed had not used its authority over bank affiliates to examine the brokers for abusive practices even though Ned [Edward Gramlich, Federal Reserve Board member] had pushed Chairman Greenspan to do so.[54]

In short, no substantive risk regulation followed the expansion of the subprime market despite the risks it carried for the system and consumers. The existing regulatory powers of the Home Ownership and Equity Protection Act were not employed either. Sheila Bair noted:

> The subprime lending abuses could have been avoided if the Federal Reserve Board had simply used the authority it had since 1994 under the Home Ownership and Equity Protection Act (HOEPA) to promulgate mortgage-lending standards across the board. The Fed was the only agency with the authority to prescribe mortgage-lending standards for banks and nonbanks.[55]

68 DISEMBEDDED

In its 2011 report, the Financial Crisis Inquiry Commission reached the same conclusion as Bair concerning the Federal Reserve's failure to use its authority to set prudent mortgage lending standards: "The Federal Reserve was the one entity empowered to do so and it did not."[56]

Regulatory drift also occurred following enactment of GLBA, the deregulatory act that allowed bank holding companies to become financial holding companies. As explained before, despite looming large in the popular press, GLBA's impact was less consequential than other deregulatory acts because by the time it was enacted, federal agencies and the courts had already "permitted banks to make significant inroads into securities and insurance sectors."[57] Nevertheless, the growth of financial holding companies was quite a consequential development, with FHCs holding 86 percent of industry assets a mere five years after GLBA had passed, and the government developed no regulatory mechanisms to mitigate the associated risks.[58] As Wilmarth noted, "The growing concentration of securities and derivatives activities within a small group of major financial institutions"—that is, FHCs—meant that "the failure of any big institution could create systemic risk and trigger a costly bailout by federal regulators."[59] That was, however, a risk that Federal Reserve did not tackle.

A third blatant case of regulatory drift concerned the "extraordinary development and expansion" of the derivatives market, which Greenspan called "by far the most significant event in finance during the past decade."[60] Starting in the 1980s, the market for a particular type of derivative, credit default swaps, began to expand. Credit default swaps, which work like insurance to protect lenders against a default risk, "helped fuel the mortgage boom, allowing lenders to spread their risk further and further, thus generating more and more loans."[61] As the 1990s came to a close, Brooksley Born, at the helm of the Commodity Futures Trading Commission (CFTC), expressed concern about "how quickly the over-the-counter derivatives market was growing, how little any of the federal regulators knew about it."[62] The market, she explained, was "opaque," a "dark market" in which "nobody really knew what was going on."[63] No regulation existed to ensure "that the parties were able to pay what they promised."[64] When Born initiated a discussion on how to regulate the derivatives market, she encountered severe opposition not only from the industry, but also from policymakers in the Clinton administration, including key members of the President's Working Group on Financial Markets. In a now infamous phone conversation, Assistant Secretary of Treasury Lawrence Summers told Born: "I have thirteen bankers

FROM POLITICS TO POLICY 69

in my office and they say if you go forward with this, you will cause the worst financial crisis since World War II."[65] Nevertheless, the CFTC went on to issue a "concept release," suggesting it was high time to consider whether modifications were needed to "enhance the fairness, financial integrity, and efficiency of this market."[66] Treasury Secretary Robert Rubin, Federal Reserve Chairman Greenspan, and SEC Chairman Arthur Levitt—members of the President's Working Group in Financial Markets—countered with a joint statement denouncing the move:

> We have grave concerns about this action and its possible consequences. The OTC derivatives market is a large and important global market. We seriously question the scope of the CFTC's jurisdiction in this area, and we are very concerned about reports that the CFTC's action may increase the legal uncertainty concerning certain types of OTC derivatives.[67]

Further, Greenspan emphasized in his testimony before the Committee on Banking and Financial Services in July 1998:

> Aside from safety and soundness regulation of derivatives dealers under the banking and securities laws, regulation of derivatives transactions that are privately negotiated by professionals is unnecessary.[68]

Later that very year, the hedge fund Long-Term Capital Management went under, prompting Born to describe it in her congressional testimony as "a wake-up call about the unknown risks in the over-the-counter derivatives market."[69] Nevertheless, the Clinton administration continued to oppose Born's bid to regulate the derivatives markets. In a November 1999 report, the President's Working Group on Financial Markets unanimously recommended the exclusion of over-the-counter (OTC) derivatives from CFTC oversight under the Commodity Exchanges Act (CEA), arguing that "sophisticated counterparties that use OTC derivatives simply do not require the same protections under the CEA as those required by retail investors."[70]

In 2000—by this time Born had resigned from her position—Congress passed the Commodity Futures Modernization Act (CFMA), which was not a deregulatory measure as popularly portrayed, but an instance of regulatory drift par excellence. CFMA clarified the legal status of swap agreements: they were shielded from CFTC and SEC regulation. Ten years

70 DISEMBEDDED

later, former Treasury Secretary Summers would finally admit that the regulatory framework for derivatives "was manifestly inadequate."[71]

Micro-Orientations in Risk Regulation

Another pillar of neoliberal risk regulation in the time of financialization was the espousal of a micro-orientation; that is, tackling risk regulation at the level of individual institutions. This new policy direction was a direct result of theories that had eroded the role and responsibility of the state in risk regulation and protection of investors and consumers. The micro-orientation in regulation was manifest in two ways. First, prudential regulation took on a decidedly micro form. Second, the government's regulatory grip further loosened as individual institutions themselves were entrusted to regulate their own risk.

A macro-prudential approach attempts to ensure "the stability of the financial system as a whole to prevent substantial disruptions in credit and other vital financial services necessary for stable economic growth."[72] Micro-prudential regulation, on the other hand, focuses on the safety and soundness of individual financial institutions, With a micro-prudential approach, an increase in a financial institution's profitability or capital "is seen as favorable, without regard to how this is accomplished."[73] Nevertheless, the *how* might have substantial consequences for the other market participants, but that question would require a macro-prudential approach looking at the well-being of a particular institution from the vantage point of how the firm is "connected with the rest of the financial system and real economy," and "the risk that a firm's distress could have on the financial sector and economy, and feedback effects to that firm."[74]

The increased reliance on micro-regulation was not unique to the US. In the years leading to the financial crisis, advanced countries used macro-prudential tools in a rather limited fashion. This was particularly true for advanced economies, where few substantive regulatory measures existed concerning size, interconnectedness, and debt growth such as size-dependent leverage limits, capital surcharges for systemically important institutions, limits on interbank exposures, and caps on debt-to-income ratio.

After the crisis, this orientation would change (see Figure 4.3 and Figure 4.4). An indication of this shift is Ben Bernanke's statement in a 2009 speech that the Federal Reserve needed to enhance its "traditional micro-prudential,

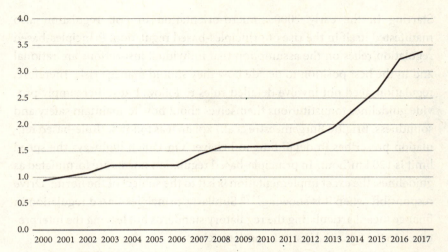

Figure 4.3 Increasing Use of Macro-prudential Tools in Advanced Countries
Eugenio Cerutti, Stijn Claessens, and Luc Laeven, "The Use and Effectiveness of Macroprudential Policies: New Evidence," *Journal of Financial Stability* 28 (2017): 203–224. Data is from the 2018 update of the Cerutti, Claessens, and Laeven (2017) macro-prudential policy dataset. For a discussion on comparative and historical growth of macro-prudential measures, see Xavier Freixas et al., *Systemic Risk, Crises, and Macroprudential Regulation* (Boston, MA: MIT Press, 2015).

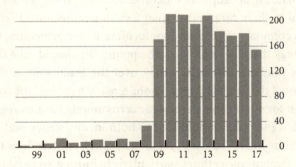

Figure 4.4 Number of Central Bank Speeches Mentioning "Macro-prudential"
BIS central bankers' speeches. The figure is from Bank for International Settlements (BIS), *Annual Economic Report 2018*, June 24, 2018, 64, https://www.bis.org/publ/arpdf/ar2018e.htm.

or firm-specific, methods of oversight with a more macro-prudential, or systemwide, approach."[75] Bernanke was not alone in touting a macro approach in the post-crisis context. The same shift in thinking about prudential regulation happened across the board in advanced countries. Looking at the data, however, reveals the relative lack of macro-prudential focus in the risk-regulation paradigm prior to 2009.

72 DISEMBEDDED

Starting in the early 2000s, micro-orientation in risk regulation also manifested itself in the rise of principles-based regulation. Principles-based regulation relies on the assumption that individual institutions are rational and in the best position to decide how they should manage risk. Therefore, regulation need not involve detailed rules to follow, but rather simply provide guidelines to institutions themselves about how to maintain safety and soundness. Brigitte Burgemeestre et al. explain it as follows: "Rule-based regulation prescribes in detail how to behave: 'On Dutch highways the speed limit is 120 km/hour.' In principle-based regulation norms are formulated as guidelines; the exact implementation is left to the subject of the norm: 'Drive responsibly when it is snowing.'"[76] Similarly, principles-based regulation in finance meant articulating the regulatory standards but leaving the interpretation to the financial institutions themselves.[77]

As the Basel II Accords were being shaped, principles-based regulation was all the rage. Basel II allowed banks a great deal of flexibility in determining their own risk-based capital requirements. Channeling this, New York Insurance Superintendent Eric Dinallo argued, for instance, that "The essential goal of regulation is not rote compliance with a long list of rules, but ensuring appropriate outcomes . . . The principles ask companies to be ethical to their core, rather than focusing on technical requirements. Indeed, if a company is generally conforming to the principles, but violates a rule in a way that does not harm the public, we should take that into account."[78] By the time Sheila Bair took over the leadership of the FDIC in 2006, she noted that financial regulations already had been moving toward a lighter touch for some time, despite concerns among various regulators and observers that the policy would lead to both inconsistency and decrease in capital requirements.[79] "Adding fuel to the fire," she noted, "was the fact that some of our foreign competitors, particularly in Europe, were taking industry self-regulation to new extremes."[80] Principles-based regulation had begun to be seen as a necessary component of US financial competitiveness.[81]

Information Provision as Risk Regulation

As policy began shifting away from hands-on, direct, substantive government oversight to an approach anchored in the assumptions of individual rationality and market discipline, information-based regulation started taking center stage. At the heart of this perspective was the belief that furnishing and guaranteeing access to accurate information was essential for risk regulation. Part and parcel of this development were reliance on disclosures, national and state campaigns to enhance financial literacy, and increased reliance on credit rating agencies, as unrelated as these elements may look at the outset.

Caveat Emptor: Risk Regulation by Disclosure

As Justice Stephen Breyer explained in his book, *Regulation and Its Reform*, disclosure is different from direct, substantive regulation: "It does not regulate production processes, output, price, or allocation of products. Nor does it restrict individual choice as much as the other classical forms of regulation."[82] Disclosure is intended to help rational actors make informed decisions, and in turn, enhance market discipline as a risk regulation method.

Disclosures are not a novel phenomenon. They are rooted in American common law, and have been "mainstream policy in the US" for quite sometime.[83] In the early twentieth century, public interest theorists like Louis D. Brandeis specifically endorsed disclosure in financial transactions, and in the aftermath of the Great Depression, disclosures gained more traction. In accepting the presidential nomination at the Democratic convention in Chicago in 1932, Franklin D. Roosevelt famously called for "letting in of the light of day on issues of securities, foreign and domestic, which are offered for sale to the investing public."[84] Provision of information "would help to protect the savings of the country from the dishonesty of crooks and from the lack of honor of some men in high financial places."[85] As Mary Graham explains, "the Securities Act of 1933 and the Securities and Exchange Act of 1934 required publicly traded companies to disclose, in standardized form and at regular intervals, detailed information about their officers and financial practices and gave the government new authority to set accounting standards."[86] However, at this point in time, disclosures were *not* considered a substitute for substantive government regulation but a supplement to it.[87] Case in point is the first major bill in the twentieth century concerning disclosure in financial transactions—the Truth in Lending Act of 1968—which declared: "The Congress finds that economic stabilization would be enhanced and the competition among various financial institutions and other firms engaged in the extent of consumer credit would be strengthened by the informed use of credit."[88] As Anne Fleming explains, the major goal of Senator Paul H. Douglas of Illinois, the bill's original sponsor, was "avoiding

74 DISEMBEDDED

deception and warning borrowers of the high cost of credit."[89] All along, Fleming elaborates, "Douglas viewed disclosure as a complement to price ceilings and other consumer protection laws, not a substitute for them."[90] Only later, in the 1980s, was disclosure considered an alternative to direct, substantive regulation, "as part of a trend to inform and educate rather than regulate."[91] As direct and substantive risk regulation on the part of government retreated and drifted, "government by disclosure has emerged as a third wave of modern risk regulation."[92] The rising prominence of disclosures in financial markets traced this trend (see Table 4.2). So pronounced has this trend been that legal scholar Lauren Willis argues that today, "the dominant model of regulation in the United States for consumer credit, insurance, and investment products is disclosure and unfettered choice."[93]

One reason for the trend toward disclosure as a risk regulation tool is that information provision aligns with the anti-statist view that had been brewing since the early 1970s. As Paula Dalley notes, "disclosure is a 'soft' form of intervention that does not directly mandate change in the underlying behavior."[94] It is "less costly and less interfering than price controls, such as the old usury laws, or other types of substantive regulation."[95] It does not dictate what can or cannot be exchanged in the market place, who can or cannot be party to the exchange or in what terms; it does not curtail consumer choice or impose costs, as substantive government regulations do. Rather, disclosure is thought to regulate risk merely by helping rational actors in their decision-making process. And for those very reasons it remains attractive to "legislators and regulators, as well as industry."[96] In Justice Bryer's words, disclosure is "viewed as augmenting the preconditions of a competitive marketplace."[97]

The rising prominence of disclosure is also linked to the political stalemate and the increasing polarization that have characterized US politics over the past four decades.[98] In this polarized political atmosphere, according

Table 4.2 Disclosure Acts and the Financial Sector

Prior to 1973	1973–1990	1991–2007
0	47	125

Source: https://www.congress.gov/. (Bill topic = finance and financial sector; Legislation = Introduced in the House or Senate; "Disclosure Act" in the title). Please note that the number of disclosure-oriented acts is underestimated here because only those that include "disclosure act" in the title were selected.

to Graham, information disclosure emerged as a common ground, as "it combined the ideas of corporate transparency and public participation often favored by Democrats with the lower cost, less intrusive, market-oriented approaches typically championed by Republicans."[99] In this sense, the politics of disclosure regulation is similar to the conditions that led to the expansion of what Suzanne Mettler calls the "submerged state"—federal policies that lie beneath the surface.[100] With sharp polarization, brokering political agreements becomes increasingly difficult, and therefore, policy and repertoires increasingly involve formats that appeal to both liberals and conservatives, according to Mettler. Thus, direct policies are pushed back and submerged policies are expanded. Although disclosure requirements are not the type of "governance unseen" Mettler analyzes, they embody a parallel trend.[101] When direct, substantive regulation came under attack, the popularity of disclosure arose as a non-intrusive, market-enhancing way to regulate risk, similar to the rise of submerged social policies.

Disclosure did not walk alone, of course, in the larger turn toward information-reliant risk regulation. Two other important trends were the increasing prominence of rating agencies, and the political endorsement and cultural espousal of financial literacy programs.

Rating Agencies

Rating agencies have played an important role in the workings of the American economy since the early twentieth century. In the early days, this role was primarily one of information provision. However, as Pierre Pénet explains, as early as the 1930s US regulators began to "incorporate ratings into public regulatory frameworks."[102] This was "a timely and affordable solution to the financial and institutional problems facing U.S. regulators during the Great Depression."[103]

In the 1940s, with the more predictable and stable framework of the Bretton Woods system in place, the significance of rating agencies and their regulatory role in the US government diminished. However, this demand revived after the Bretton Woods system collapsed in the late 1970s, primarily due to the increased movement of capital and the rise of new, complex financial instruments.[104] "Deregulation and internationalization," as Pénet elaborates, "increased the propensity of market actors to use expert knowledge in investment decision-making," making rating agencies "pivotal

Table 4.3 Mention of Rating Agencies in the News

	1975–1990	1990–2007
Moody's	3894	10K+
Standard & Poor's	7367	10K+

Source: LexisNexis: US Newspapers, Business News.

knowledge intermediaries for lending and borrowing transactions"[105] (see in Table 4.3 the increasing mention of rating agencies in the news).

In 1975, the SEC officially named the three biggest rating agencies—Moody's, Standard and Poor's, and Fitch—as a Nationally Recognized Statistical Rating Organization, endowing them with legal status. It was around this time that rating agencies became part of a new risk regulation regime that relied on market discipline and individual rationality. The information that was provided by the major rating agencies was used as the indicator of safety and soundness of individual institutions and products. As Pénet clarifies, in this latter period, the espousal of rating-based regulations was not to "tackle the problem of speculation and restrict the scope of appropriate investment practices."[106] Rather, aligned with the ideas of limited government, market discipline, and individual rationality, rating agencies became "active guarantors of more open and integrated markets."[107] This shift is critical. Just as was the case with disclosures which, beginning in the 1980s, began to be seen as an alternative to the substantive, macro-structural risk regulation framework that they were previously considered to be in aid of, rating agencies have become not merely a supplement to, but a core element of, a micro-oriented, information-based risk regulation regime.

As Richard Cantor and Frank Pecker note, ratings reliance extended to "virtually all financial regulators, including the public authorities that oversee banks, thrifts, insurance companies, securities firms, capital markets, mutual funds, and private pensions."[108] Meanwhile, the credit rating agencies themselves understood all too well the limitations of their information for risk assessment, as the standard disclaimer in Standard & Poor's credit ratings revealed: "[A]ny user of the information contained herein should not rely on any credit rating or other opinion contained herein in making any investment decision."[109]

Financial Literacy

Finally, consumer education—specifically, financial literacy programs—also constituted an integral element of an information-based approach to risk regulation in the era of neoliberal financialization. As financial markets have become more complex, the emphasis on literacy has increased; and, as Willis notes, "policymakers have embraced financial literacy education as a necessary corollary to the disclosure model of regulation."[110] The political and cultural espousal of financial literacy went hand in hand with the rejection of paternalistic government regulation and the sacralization of "responsible" individuals and families. The vision was one of "educated consumers handling their own credit, insurance, and retirement planning matters by confidently navigating the bountiful unrestricted marketplace."[111] National bestseller lists started featuring personal finance books, and financial experts began gaining celebrity status. A clear indication of the growing cultural acceptance of financial literacy came in 2002 when CNBC launched *The Suze Orman Show*, drawing in a quarter of a million viewers on its premiere night. *Rich Dad Poor Dad*, a book that promises to educate its readers in matters of money and personal finance, has sold over thirty-five million copies worldwide since its initial publication.[112]

The adoption of financial literacy as a tool that would empower rational individuals as risk managers of self into the governing logic of the state manifested itself in the attention paid to it in the halls of Congress. In February 2002, the Senate Banking, Housing, and Urban Affairs Committee held a two-day hearing to consider "the state of financial literacy and education in America."[113] All three witnesses on the first day—Treasury Secretary Paul H. O'Neill, Federal Reserve Chairman Greenspan, and SEC Chairman Harvey L. Pitt—trumpeted financial literacy as an integral part of risk regulation in a financialized economy. "For an increasingly complex financial system to function effectively," Greenspan said, "widespread dissemination of timely financial and other relevant information among educated market participants is essential if they are to make the type of informed judgments that promote their own well-being and foster the most efficient allocation of capital."[114] Pitt noted that "ours is a disclosure-based system. And it is our job to promote clear, accurate, and timely disclosures—proactively. Once investors are fully informed, we leave it to them to evaluate the merits of an investment."[115] O'Neill agreed: "More directly to the subject of financial literacy, it is more and more imperative, it seems to me, that every American citizen be financially literate."[116]

78 DISEMBEDDED

On the hearing's second day, consumer advocates were more measured in their praise of financial literacy.[117] Steven Brobeck, executive director of the Consumer Federation of America, recounted the structural problems consumers—especially those with modest means—face, such as having little to no savings and falling prey to risky loans. Financial education is not enough, he said, insisting that "only a sensible combination of financial education and regulation can help ensure that consumers manage, spend, borrow, and save their money adequately."[118]

However, the government's faith in financial literacy did not waiver— if anything, it intensified. In 2003, the Financial Literacy and Education Commission was established to "improve the financial literacy and education of persons in the United States through development of a national strategy to promote financial literacy and education" under the Fair and Accurate Credit Transactions Act.[119] In May 2006, the Senate Banking, Housing, and Urban Affairs Committee held another hearing on financial literacy.[120] This time, the Federal Reserve had a new chairman in Ben S. Bernanke, but the message was very much the same: the financial services market is increasingly diverse and complex, and consumers need good information "to choose wisely from the variety of products and providers available."[121] Acknowledging educational disparities, Bernanke said that consumers who have the skill to make informed decisions will be better off than those who do not. Therefore, he said, "regulators have an important role in helping to ensure that financial service companies provide necessary information to their customers, but such information is of value only to the extent that it can be understood and applied by potential users of these services."[122] Soon, financial literacy was integrated into high school curricula in states across the country and, in 2012, President Barack Obama declared April "National Financial Capability Month" as part of the White House's renewed drive to provide all Americans with the tools to navigate the financial system.

Conclusion

To reiterate, the change in the regulatory relationship between the state and economy was by no means limited to deregulation. Specifically, the notion that neoliberalism led to deregulation, which then led to excessive risk-taking and ultimately leading to a full-blown crisis, is reductive. To move beyond that narrative, we must first attempt to get a more complete view of the

FROM POLITICS TO POLICY 79

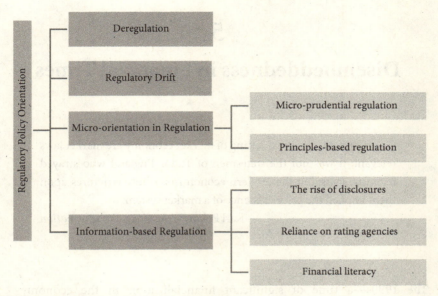

Figure 4.5 Regulatory Policy and Finance

policy and institutional changes that have taken place since the 1980s. This is what this chapter has attempted to do. Not only regulatory retreat but also regulatory drift was on the action menu of the neoliberal state, along with the espousal of a micro and information-based approach to risk regulation (see Figure 4.5).

In the next chapter, I will discuss how the neoliberal risk regulation was connected to the disembeddedness of the economy, and specifically what it meant in terms of systemic risk and consumer financial protection.

5

Disembeddedness in Financial Times

> Only in the institutional setting of market economy are market laws relevant; it was not the statesmen of Tudor England who strayed from the facts, but the modern economists, whose strictures upon them implied the prior existence of a market system.
> —Karl Polanyi, *The Great Transformation*

The 1990s—a time of significant financialization in the economy— appeared, on the surface, to be a time of growth and prosperity. Inflation was under control, poverty was in decline, and productivity had reached "levels that exceeded even those of the boom following World War II."[1] As Joseph Stiglitz observed, "Capitalism American-style seemed triumphant."[2] In the face of what was perceived to be an extremely strong economy with a vibrant financial sector, questions about risk protection, equitable distribution of income and wealth, or sustainability of economic growth did not gain much salience. The prevailing political economy of the time could be termed "vulgar," borrowing a phrase used by Marx and Engels to critique much of the nineteenth-century political economy; it dealt "with appearances only," and not with the underlying machineries of capital accumulation or distribution.[3] It wasn't until the first decade of the twenty-first century, as we hurtled toward an impending crisis and recession, that some of the structural issues became subject to scrutiny, and the political economy of the 1990s, a decade which was deemed "roaring," was dissected and debunked. In the aftermath, calls were made to enact reform and to revive the principles of embedded liberalism. This brings us back to the question: How did the American economy become so disembedded in the first place? What was the nature of the risk protection deficit, and what regulatory frameworks contributed to its existence?

Disembedded. Basak Kus, Oxford University Press. © Oxford University Press 2024.
DOI: 10.1093/oso/9780197764862.003.0005

The Regulatory Underpinnings of Disembedded Finance

As discussed earlier, by the onset of the 2000s, the financial sector looked very different from just two decades earlier. In part due to various deregulatory policies implemented in the early 1980s, financial markets had grown and diversified, incorporating new actors and instruments. Both banking and non-banking financial institutions were more interconnected than ever, with some growing so large they became what is often referred to as "too big to fail." And again, as previously articulated, despite these significant changes, regulation designed to address risk had failed to keep pace with the new realities of the financial sector, and had in fact, drifted away. The political movement against direct and substantive regulation combined with the faith placed in market discipline and rational self-conduct had led to a new regulatory framework with a decisively micro and information-based approach to regulating risk in the financial marketplace. This approach focused primarily on the "safety and soundness" of individual institutions, increasingly relying on those very institutions themselves to decide *what* was safe and sound and *how* to achieve it. Concurrently, it embraced the notion that the government's most effective role in risk regulation was to ensure market actors could access and comprehend information. This was to be achieved through disclosures, credit ratings, and enhanced consumer literacy. It is in this context that a significant deficit in risk protection emerged in America's financialized economy—a phenomenon that I have termed "disembedded financialization."

The Limitations of a Micro-Oriented Approach

Micro-prudential regulation focuses on key indicators such as capital adequacy, asset quality, management capability, earnings, liquidity, and sensitivity to market risk (CAMELS) at the level of individual institutions. There are several notable limitations to approaching safety and soundness at the firm level, however. First, while necessary, these measures, when viewed in isolation, may not necessarily imply or guarantee stability during times when other institutions in the field are showing stress. That is, while they might be taken as valid indicators of safety and soundness during normal times, during an industry-wide downturn, they may not mean much. Second, the micro-prudential approach does not question the means through which institutions meet these requirements. It overlooks whether these strategies, although beneficial to the individual institution, could contribute to systemic instability. To quote Kadija Yilla and Nellie Liang, "The ability of a bank to increase its capital to meet regulatory requirements is seen as favorable, without regard to how this is accomplished."[4] Thirdly, as Adam Levitin pointed out, the focus of micro-prudential regulation on the safety and soundness of individual institutions could potentially conflict, and often has, with other protective objectives.[5] Notably, actions that are considered advantageous to an institution's safety and soundness could potentially conflict with consumer financial protection. The prioritization of the firm's profitability above all else can sometimes validate practices that are "unfair, deceptive, and abusive" to consumers as long as they are profitable.[6]

In any case, while micro-prudential regulation itself was not a comprehensive framework to analyze safety and soundness to begin with for the very reasons elaborated just now, it had lost some teeth over time, as risk regulation transitioned away from rules-based regulation toward principles-based regulation in the years leading up to the crisis. Instead of prescribing what regulated parties must do and how they must do it, regulators began to approach risk regulation by issuing broad guidelines (principles), allowing rational, self-interested firms to determine how these guidelines would be met. This often resulted in key decisions being made from the vantage point of what is profitable and/or less burdensome for the firm, without necessarily considering the complex environments in which these institutions operated.[7] Sheila Bair directly addressed this issue in her testimony before the State Banking committee regarding Basel II Advanced Approaches, which, in the spirit of principles-based regulation, "allow[ed] banks to determine their risk-based capital requirements by using their own estimates of key risk parameters as inputs to formulas developed by the Basel Committee."[8] Bair argued that "banks may tend to hold less capital than is optimal for prudential purposes," especially because "when calculating economic capital needs, banks do not consider the substantial costs that their potential failure would impose on other parts of the economy."[9] Similarly, Diana Taylor, Superintendent of New York State Banking Department, cautioned in her testimony that the flexibility that Basel II's Advanced Approaches allowed banks in determining their own risk-based capital requirements would undermine the safety and soundness of financial institutions, and the stability of the system. She pointed to the results of the then most recent Quantitative Impact Study, undertaken by the Basel Committee, which showed "drastic drops in required capital," arguing that this was a concerning trend because "sufficient capital levels are a prerequisite in maintaining the safety and soundness of an institution."[10] The principles-based regulatory framework also raised concerns from a consumer protection angle. Travis B. Plunkett, Legislative Director of Consumer Federation of America, argued that "industry representatives who advocate a principles-based approach to regulation often have weakened consumer protections as their real goal" because the approach "moves decisions about what constitutes non-compliant behavior out of the relatively transparent public rulemaking process into backroom negotiations between the regulator and the regulated entity," often leading to "lax enforcement."[11]

The Limitations of an Information-Based Approach

Relying on the provision of and access to information as a tool for risk regulation also played its part in creating a risk deficit. As discussed before, disclosure is supposed to regulate risk in a way that is in line with the idea of free markets. It does not outlaw products or prohibit exchange. It does not intervene with economic freedoms or impose costs. As Omri Ben-Shahar et al. note, "It lets sellers sell and buyers buy, as long as buyers know what sellers are selling,"[12] and precisely for this reason, its capacity as a mode of risk regulation remains limited.

First, the premise that information can be made available to all the parties in a transaction is questionable. It is well established that information asymmetries exist—that is, vital information may be available to one party, and not the other. Second, as Mary Graham explains, if information is "distorted, incomplete or misunderstood," it would certainly not lead to safe and sound decisions and might in fact increase risk rather than help mitigate it.[13] The information provided by rating agencies is a case in point. During the crisis, Moody's, S&P, and Fitch were all criticized for assigning highly favorable ratings to products that were later deemed junk. Starting in the 1970s with Moody's, the major rating agencies in the US embraced the "issuer fee" business model. In this model, "the evaluated entity selects a rating agency and establishes a commercial relationship with it."[14] This could, and did, create collusion. Issuers were able to shop for an agency that would rate them and their products favorably. As the rating agencies competed to get them as clients, the accuracy of their evaluations was compromised.

84   DISEMBEDDED

There are also challenges tied to organization and implementation. As Willis points out, while the law acknowledges that consumers need to have written disclosures to make informed decisions, it does not provide these disclosures until a stage where, realistically, many consumers can't compare prices anymore.[15] This is particularly true in the mortgage sector, where disclosures occur "after the application fee is paid," which makes it challenging for "borrowers on a limited budget" to abandon their current application and consider other options.[16] For information access and provision to effectively serve as a regulatory tool, a complex series of interconnected actions must be executed without flaw, requiring all parties involved— "lawmakers, disclosers, and disclosees"—to proficiently perform their respective roles.[17]

And perhaps most critically, whether and the extent to which the buyers *can know* what transaction they are becoming party to is open to question. When the product or the market process in question is complex, which is the case with most everything exchanged in financial markets, there is no guarantee that individuals will be able to assess and understand the full extent of the risk they are taking, even if they have access to information. They simply may not be able to because they do not have the kind of literacy that this requires. As Ben-Shahar et al. note, "financial and medical privacy notices are generally written at a college level," while "only a tiny percent of the population can understand ordinary contractual language."[18] Elizabeth Warren, for these very reasons, calls it a "disclosure hoax," the idea that disclosure can be an effective consumer protection tool in financial markets: "Mortgage-loan documents, payday-loan papers, car-loan, and credit card terms—all these and other lending products have become long and jargon-filled, often proving entirely incomprehensible to those with law degrees—much less to those whose specialty is not reading legal documents."[19]

Financial literacy is often argued to be a panacea to these issues; however, it is hardly so. Even if individuals had the necessary literacy, there are other psychological or behavioral factors that affect the way they are able to relate to information. As David Moss articulates, there are "a large number of systematic biases that adversely affect the way most of us perceive and interpret risk" ranging from "misapplications of simple heuristics" to "optimistic bias and illusions of control."[20] There is no guarantee that market actors will avoid risk, even if they are literate to understand what constitutes it, because it is supposed to be the "rational" thing to do. For all these reasons, disclosures and other informational tools, such as credit ratings or financial literacy enhancing programs, are not necessarily or fully effective tools to mitigate systemic risk or protect consumers.

The Fragmented Regulatory Structure of US Finance

The regulatory approach to risk regulation that was embraced in the decades leading to the crisis had many pitfalls in terms of risk protection. However, it is also crucial to note that the disjointed regulatory framework within which these risk regulation objectives were sought further exacerbated the deficit in risk protection. As of the onset of the economic crisis, the oversight of the financial system was scattered across multiple federal and state-level agencies, competing over turf (see Figure 5.1). This fragmented structure sets the US apart from many of its advanced economy counterparts, such as Canada, Germany, Switzerland, the UK, Australia, and France, which all maintain a more unified regulatory structure.[21] This fragmentation in the US regulatory structure can be traced back to historical patterns of state formation. As Elizabeth Kimberly Pernell argues, political and regulatory institutions in the US "embodied the principle of local sovereignty" central to which is the belief that "the general interest would be best served by local communities determining local affairs in active competition with rival local groups."[22] In other words, the American political and regulatory architecture embraced

OCC	OCC	OCC	OCC	OCC	OCC	OCC
	FRS	FRS	FRS	FRS	FRS	FRS
		FHLBB	CEC	CFTC	CFTC	CFTC
		GFA	FDIC	FDIC	FDIC	FDIC
			FSLIC	NCUA	NCUA	NCUA
			BFCU	OTS	OTS	OTS
			SEC	OFHEO	SEC	SEC
			FHLBB	SEC	OFHEO	FHFA
				FHFB	FHFB	PCAOB
					PCAOB	

Late 1800s---------------------------------------1930s------------------1970s-------------------------------- Late 2000s

Figure 5.1 The Development of the Regulatory Architecture of American Finance

Adapted from Alejandro Komai and Gary Richardson, "A Brief History of Regulations Regarding Financial Markets in the United States: 1789 to 2009," Working Paper 17443, https://www.nber.org/papers/w17443.

86   DISEMBEDDED

"a deconcentrated structure" where "power was divided among many independent groups with distinct interests, and where power to direct local affairs remained in local hands."[23]

From a risk protection perspective, however, the fragmented architecture, which is often depicted as an alphabet soup, or in the words of Treasury Secretary Henry Paulson as "a hopelessly outmoded patchwork quilt built for another day and age . . . rife with duplication, gaping holes, and counterproductive competition among regulators"—seems to pose challenges.[24] It opens up the question: "Do scattered posts make a fence?" as Senator Warren put it.[25] For one, it leads to turf wars among regulatory agencies. This was especially the case because financial products and activities were regulated based on the identity of the issuer rather than the type of the product. This meant that large firms with different financial entities could go to a number of different agencies based on which regulator they found more lenient. As a result, not only was it not clear what was in whose jurisdiction, but with financial institutions shopping for the regulator they found easy to deal with, and the agencies competing to expand their constituency—it led to a regulatory arbitrage, and a regulatory race to the bottom.[26] Moreover, as the products available to consumers multiplied and became more complex in nature, the fragmented regulatory architecture seemed to be less fitting to the market it was supposed to regulate. Credit products being regulated based on the identity of the issuer rather than the type of the product meant, for instance, that they could be issued by an institution that was not subject to regulation.

Disembeddedness as Deficit in Risk Protection

For reasons described so far, the American economy remained subject to a deficit in risk protection in the decades leading to the crisis. This was observed in terms of the government's mitigation of systemic risk in a highly financialized economy (systemic risk protection), as well as the state's mitigation of risks that consumers faced in a financializing economy (consumer financial protection).[27]

Deficit in Systemic Risk Protection

It is not uncommon for financial markets to experience shocks, small and large, originating within the sector or in the main street. Systemic risk is not financial instability as such. It has "a certain breadth" and "a certain depth," as Xavier Freixas et al. explain.[28] It refers to "the risk or probability of breakdowns in an entire system, as opposed to breakdowns in individual parts or components."[29] In other words, it is a case of financial instability "so widespread that it impairs the functioning of a financial system to the point where economic growth and welfare suffer materially."[30]

The designation of a systemically risky institution is made from this angle—on the theoretical grounds that its failure "to meet its obligations to creditors and customers would have significant adverse consequences for the financial system and the broader economy."[31] Christian Brownlees and Robert Engle operationalize it as "a function of the size of the firm, its degree of leverage, and its expected equity loss conditional on the market decline."[32] In stable times, should the value of a firm's equity fall dramatically to a "small fraction of its outstanding liabilities," the firm in question may encounter one of several consequences: acquisition, orderly bankruptcy, or in a more optimistic scenario, the ability to raise new capital.[33] However, "if this capital shortage occurs at a time when the financial sector is already financially constrained, then the government faces the question of whether to rescue the firm with taxpayer money as other avenues are no longer available."[34] As Viral Acharya et al. explain, each financial institution's contribution to systemic risk can thus be measured in terms of its "propensity to be undercapitalized when the system as a whole is undercapitalized."[35] With respect to the systemic risk individual institutions pose, in other words, interdependency matters, as well as the size of the institution and the overall state of markets (see the systemic risk contributions of major financial institutions circa 2007 in Table 5.1). And this precisely speaks to limitation of the micro-focused risk regulation that existed leading up to the crisis, whose goal was to limit each institution's risk "in isolation," as Acharya et al. argue (see in Figure 5.2 expanding systemic risk in US financial markets, and in Figure 5.3 the increasing probability of crisis).[36]

Systemic risk became the key focus of regulatory reform efforts in the aftermath of the financial crisis, but up until the crisis it was hardly a salient issue on the radar of the regulators. In fact, the government had consciously refrained from imposing direct, substantive tools to mitigate systemic risk in the substantially altered financial markets. As noted, policymakers at the highest levels resisted elevating systemic risk "to the status of an official macroeconomic policy objective."[37] In retrospect, this lack of focus is striking. While different methodologies might operationalize and measure it differently, the trend is clear: from the early 2000s leading up to the crisis, the level

Table 5.1 Systemically Risky Institutions, Rankings (End of 2007)

	The Systemic Risk Contribution, SRISK%
Citigroup	15.48
Morgan Stanley	8.88
Merrill Lynch	8.82
Freddie Mac	7.8
Goldman Sachs Group	7.44
Fannie Mae	7.35
JPMorgan Chase & Co	7.28
Lehman Brothers	5.77
Bank of America	5.55
Bear Stearns	3.69

Source: The Systemic Risk Contribution, SRISK%, is "the percentage of financial sector capital shortfall that would be experienced by this firm in the event of a crisis." See V-Lab, Systemic Risk Analysis, https://vlab.stern.nyu.edu/docs/srisk.

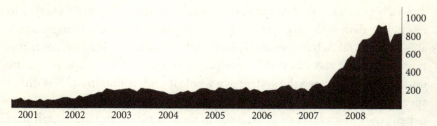

Figure 5.2 United States Financials Total SRISK (US$ billion): 2000–2009
https://vlab.stern.nyu.edu, accessed on January 15, 2020. The capital shortfall that would be experienced by each firm in the event of a crisis is summed to provide a measure of systemic risk for the entire financial sector. For further discussion see Robert F. Engle and Tianyue Ruan, "How Much SRisk Is Too Much?" *SSRN* (2018), 3, https://papers.ssrn.com/sol3/papers.cfm?abstract_id=3108269.

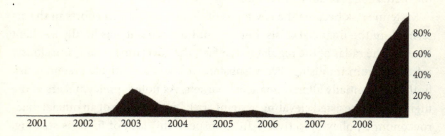

Figure 5.3 Probability of Crisis
https://vlab.stern.nyu.edu, accessed on January 15, 2020.

of systemic risk in the US financial sector had been increasing, and the probability of crisis was rising.

Deficit in Consumer Financial Protection

Protective deficit was also observed in terms of consumer financial protection. Americans' participation in financial markets increased substantially in the last quarter of the twentieth century. For one, Americans turned to credit markets at an increasing rate. According to data from the St. Louis Federal Reserve, gross household debt which was at 15 percent of the GDP in 1946 had reached close to 100 percent by 2008.[38] Household mortgage debt, which was about one-third of the GDP in the 1980s, amounted to more than 70 percent of the GDP by 2008 (see Figure 5.4).[39] The reasons for the turn to debt have been analyzed extensively in the past decade. Scholars seem to agree that one reason was the stagnating wages and soaring income inequality in places where the social welfare system was not generous, and redistributive effort was limited.[40] In the case of the US, despite the rising socio-economic insecurity, characterized by stagnant wages, widening income, and wealth inequality, the state did not effectively step in with needed social insurance and redistribution. As the state

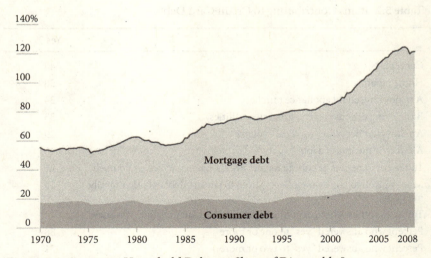

Figure 5.4 Aggregate Household Debt as a Share of Disposable Income
Hutchins Center on Fiscal and Monetary Policy at Brookings and Yale School of Management Program on Financial Stability, *Charting the Financial Crisis: US Strategy and Outcomes*, 2020.

90 DISEMBEDDED

retreated and drifted away from tackling socio-economic risks directly, socio-economic risk management increasingly has been constructed as an individual endeavor to be addressed with market-based tools. Many Americans have found that many of their needs are unattainable without loans. Credit has become essential in maintaining the basic necessities of a middle-class lifestyle and has helped mitigate the impact of rising income inequality (see Table 5.2).

At the same time, participation in stock markets increased. In 1952, less than 5 percent of the US population owned stocks; in 1980, 13 percent did, and by the time the crisis started it was almost 60 percent.[41] To be sure, stock ownership through active individual investment is concentrated in the hands of those with high income. One does not need to participate in the stock markets, or broadly in the financial system, by being an active investor, however. Retirement, one of the most important aspects of socio-economic security, has been financialized in the US whether one seeks to participate in financial markets or not. In the beginning of the 1990s, about 60 percent of full-time workers in the US still had defined-benefit plans, such as pensions. By the time the crisis started, only one-third of Americans did. Retirement planning had turned to defined-contribution plans (such as 401K) for more than half of the full-time work force.

Table 5.2 Items Contributing to Credit Card Debt

	Yes %
Car repairs	48
Home repairs	38
A major household appliance purchase	34
Basic living expenses (rent, groceries, utilities)	33
An illness or necessary medical expense	29
A layoff or the loss of a job	25
Tuition or expenses or college for a child, spouse, a partner, or yourself	21
Money given to family members is used to pay the debts of other family members	19
Tuition or other school expenses for a child high-school age or younger	12
Percent who answered "yes" to one or more	88
Percent who answered "yes" to two or more	71

Source: Data is from https://www.responsiblelending.org/credit-cards/research-analysis/DEMOS-101205.pdf, 10.

The period within which Americans were becoming enmeshed with financial markets as consumers was one that was shaped by neoliberal creed when it came to regulation and risk mitigation. It envisioned a diminished role for the state in consumer protection, leaving it to the rationality of the private decision makers and market discipline. This was, in many ways, an overturn of the postwar consumer protection regime. From the Progressive era until the 1980s, barring a brief pause in the 1920s, the US government had consistently strengthened consumer protection in various ways. The establishment of the Food and Drug Administration and the passage of the Pure Food and Drug Act; the Meat Inspection Act; and anti-trust legislations, including the Clayton Antitrust Act and the Federal Trade Commission Act, all in the early 1900s, marked substantial strides in amplifying consumer protection in the marketplace. As Lizabeth Cohen notes, these legislative measures were widely embraced and endorsed by an increasingly mindful consumer population who had already begun "to assert their power in the marketplace" by staging boycotts against merchants whose pricing they deemed unfair.[42] The New Deal involved a legislative focus on business regulation and consumer protection. One of the important developments was the creation of consumer divisions within New Deal agencies, indicating, as the president noted, that the "problems of consumers" were now being "thoroughly and unequivocally accepted as the direct responsibility of government," as Cohen put it.[43] The passage of the Federal Food, Drug, and Cosmetic Act—a set of laws which endowed authority to the FDA to oversee the safety of food, drugs, and cosmetics; and of the Wheeler–Lea Act of 1938, which aimed to prohibit unfair competition and false advertising, were significant achievements.

The issue of consumer protection in the marketplace became even more salient in the 1960s and 1970s, featuring prominently on both Congressional and White House agendas. As Caroline Edwards notes, a time of "legislative experimentation in modern consumer protection had begun and confidence that government could protect consumers' interests soared."[44] In 1962, President Kennedy gave his Consumer Bill of Rights. This was a remarkable moment, as Fleming highlights, because it called "for the federal government—'the highest spokesman for all the people'—to act on behalf of consumers instead of ceding the role of consumer protector to the states."[45] Consequently, the federal government escalated its efforts, leading to a surge in consumer legislation. Presidents Johnson and Nixon continued to embrace consumer protection at the federal level, establishing, as Cohen points out, "much of the infrastructure for modern consumer protection—the

92   DISEMBEDDED

Water Quality Act of 1965, the National Traffic and Motor Vehicle Safety Act of 1966, the Fair Packaging and Labeling Act of 1966, the Consumer Product Safety Act of 1970 (and the establishment of the Commission in 1972), and the Equal Credit Opportunity Act of 1974, to name only a few."[46]

The development of the Uniform Commercial Code (UCC) also took place in this context, spotlighting the imbalances and injustices that consumers, especially those with limited means, faced in the marketplace. Edwards recounts how Congressional hearings unveiled widespread fraud and deception in consumer loans and credit sales, seemingly targeting individuals with modest means, compelling them to pay "higher cash prices and higher finance charges for goods and services than did members of the middle class who were believed to have access to merchants offering more favorable prices and terms."[47] As detailed in a law review article from the late 1960s, credit transactions involving lower-income consumers were "marked by ignorance on the part of the buyer, enticement, the bait of easy terms, fraudulent practices, shoddy merchandise, unreliable dealers, garnishment, and oppressive collection methods."[48] The development of the UCC was seen as a partial remedy "to address lopsided bargains and the sale of defective merchandise" and more broadly a step toward better consumer protection.[49] Enacted by state legislatures in the early 1960s, the UCC led to courts becoming more cautious about predatory and abusive practices against consumers, particularly in instances where there seemed to be a clear power disparity characterized by the consumers' lack of information or choice.[50] Although the UCC eventually held up the ideal of freedom of contract, it recognized what came to be known as "the doctrine of unconscionability"— the principle that "disparity of bargaining power exists in the marketplace and that freedom of contract must be limited in the interests of fairness, at least in extraordinary circumstances."[51] As Fleming articulates, the doctrine of unconscionability was seen as part of a new area of the law—"the law of the poor."[52] In short, despite the limitations of the existing consumer protection laws in terms of addressing the various predatory practices and injustices that existed in the marketplace, the notion that consumer protection was the responsibility of the government and needed to be addressed with direct and substantive risk regulation, seemed to have taken hold throughout the 1960s and 1970s.

With the rise of neoliberal risk regulation in the late 1970s, the contours of consumer protection began to shift. Consumer protection began to be seen as something that could be tackled by rational individuals themselves.

Rational consumers were expected to be "responsible" adults who would be able to make sound decisions for themselves and their families. According to the neoliberal risk regulation framework, restricting what can be bought and sold in the marketplace would not be an effective way to protect the consumer; it would only limit consumer choice. Moreover, the cost of increased regulatory burdens would then be shifted onto consumers in the form of higher prices. The neoliberal risk regulation framework instead endorsed empowering consumers with adequate information. In the case of consumer financial protection, as Lauren Willis argues, disclosure regulations emerged as the predominant regulatory approach to risk protection.[53] Coupled with financial literacy programs and other market devices supplying information, disclosures were supposed to enable individuals and households to navigate markets and keep themselves from harm's way.

For reasons articulated earlier, however, for many individuals and households there was no way of telling a bad product from a good one; a fair contract from a predatory one. Those who took on mortgages, for instance, regardless of how much debt they had taken on relative to their annual income or assets, had every reason to believe that they were in a good financial position in a booming housing market. The contracts they signed were long and complex. Then-Harvard Law professor Elizabeth Warren—who would later fight to create the consumer financial protection bureau in the aftermath of the crisis and become a senator from Massachusetts—argued at the time: "Plain and simple, consumers cannot compare financial products because the financial products have become too complicated. In the early 1980s, the average credit card contract was about a page long. Today, it is more than 30 pages. It would take hours to parse these contracts, and even then, I'm not sure what the customer would know. I am a contract law professor, and I cannot understand some of the fine print."[54]

Various studies conducted as the economy was heading to the crisis, and in the years after, showed that many families who received subprime mortgages with higher rates and punishing terms could actually qualify for prime loans, but were somehow steered toward subprime loans. This explains how, from 1994 to 2005, in a matter of one decade, the subprime home loan market would grow from $35 billion to $665 billion, constituting more than 20 percent of the total mortgage market.[55] Even loans that would later be deemed as "predatory" were not regulated out of the market, but were sold as legitimate market exchange—access to finance made available at higher prices to customers lacking in creditworthiness. Risk premium in this particular

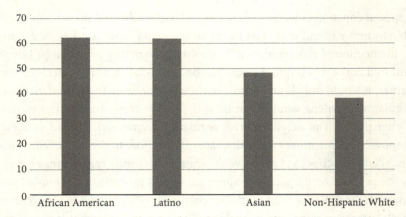

Figure 5.5 Incidence of High-Risk Loan Features (2004–2008 origination)
Gruenstein Bocian et al., *Lost Ground, 2011*, one or more high-risk feature.

way was not distributed evenly, however. As the research of the Center for Responsible Lending showed (see Figure 5.5), "borrowers in minority groups were much more likely to receive loans with product features associated with higher rates of foreclosures, specifically higher interest rates, hybrid and option ARMs, and prepayment penalties."[56]

As Ellen Schloemer et al. argue, in a report also published by the Center for Responsible Lending, foreclosure "is a last resort, often coming in the wake of unemployment, illness, divorce, or other personal event that causes a drop in income."[57] However, the "tsunami of dispossession," which hit the United States, as Martin et al. describe it,[58] could hardly be explained by these factors. The core issue was not "a change in income, but rather an unmanageable increase in the amount of the mortgage payment or the realization that the mortgage was not affordable in the first place."[59]

While the representatives of various anti-regulation lobbies repeatedly blamed the foreclosures and delinquencies on consumer ignorance—on individuals and families who were not responsible and literate enough in taking on these loans—the comparison in the outcomes of subprime and the Federal Housing Administration (FHA) loans is telling (see Figure 5.6). As Schloemer et al. illustrate, FHA loans, similar to subprime loans, cater to borrowers with low income, limited employment history, or less than good credit scores. However, they also differ in significant ways: "FHA loans are predominantly fixed-rate, amortizing loans and establish escrow accounts for taxes and insurance . . . and [provide] more consumer protections and lower costs during the origination process."[60] While the subprime loans originated in 2000 had a 12.9 percent foreclosure rate within five years, FHA loans had a 6.29 percent foreclosure rate.[61]

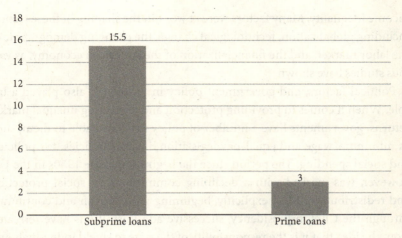

Figure 5.6 Percentage of Mortgages in the Foreclosure Process, 2009
Source: Data is from the Mortgage Bankers Association, quoted in Katie Jones, *Preserving Homeownership: Foreclosure Prevention Initiatives* (Washington, DC: Congressional Research Service, May 14, 2015), https://fas.org/sgp/crs/misc/R40210.pdf, 3.

The non-housing credit market also put consumers at risk—particularly poor households who had a much bigger footprint in non-housing debt, compared to housing debt.[62] In this case, the issue could not be written off as consumers irresponsibly taking on mortgages for houses that they couldn't afford, as some of the talking heads on TV often claimed during the financial crisis. This was clearly a case of piling on debt to make ends meet. According to the Center for Responsible Lending, credit card debt had almost tripled between 1989 and 2005, becoming for many households "the new 'safety net' for managing essential expenses."[63] High-interest borrowing, such as loans from payday lenders or pawnshops, had also expanded. According to the Center for Responsible Lending, "Over 90 percent of payday lending revenue comes from borrowers caught in a cycle of repeat payday loans," and every year there are twelve million such borrowers.[64] Payday lenders are concentrated in "neighborhoods with the largest shares of African Americans and Latinos as compared to white neighborhoods."[65]

Deficit in Social Protection in the Time of Financialization

Although it is not the main focus of this analysis, it should be noted that deficit in social protection was also an important aspect of disembedded financialization. The period since the early 1980s in the US has seen stagnant wages for nonsupervisory workers in the private sector and increasing

96 DISEMBEDDED

income inequality. Many factors were at work in the shaping of these trends, including globalization, technological change, the changing demographic of the labor market, and the financialization of the American economy, as various studies have shown.[66]

Political factors, and government policy in particular, also played a big role. When it comes to providing protection and correcting unequal market returns, governments have a number of policy tools available to them, such as minimum-wage and equal-pay legislation, income policies, tax policies, and social spending. The period since the beginning of the 1980s in the US, however, was marked with a declining commitment to social protection and redistribution. Most explicitly, beginning with Reagan and continuing through the Clinton presidency, successive administrations have retreated from the idea that it is the responsibility of the state to shield individuals and households from the material risks and distributional injustices that economic structures produce. Credit reliance became pervasive in this context, largely as a mechanism which allowed households to supplement their income and meet their consumption needs or aspirations. As Colin Crouch puts it, "the basis of prosperity shifted from the social democratic formula of working classes supported by government intervention to the neoliberal conservative one of banks, stock exchanges and financial markets."[67] During the postwar era of "embedded liberalism," governments intervened to provide citizens with economic security and even prosperity, but in the era of neoliberalism, citizens have begun to turn to banks and other financial institutions to make ends meet or to enhance their lifestyles. In other words, "financial citizenship has taken hold where social citizenship has been undermined."[68] Access to credit made it possible to enjoy a wide variety of products and services that workers could not otherwise afford. It compensated for stagnant wages, and it blurred once sharp class boundaries. This pattern of credit-reliant welfare was hardly sustainable, however. The high levels of indebtedness put families under heightened risk.

Conclusion

One of the key objectives of this book is to describe the disembeddedness of America's financialized economy. Conceptualizing disembeddedness in terms of deficit in risk protection, this chapter discussed how the policies and tools that constituted neoliberal risk regulation created a deficit in systemic risk protection and consumer financial protection. Neither high levels of systemic risk, nor the ways in which consumers found themselves subject to predatory and unconscionable practices as they participated in financial markets, are natural and inevitable aspects of markets. Nor were they the doing of several greedy CEOs. They directly resulted from the specific tools and policies that American governments embraced in some three decades leading up to the crisis. Those policies, as argued in Chapter 3, are not limited to deregulation. Therefore, depicting the road to the crisis as one paved by individual institutions taking excessive risks in a deregulated environment brought about by neoliberal ideas is incomplete, if not entirely inaccurate. Shifting the focus from risk-taking at the individual level to risk protection deficit at the structural level helps us see disembeddedness as a characteristic of the state–economy relationship in the US.

6

The Crisis

> In a crisis "responses" might point toward mutually exclusive solutions.
>
> —Karl Polanyi, *The Great Transformation*

Ten years after President Clinton announced the record budget surplus at the White House press conference in September 1998, the outlook on the American economy was quite different. The financial crisis and the recession—now referred to as the Great Recession—constituted the longest and deepest downturn since the Great Depression of the 1930s. In fact, by some measures, it was worse than its predecessor (see Figure 6.1). "As a scholar of the Great Depression, I honestly believe that September and October of 2008 was the worst financial crisis in global history, including the Great Depression," Ben Bernanke remarked in 2014, his last year as chairman of the Federal Reserve.[1]

The crisis posed two major questions, one of which required an immediate answer: What needs to be done to stop the bleeding? The answer was a series of fast-paced relief and recovery programs. The second question went straight to the heart of America's disembedded financialized economy: What needs to be done to reform the system—its institutions and policies—that failed so spectacularly? While the immediate intervention was visible in the relief delivered—how, how much, and to whom—the reform process took longer and was more complex to legislate. Whether and to what extent the measures were successful in re-embedding America's financialized economy are a matter of debate.[2]

Relief and Recovery: Technocratic Realism, Cautious Keynesianism

The US government's initial response was to figure-it-out-as-you-go, which involved various emergency initiatives. At this stage, the Federal Reserve

Disembedded. Basak Kus, Oxford University Press. © Oxford University Press 2024.
DOI: 10.1093/oso/9780197764862.003.0006

Figure 6.1 Great Recession: Economic Indicators
GD: Great Depression; GR: Great Recession.
Source: GDP data from the Bureau of Economic Analysis (Q1); unemployment data from the Bureau of Labor Statistics; stock market data from the data set in R. Shiller, "U.S. Stock Markets 1871–Present," http://www.econ.yale.edu/~shiller/data/ie_data.xls; data on household wealth from Hutchins Center on Fiscal and Monetary Policy at Brookings and Yale School of Management Program on Financial Stability, *Charting the Financial Crisis: US Strategy and Outcomes*, 2018.

played a significant role, providing relief to financial markets through large quantities of reserves. However, many of the risk-mitigation tools that the Treasury, the Federal Reserve, and the Federal Deposit Insurance Corporation had at their disposal were aimed at depository institutions. Although non-bank financial institutions were a significant part of the American financial system, and were "very fragile" in the words of William Dudley, former president of the Federal Reserve Bank of New York, "there was very little in the tool kit that the regulatory authorities had to respond as circumstances deteriorated."[3] According to Patricia Mosser, a senior economist and veteran of the New York Federal Reserve, the exclusion of non-banks was a major issue because central bank lending at this juncture was supposed to substitute "for the breakdown in private lending relationships until the system [could] stabilize itself."[4] Due to these circumstances, in March 2008, for the first time since the Great Depression the Federal Reserve exercised its emergency powers as per section 13(3) of The Federal Reserve Act to provide loans to non-banking entities.[5] Within a few months, a more systematic program followed, combining relief, recovery, and reform measures, which extended relief to financial and non-financial institutions, and to a limited extent, to American households (see Table 6.1).

100 DISEMBEDDED

Table 6.1 Government's Response to the Financial Crisis

Relief & Recovery	Reform
Federal Reserve relief to bank and non-bank institutions The Housing and Economic Recovery Act, 2008 The Emergency Economic Stabilization Act, 2008 The Economic Stimulus Act, 2008 The American Recovery and Reinvestment Act, 2009	Credit Card Act, 2009 Dodd–Frank Wall Street Reform and Consumer Protection Act, 2010

Relief

Early in 2008, public opinion was clearly opposed to the federal government's helping Wall Street. Sixty-one percent of those participating in a Gallup survey in March 2008 said they did not support the federal government's taking steps to help prevent major financial institutions from failing.[6] Pew Research Center polls conducted a few months later similarly showed a large percentage of Americans were "angry," "scared," "confused," and "very concerned" about "letting those who are responsible off the hook," even among those who backed a bailout (see Table 6.2).[7]

As Simon Johnson and James Kwak elaborated, government choices at this juncture "lay on a spectrum between two main options." On the one end of the spectrum, there was the "blank check option" whereby the government would "keep financial institutions afloat and prevent a systemic collapse by simply giving them the money they needed (by investing new capital, overpaying for banks' assets, or insuring those assets at below-market rates)," and on the other end, the "takeover option" whereby the government

Table 6.2 Public Opinion about Relief and Recovery Measures

Do you favor or oppose the federal government taking steps to help prevent major Wall Street investment companies from failing?	Oppose: 61%
Feeling about government committing billions to secure nation's financial system	Angry: 61%
Public concern about "letting those who are responsible off the hook"	Very concerned: 72%

Source: For the first question, see Jacobe, "Six in 10 Oppose Wall Street Bailouts." For the second and third questions, see Pew Research Center, "Small Plurality Backs Bailout Plan."

would put the failing institutions under receivership.[8] In the first case, "managers [would] keep their jobs, shareholders [would] keep some value, and creditors [would be] kept whole," and "the taxpayers [would] bear most of the losses"; whereas in the second option, "managers [would] lose their jobs, shareholders [would be] wiped out, and any remaining losses [would be] shared between taxpayers and creditors."[9]

The government stayed close to the first option. In October 2008, President George W. Bush signed the Emergency Economic Stabilization Act, creating the Troubled Asset Relief Program (TARP) and authorizing the Treasury to spend $700 billion in a financial rescue plan that entailed purchasing troubled assets held by financial institutions, injecting capital into banks, providing loans to the auto industry, and assisting the global insurance company AIG. The relief to the banking sector was massive by any comparative and historical standard: $250 billion was earmarked to launch the Capital Purchase Program,[10] and about half of that money went to nine big banks: Goldman Sachs Group, Morgan Stanley, JPMorgan Chase, Citigroup, Wells Fargo, State Street, Bank of New York Mellon, Bank of America, and Merrill Lynch. The banks' participation in the capital purchase program was not voluntary. Treasury Secretary Henry Paulson informed the banks that they would be "vulnerable and exposed" if they were to opt out.[11]

In contrast, the relief extended to homeowners proved to be quite restricted. In July 2008, Congress passed the Housing and Economic Recovery Act (HERA) to bail out the government-sponsored entities Fannie Mae and Freddie Mac, stabilize the mortgage market, and prevent a further drop in home prices. As part of HERA, the HOPE for Homeowners program was established to aid struggling borrowers in refinancing their homes through affordable FHA-insured mortgages. Additionally, the Neighborhood Stabilization Program was introduced. This initiative aimed to support states and local governments by offering grants to "purchase foreclosed or abandoned homes and to rehabilitate, resell, or redevelop these homes in order to stabilize neighborhoods and stem the decline of house values of neighboring homes."[12] Another measure of relief came from TARP, which introduced the Making Home Affordable program (MHA) in February 2009. This program encompassed the Home Affordable Modification Program and the Home Affordable Refinance Program. Nonetheless, the funding allocated to housing programs constituted a minor fraction of the overall TARP budget (see Figure 6.2). This led to criticism of the government's actions, with many asserting that it prioritized rescuing failing financial institutions

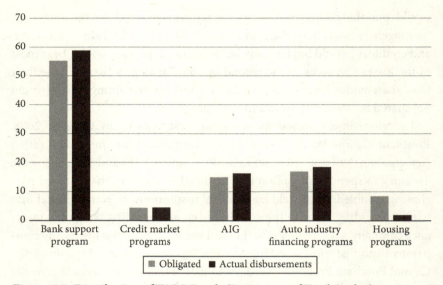

Figure 6.2 Distribution of TARP Funds (Percentage of Total Outlay)

Author's calculation based on data as of June 2013 from Baird Webel, "Troubled Asset Relief Program: Implementation and Status," Congressional Research Service, 2013, https://sgp.fas.org/crs/misc/R41427.pdf.

over providing adequate support to homeowner.[13] By 2010, the number of foreclosures had surged to ten million, and millions of homeowners were under water with negative equity.[14]

According to the leading policymakers, most notably Treasury Secretary Paulson, the notion that the US government had not helped homeowners was misguided; placing Fannie Mae and Freddie Mac under conservatorship had significantly benefited homeowners, helped prevent housing prices from declining further, and stabilized the lenders, ensuring the resumption of credit flow (see Figure 6.3).[15] Neel Kashkari, a senior Treasury official and TARP administrator, made an analogous argument, stating that the US government could not merely allocate the $700 billion in relief directly to homeowners instead of banks. He described the situation as a "massive heart attack" in the US economy, elaborating that just as a heart attack deprives critical organs of blood and requires the surgeon to pay immediate attention to the heart, the government needed to prioritize stabilizing the core financial system over directly aiding individual homeowners.[16]

As Polanyi rightly observed, during a time of crisis, the potential solutions that are presented may appear in conflict with each other, or

Figure 6.3 US Government's Housing Programs
Hutchins Center on Fiscal and Monetary Policy at Brookings and Yale School of Management Program on Financial Stability, *Charting the Financial Crisis: US Strategy and Outcomes*, 2020.

"mutually exclusive."[17] The trade-off presented by major policymakers regarding relief might not mirror the actual situation. There was no consensus that the government's decision to prioritize rescuing lenders meant that they could not help borrowers more substantially. Indeed, the view that helping homeowners would "prevent further damage to home values and communities" and would also serve to "stabilize the economy as a whole" was on the table.[18] The reason for not launching a more robust relief for homeowners seems to have been shaped by political factors, possibly influenced by high-income and Republican voters' reluctance to assist homeowners they deemed "undeserving." This sentiment was fueled by the belief that "foreclosure prevention should be worked out between lenders and borrowers without government interference," and that offsetting the losses of "people who knowingly took on mortgages that they could not afford" is not a good use of taxpayers' dollars.[19]

The biggest opposition to the relief and recovery programs in general, and relief for homeowners in particular, came from the conservative Tea Party movement within the Republican Party (see Figure 6.4). Rick Santelli, an editor for *CNBC Business News*, captured the popular opposition in a rant on TV that ignited the movement:

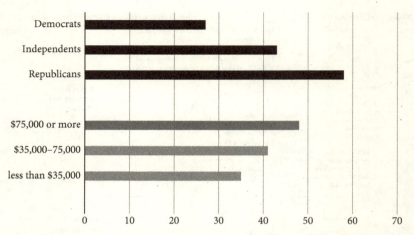

Figure 6.4 Percentage Opposing Federal Government's Steps to Prevent Home Foreclosures (By Party Affiliation; Income Level)
Jacobe, "Six in 10 Oppose Wall Street Bailouts."

How about this, President and new administration? Why don't you put up a website to have people vote on the Internet as a referendum to see if we really want to subsidize the losers' mortgages; or would we like to at least buy cars and buy houses in foreclosure and give them to people that might have a chance to actually prosper down the road, and reward people that could carry the water instead of drink the water? . . . This is America! How many of you people want to pay for your neighbor's mortgage that has an extra bathroom and can't pay their bills? . . . We're thinking of having a Chicago Tea Party in July. All you capitalists that want to show up to Lake Michigan, we're going to be dumping in some derivative securities.[20]

Recovery

The politics around the economic stimulus package were also contentious. Adopting a Keynesian approach, the government sought to offset the decrease in private consumer spending with an increase in public spending to tackle unemployment and stop further economic decline. The key question was how big to go. In 1932, John Maynard Keynes had urged President Roosevelt to prioritize recovery through government spending: "During a major downturn only large increases in government expenditures can resuscitate the economy," he wrote in a letter.[21] But in the US, pursuing such a course is easier said than done. Public discourse around government spending evokes fears of big government and swelling deficit. In a 2011 national poll, for instance, only 38 percent of those surveyed agreed that "government spending is critical during an economic downturn, even if the government is already running a deficit because government has the unique ability to stimulate the economy through public investment and infrastructure improvement projects that lower unemployment and encourage consumer spending."[22] Instead, the majority of those surveyed (56 percent) held that "government spending when the government is already running a deficit is the wrong approach during an economic downturn because it is only a temporary solution that increases long-term debt."[23] This aversion to government spending explains to some extent why the initial Economic Stimulus Act that the Republican President George W. Bush signed on February 13, 2008, did not go big on spending. Although it found bipartisan support as a stimulus effort, the $152 billion it allocated, amounting to only 1 percent of the GDP, had little impact on the economy.

A year later, President Barak Obama signed the American Recovery and Reinvestment Act which allocated an economic stimulus of $787 billion—roughly 5.5 percent of the GDP. The act, according to Christina Romer, then chair of the Council of Economic Advisors, was "the boldest countercyclical fiscal action in American history."[24] It also was comparatively large among other advanced nations (Figure 6.5). The act focused on creating jobs,

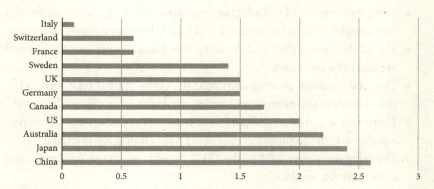

Figure 6.5 Fiscal Stimulus in Advanced Nations (% of GDP)

Executive Office of the President of the United States, "The Economic Impact of American Recovery and Reinvestment Act," *First Quarterly Report*, September 10, 2009, https://eml.berkeley.edu/~dromer/papers/CEA_ARRA_Report_Final.pdf. Data captures the magnitude of the fiscal stimulus that took effect in 2009 as a share of the GDP.

106 DISEMBEDDED

jumpstarting the economy, and maintaining spending on education and health programs through federal transfers to state governments.

The results were relatively successful (see Figure 6.6 and Figure 6.7). From 2009 to 2010, the GDP grew significantly, and unemployment began to fall. Compared with other financial crises, the Great Recession was shorter and the recovery was faster.

Regulatory Reform

While relief and recovery measures were implemented rather swiftly, regulatory reform took more time and deliberation. This is not surprising. Post-crisis policy reform remains a deeply political process. Key actors interpret and negotiate what happened, why it happened, and what needs to be done about it.[25] Competing articulations of the crisis live side-by-side, and policy proposals take shape in light of voter preferences, interest group demands, and what seems feasible given the rules and procedures of Congress's legislative process. In this case, the diagnoses of the administration, financial industry representatives, and consumer representatives varied, as did their solutions. In June 2009, the Obama administration's Treasury Department circulated a white paper that acknowledged outright the shortcomings of substantive government regulation and the breakdown of market discipline. Specifically, the document noted the following:[26]

- The government did not adequately address the dangers that came with the collapse of large, intertwined, and highly leveraged financial entities.
- The established capital and liquidity benchmarks were insufficient and needed to be increased.
- The securitization process disrupted the conventional relationship between lenders and borrowers, leading to persistent conflicts of interest.
- There was a substantial deterioration in credit underwriting criteria, notably within the subprime and other home mortgage domains.
- The regulatory oversight of the OTC derivatives sector, encompassing CDS markets, was lacking.
- Investors excessively depended on credit rating agencies, which often miscalculated the risks tied to the products they rated.
- Regulatory bodies failed to sufficiently protect consumers from the risks that financial markets placed upon them.

THE CRISIS   107

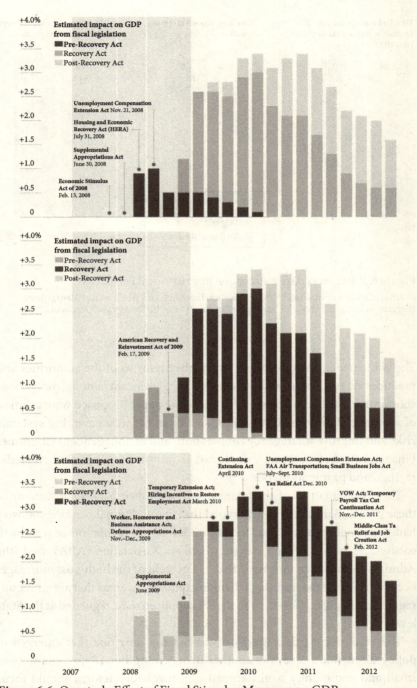

Figure 6.6 Quarterly Effect of Fiscal Stimulus Measures on GDP
Hutchins Center on Fiscal and Monetary Policy at Brookings and Yale School of Management Program on Financial Stability, *Charting the Financial Crisis: US Strategy and Outcomes*, 2020.

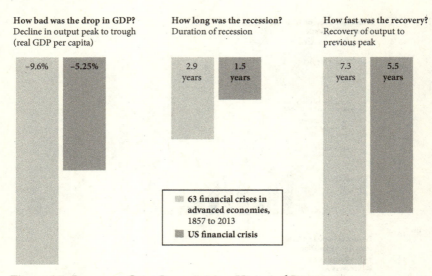

Figure 6.7 Recovery: Great Recession in a Historical Perspective
Hutchins Center on Fiscal and Monetary Policy at Brookings and Yale School of Management Program on Financial Stability, *Charting the Financial Crisis: US Strategy and Outcomes*, 2020.

The white paper recommended "substantive reforms of the authorities and practices of regulation and supervision."[27] Significant among the various substantive regulatory changes that the white paper proposed were creation of a Financial Services Oversight Council "to identify emerging systemic risks and improve interagency cooperation" and an independent Consumer Financial Protection Agency dedicated to "consumer protection in credit, savings, and payments markets."[28]

The representatives of the financial sector pushed back against many of these points. Bankers, for one, argued that the traditional banking industry had been well regulated, but the failure lay in the regulation of non-bank entities. As evidence, the American Bankers Association (ABA) used "the Administration's own numbers" that "94 percent of the high-cost mortgages occurred outside the traditional banking industry in areas that are either unregulated, lightly regulated, or in theory supposed to be regulated at the State level."[29]

The bank/non-bank distinction was not the only one that emerged in policy discussions. Size was another demarcating line. Representatives of small and community banks argued that regulatory reform should focus on large and complex financial firms. Michael Menzies, chairman of the

Independent Community Bankers Association (ICBA), a vocal proponent of this point, argued that the crisis was "driven by a few unmanageable financial entities that nearly destroyed our equity markets, our real estate markets, our consumer loan markets and the global finance markets, and cost American consumers over \$7 trillion in net worth" and urged the Obama administration to take the necessary steps to curb the "risky and irresponsible behavior by large or unregulated institutions."[30]

These differences notwithstanding, the financial sector was in agreement, broadly speaking, that the government had to address the systemic risk in the financial system, and supported designating the Federal Reserve Board as an oversight authority on the condition provided that it did not become "an additional super-regulator."[31] The banking industry argued that the role of the Federal Reserve as a systemic risk oversight regulator should be one of "identifying potential systemic problems and then putting forth solutions" rather than regulating specific institutions.[32]

The discussion around consumer financial protection was more contentious. The idea to create a consumer financial protection agency had been originated by Elizabeth Warren, chair of the Congressional Oversight Panel of the Troubled Asset Relief Program. In a 2007 article, "Unsafe at Any Rate," Warren emphasized the necessity of such a regulatory agency with this comparison: "It is impossible to buy a toaster that has a one-in-five chance of bursting into flames and burning down your house. But it is possible to refinance an existing home with a mortgage that has the same one-in-five chance of putting the family out on the street."[33] The Obama administration's white paper had also promoted the idea, but neither the House nor the Senate initially embraced it.

Early on, the representatives of the banking industry uniformly opposed the creation of a new consumer protection agency, arguing that it would only limit consumer choice and increase the cost of financial products. Steve Bartlett, the President and CEO of the Financial Services Roundtable, acknowledged the importance of "strengthened consumer protection" as "an essential component of broader regulatory reform"; however, he "strongly oppose[d] the creation of a separate, free-standing Consumer Financial Protection Agency" arguing that it would "bifurcate consumer protection from safety and soundness," and instead recommended "better disclosures for consumers."[34] The American Financial Services Association, representing "every segment of the consumer credit marketplace,"[35] argued that "setting up a new government agency would cost taxpayers more money at a time

110   DISEMBEDDED

when they are already struggling to stay afloat financially," suggesting instead better enforcement or improved financial literacy as a solution.[36] John Courson, speaking for the Mortgage Bankers Association, contended that this approach might "actually weaken consumer protections by disbursing regulatory power and removing consumer protection from the mainstream of the [existing] regulators' focus."[37]

In the debate about the consumer protection agency, size emerged as a defining issue, as well. Small and independent bankers continued to point their finger at large, complex organizations, with ICBA Chairman Menzies asserting that controlling too-big-to-fail institutions was "the only way to truly protect consumers, our financial system, and the economy."[38] He argued:

> We can have all the product legislation in the world and do everything possible to protect the consumer, but the greatest damage to the consumer was the failure of a system because of concentrations and excesses across the board, of a Wall Street vehicle that gathered together substandard, subprime, weird mortgages that community banks didn't make, created a warehouse to slice and dice those entities, make huge profits selling off those items, and have very little skin in the game, very little capital at risk, leveraged in some cases, according to *Harvard Business Review* this week, 70 to 1.[39]

The Consumer Bankers Association concurred, emphasizing that a new consumer protection agency would disproportionately affect small and independent banks which had very little to do with the crisis. Steven Zeisel, the association's representative, warned that "the proposal would subject retail banks to the consumer laws of fifty states," creating undue burden, and as a result, some banks would avoid operating in some states, ultimately leading to "fewer and more expensive choices for consumers as a result of the decreasing competition."[40] Larger banks on the other hand shifted the blame to non-bank institutions as the root of consumer problems. ABA President Edward Yingling contended that the proposed agency would neglect the non-bank sector, "where the great majority of the problem has been."[41]

Unsurprisingly, consumer advocacy groups were fervent supporters of an independent federal agency solely dedicated to protecting consumers. They argued that consumers' perspective and interests in the financial marketplace had not been taken seriously. John Taylor, President and CEO of the

National Community Reinvestment Coalition, expressed astonishment at seeing "all these bankers appointed to [Fed's] Consumer Advisory Council" supposedly to provide a consumer perspective, while they already had a separate council—Bankers Council, comprised entirely of bankers.[42]

One major issue for the consumer advocates was the conflation of safety and soundness with consumer protection, and more critically, with the prioritization of the former at the expense of the latter. They pointed out that regulations focusing on the safety and soundness of individual financial institutions had not provided much protection for consumers, especially because profitability was the measure of safety and soundness, and an activity that was highly profitable to a financial institution could be quite abusive to consumers. Travis B. Plunkett, Legislative Director of Consumer Federation of America, advocated for ensuring that consumer protection "no longer be subjugated to safety and soundness regulation at regulatory agencies."[43] He argued:

> Combining safety and soundness supervision with its focus on bank profitability in the same regulatory institutions as consumer protection magnified an ideological predisposition or anti-regulatory bias by Federal officials that led to unwillingness to rein in abusive lending before it triggered the housing and economic crisis.[44]

That consumer protection remained "an orphan mission" in a fragmented regulatory architecture facing the danger of "fall[ing] between the cracks," as Adam Levitin puts it, was another concern that was voiced by the consumer advocates.[45] It was supposedly "everyone's responsibility" but had in fact become "no one's responsibility."[46] Plunkett argued that federal agencies "appeared to compete against each other to keep standards low and reduce oversight of financial institutions." Edmund Mierzwinski, the Consumer Program Director of US Public Research Interest Group, similarly remarked: "The idea of a new regulator that has only one job, protecting consumers, is one of the best ideas this Congress has had. It will not have conflicts of interest. It will not have two jobs to do. It will focus on consumer protection."[47]

Several community groups made sure to emphasize that consumer protection was also a matter of racial justice. Nancy Zirkin, Executive Vice President of the Leadership Conference on Civil Rights (LCRR), remarked that her organization supported the idea of a Consumer Financial Protection

112 DISEMBEDDED

Agency "because it is the key to protecting the civil rights of the communities that LCCR represents."[48] Homeownership, she noted, had "always been one of the key goals of the civil rights movement" and while some progress had been made since the 1960s, "predatory lending has been the latest obstacle standing in the way."[49]

Consumer advocates also criticized the fact that financial institutions were responsible for paying fees to the federal regulatory agencies overseeing them. They contended that this financial dependency on the very institutions they were meant to regulate undermined consumer protection[50]. This concern was compounded by the system's allowance for "regulatory shopping," where financial institutions could choose their main regulators. Such a structure created incentives for federal regulators to be lenient with rules and enforcement in hopes that financial institutions would select them, thereby enhancing their revenue stream. The situation not only manifested a clear conflict of interest but also led to a troubling compromise, where regulators might neglect consumer interests to foster positive relationships with the very financial institutions they were tasked with supervising.

Finally, consumer interest groups advocated for strengthening the role of the states in consumer financial protection. The US Public Interest Research Group, for instance, suggested that federal law should serve "as a floor of consumer protection and allow the states to go higher."[51] Similarly, the Consumer Federation of America argued that states should not be competing "to attract institutions based on weak consumer protection standards or anemic enforcement of consumer rules," and the law "should . . . set minimum national credit standards, which states could then enforce."[52]

Dodd–Frank

The road to enactment of the Dodd–Frank Wall Street Reform and Consumer Protection Act was politically bumpy. American policymaking takes place in a fragmented structure, as passage of a bill requires successive affirmative votes at "veto points."[53] This characteristic not only slows down the legislative process, but also makes large legislative measures—of which Dodd–Frank was one—particularly difficult to undertake. The fragmentation also yields significant political power to individual members of Congress, according to Sven Steinmo, and makes the whole system particularly susceptible to special interests.[54] Although party unity has been increasing for several decades, signifying that party members are toeing the party line more and more, individual elected officials may still act out when special interests strongly push them, and the structure makes that possible. Therefore, ambitious legislative attempts are open to intense negotiation. In addition, political polarization, on the increase since the 1980s and particularly intense since the early 2000s, is another feature of American legislative space that makes passing ambitious bills more difficult.

These features were on full display on the road to Dodd–Frank. The political battle over the act was fought in a fragmented policy environment, infused with pressure from powerful interest groups and repeatedly fraught by stalemates. Therefore, the bill's sponsors often were forced into paths of relatively less resistance.[55] The challenges posed by powerful individual members came from both sides of the aisle, and many critical ones from Democrats. The New Democratic Coalition in the House—a caucus of moderate Democrats who remained close to the financial sector, particularly banks—wielded a great deal of power in this case. Thirty-one new Democrats were elected to the House in 2006 and twenty-one more in 2008, which as Robert Kaiser observes, "altered the political coloration of the Democratic caucus in the House, and of the Democratic membership of Frank's committee."[56] These newly elected Democrats were notably less liberal and had closer ties to the finance sector compared to their older colleagues.[57] In addition, the financial industry mounted strong interest group opposition to the bill. News reports estimated that the industry spent more than $1 billion on lobbying to defeat the bill (see Table 6.3).[58]

Despite these hurdles, Dodd–Frank passed with some important accomplishments from a risk regulation perspective. It created the Financial Stability Oversight Council (FSOC) to monitor systemic risk, developed a resolution procedure for large financial companies, put in place stricter capital requirements, brought derivatives markets under regulatory oversight, established the Volcker rule that prohibited commercial banks from engaging in proprietary trading or investing in hedge funds or private equity funds, and despite the intense opposition described, the act succeeded in creating the Consumer Financial Protection Bureau (CFPB) to ensure consumers are subject to fair, transparent transactions in relation to loans (mortgages, student loans, and credit cards to name a few) and other financial products. The CFPB's jurisdiction was also extended to include non-bank entities, such as mortgage brokers and payday lenders.

114 DISEMBEDDED

Table 6.3 Lobbying against Dodd–Frank

Money for lobbying by top financial industry spenders	
US Chamber of Commerce	$136.3 million
American Bankers Association	$9.0 million
JP Morgan Chase	$8.1 million
Wells Fargo	$6.8 million
Goldman Sachs	$3.5 million
Money for lobbying by top consumer protection spenders	
The American Federation of State, County and Municipal Employees	$2.7 million
Center for Responsible Lending	$595,000
US Public Interest Research Group	$236,800
Consumer Federation of America	$50,000
Americans For Financial Reform	$0

Source: Data used in the table is from Rivlin, "How Wall Street Defanged Dodd–Frank."

The establishment of CFPB was easily Dodd–Frank's most contested measure, for at least two reasons. First, in the history of US consumer protection, this was the first time the government fully recognized its responsibility in the financial marketplace. Previously, consumer financial protection was divided among several agencies—the Office of the Comptroller of the Currency (OCC), the Office of Thrift Supervision (OTS), the FDIC, the Federal Reserve, the National Credit Union Administration, and the FTC—none of which regarded consumer protection as its primary objective. With the establishment of the CFPB, consumer protection responsibility was consolidated.

Second, the establishment of the CFPB represented an expansion of the regulatory state, and as such ran against the limited government direction US regulatory policy had assumed since the early 1970s.[59] In early discussions of Dodd–Frank, Senator Chris Dodd recounted that several Democratic and Republican legislators looked at him like he was crazy when he noted that "the basis of this bill ought to be restoring consumer confidence and consumer protection."[60] Even to the consumer advocacy groups mobilizing to make CFPB a reality, it seemed like "a David and Goliath fight."[61] Not until halfway through the process toward Dodd–Frank would the creation of the CFPB become a real political possibility.

Several factors played a role in making the CFPB a reality. The first one was the financial sector's internal division. Popular accounts often portray the business community—and the financial sector in particular—as a monolithic interest group; however, scholarship contradicts that idea. Not only are there fragmentations, but they also seem to have increased over time.[62] As Cornelia Woll notes, "Finance is composed of a multitude of sectors, institutions of very different sizes, and a myriad of stakeholders, often with opposed interests, and the likeliness that different parts of the financial industry will lobby on opposing sides of most policy issues is relatively high."[63] At the onset, opposition to Dodd–Frank within the financial sector was unified, but as the political battle unfolded, divisions became apparent. From the very beginning, bankers insisted on highlighting the role of non-bank institutions in the crisis. Similarly, small and independent community banks went to great lengths to distance themselves from large institutions. The tension between the ICBA and the ABA was obvious to the act's sponsors, who did not hesitate to exploit it. Speaking to the National Press Club on July 27, 2009, Barney Frank said this about the community banks:

> And to the community banks, yes, they have been unfairly traduced because they weren't the problem. But, they have to be careful not to allow themselves to be used by some of their big, big brothers who would like to have them shelter them. We can set up a consumer protection agency that will respect all of the community banks. They were not the perpetrators of the abuses, they will not be the subjects of the corrections. And they need to work with us to help us do that. So, we are ready to go forward with a set of regulations that respond to these innovations that we believe will give us the benefit of the innovations and diminish the abuses. And our models are Theodore Roosevelt, Woodrow Wilson, and Franklin Roosevelt.[64]

Once it was agreed that the CFPB's jurisdiction would extend only to banks whose assets exceeded $10 billion, that "nonbank financial firms, for the first time, [would] be subject to the same lending rules and standards that community banks must follow," that "in all of its rule making, the bureau also would have to specifically consider the benefits and costs a new consumer-protection rule would have on banks with less than $10 billion in assets, and to rural bank customers," and "before proposing any rule that would significantly affect community banks, the bureau [would have to] convene a panel to gather input directly from community banks" among other things, the

116 DISEMBEDDED

small and independent banks threw their support behind the proposed bureau.[65] A year after Frank's speech at the National Press Club, days to Dodd–Frank becoming law, Dodd "thank[ed] the ICBA for stepping up and making that case for us [about how the overwhelming majority of the 8,000 small banks in this country do well under this bill]."[66] He noted that "the American Bankers Association had been vehemently opposed to this legislation and tried to convince people they represented all banks in the country," but the ICBA begged to differ.[67]

Another important factor in the CFPB's success was consumer mobilization. Unlike others in recent history, this consumer mobilization took a united front under the umbrella of the Americans for Financial Reform (AFR) a coalition of "more than 200 civil rights, consumer, labor, business, investor, faith-based, and civic and community groups."[68] According to Lizabeth Cohen, the mobilization of the consumers in response to the crisis could be considered the "fourth wave of consumer activism" in the twentieth century, the first being the Progressive era early in the century, the second from the Great Depression through the 1940s, and the third during the 1960s and 1970s.[69]

As noted, many of the organizations and associations that made up the AFR were not specifically consumer interest groups. Within its ranks, AFR included labor groups, racial justice groups, and faith-based groups, to name a few. For many of these groups, the issue was not narrowly financial regulation. Likening the mobilization for financial reform "to her early days as a civil rights activist," Heather Booth, the director of AFR, remarked, "I view this as a continuation of that struggle. This is about people's everyday life—whether you can keep your home, whether you have credit, whether your kids have any promise of a future. That's similar to other fights for democracy and fairness."[70]

A third factor was public support. Polling data released by the Consumer Federation of America from September 2009 showed that "57% of those polled supporting the idea of creating a new federal agency to protect consumers."[71] As Lisa Kastner notes, various polls showed that "even in conservative democratic districts and swing states, a majority of voters were in favor of a new agency."[72] In an environment where a not insignificant chunk of the public felt that taxpayer money was wasted on bailing out financial institutions that had acted in bad faith, a consumer protection agency remained a populist cause.

Conclusion

To recap, the US government's relief and recover measures were largely successful in reigniting growth, lowering unemployment, and stabilizing home prices. Comparatively, real GDP growth fared better in the US compared to other major economies (see Figure 6.8). Nevertheless, many Americans continued to believe that most of the stimulus bill's funds were wasted (see Table 6.4).

As for Dodd–Frank, its achievements are a matter of debate. Some see the legislation as a radical extension of big government that led to increased regulatory burden, as well as the development of two new regulatory agencies. A week before Dodd–Frank became law of the land, a *Wall Street Journal* editorial opined: "Dodd–Frank, with its 2,300 pages, will unleash the biggest wave of new federal financial rulemaking in three generations. Whatever else this will do, it will not make lending cheaper or credit more readily available."[73] Referring to the estimates by the law firm of Davis Polk & Wardwell LLP, the article went on to state that the law would "require no fewer than 243 new formal rule-makings by 11 different agencies."[74]

Others hold that as an attempt to re-embed America's financialized economy it did not go far enough, especially considering the window of

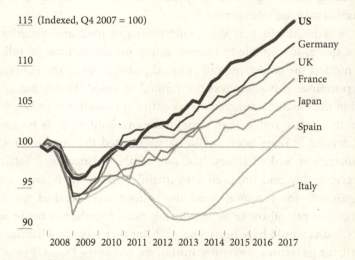

Figure 6.8 Real GDP Ten Years Later
Hutchins Center on Fiscal and Monetary Policy at Brookings and Yale School of Management Program on Financial Stability, *Charting the Financial Crisis: US Strategy and Outcomes*, 2020.

118   DISEMBEDDED

Table 6.4 Public Perception: How Much of the Money Spent Under the Stimulus Bill Has Been Wasted?

Nearly all	21%
Most	24%
About half	29%
Little	21%
None	4%
No opinion	1%

Source: As seen in the figure, 74 percent of adults polled thought that half or more of the funds were wasted. See CNN, "Opinion Research Poll," January 25, 2010, http://i2.cdn.turner.com/cnn/2010/images/01/25/rel1g.pdf. A more recent poll conducted by the Pew Research Center shows that Americans are still skeptical of stimulus spending, with 41 percent disapproving of the 2009 stimulus package. See https://www.pewresearch.org/politics/2012/02/23/auto-bailout-now-backed-stimulus-divisive/.

opportunity the major economic crisis had opened. Unlike the regulatory reforms following the Great Depression, this latter position argues, Dodd–Frank only brought an expansion in regulatory oversight—a set of upgraded rules governing essentially the same cosmos of bank and non-bank financial institutions.[75] And yet others criticize the act, as well as the process that led to its passage, for being a case of top-down reform embodying an uncritical espousal of managerial expertise.[76]

There is no doubt that the country's fragmented and polarized legislative space, susceptible to interest group influence, took its toll, rendering modest the objectives and political possibilities of the government's crisis response. This effect was not limited to Dodd–Frank, but could be found in the Obama administration's entire approach, which was to work within the system rather than structurally overhauling it, as Johnson and Kwak argued.[77] Years later, Sheila Bair lamented the course the Obama administration took: "If they had put all the mismanaged institutions into receivership and imposed accountability, fired the boards, fired the management—for instance, fired the yahoos who worked for AIG in London that put all those money-losing deals together to begin with—I think Obama would have been a hero."[78] But that was not what happened. Overall, the government's reform initiatives, including Dodd–Frank, left "a dizzying number of details to regulatory discretion."[79] The end result was the financial sector's launching and funding a systematic effort to get the interpretation it wanted (see Table 6.5).

THE CRISIS 119

Table 6.5 Post-legislative Lobbying against Dodd–Frank

Number of Lobbyists Top Financial Industry Spenders Sent to Capitol Hill to Weaken Dodd-Frank	
US Chamber of Commerce	183
American Bankers Association	90
JP Morgan Chase	60
Wells Fargo	51
Goldman Sachs	22

Number of Lobbyists Top Consumer Protection Groups Sent to Capitol Hill to Defend Dodd-Frank	
The American Federation of State, County and Municipal Employees	10
Center for Responsible Lending	6
US Public Interest Research Group	2
Consumer Federation of America	2
Americans For Financial Reform	0

Source: Data used in the table is from Rivlin, "How Wall Street Defanged Dodd–Frank."

One way to gauge the success and scope of Dodd–Frank's reforms in terms of re-embedding the financialized economy is by looking for concrete changes in the workings of the financial institutions, in terms of the precarities they may create for other financial institutions, for consumers of financial products and services (such as borrowers and investors), and more broadly for the larger economy. Specifically, we can ask whether the act has brought about concrete changes in systemic and consumer risk protections that can be observed in terms of indicators such as the degree of concentration in the financial sector, the nature of household indebtedness, or the extent to which predatory practices have been prevented. Several measures under Dodd–Frank—including the establishment of the FSOC to monitor systemic risk, the resolution procedure for large financial companies, the regulatory oversight of the derivatives markets, and the foundation of the CFPB—were surely major developments that housed the possibility to realize these outcomes. At the systemic level, the creation of the FSOC brought non-bank financial institutions under regulatory oversight, and increased banks' capital and liquidity buffers, to name a few significant reforms. Under Dodd–Frank, the FSOC had the authority to determine whether "a non-bank financial company's material financial distress—or the nature, scope, size, scale, concentration, interconnectedness, or mix of its activities—could

120 DISEMBEDDED

pose a threat to US financial stability."[80] Companies that the Council designated as systemically important were to be subject to "consolidated supervision by the Federal Reserve and enhanced prudential standards."[81] In recent years, however, the regulatory oversight of the FSOC has shrunk. Several large non-bank financial institutions that the FSOC had deemed systemically important in the aftermath of the crisis were able to fight the "systemically risky" designation in the courts and are no longer thus considered, and hence have been enjoying regulatory relief. Since the passage of Dodd–Frank, concentration in the banking sector has also not declined, but in fact has increased. Consumer financial protections have similarly eroded in recent years. According to a report by the Consumer Federation of America, law enforcement activity at the CFPB has dropped significantly since 2017[82] (see Table 6.6). These erosions happened at a time when household debt—including mortgage, credit cards, auto loans, and student loans—has continued to increase.[83]

Table 6.6 Enforcement at CFPB

	Directors		
Restitution	Cordray	Mulvaney	Kraninger
Enforcing the equal credit opportunity act			
number of cases	11	0	0
total consumer relief	$618,726,890	0	0
Student lending			
number of cases	15	0	0
total consumer relief	$712,530,184	0	0
Enforcing fair credit reporting			
number of cases	24	2	0
total consumer relief	4390157992	0	0
Enforcing mortgage-related cases			
number of cases	61	2	0
total consumer relief	$2,969,543,550	$268,869	0
All cases			
number of cases	201	11	5
total consumer relief	$11,980,130,720	$345,094,707	$12,028,522

Source: Data used is from C. L. Peterson, "Dormant: The Consumer Financial Protection Bureau's Law Enforcement Program in Decline," *Consumer Federation of America*, February 11, 2019.

THE CRISIS   121

This is not entirely surprising. Johnson and Kwak had reflected in their 2011 book in relation to the potential of the CFPB, "Any regulatory agency is only as effective as the people who staff it, and there is always the possibility that a future, pro-finance president will appoint a head of the CFPB who is opposed to consumer protection."[84] Their words, which proved to be prescient, speak to a larger issue in terms of the nature of the post-crisis reform process and the promise it carried for re-embedding the financialized economy. As K. Sabeel Rahman notes, questions of regulation are inherently about democratic citizenship.[85] Responses to regulatory blunders affecting not only the economy but also the social body cannot attain embeddedness if they merely rely on a technocratic vision focused on fixing the rough edges, rather than aiming at a structural transformation that involves citizens. In fact, any such uncritical stance on the part of policymakers may well ignite a variety of reactionary and protectionist movements—which in this case, as in the past, is what did occur. "Rather than viewing regulation as a matter of closing market failures, promoting efficiency, and focusing on techniques of expert and technocratic judgment," as Rahman notes, we need to see it "as a project of counteracting imbalances of power in the modern economy, and of creating a more inclusive, balanced, and productive form of democratic contestation and collective problem-solving."[86]

7

In Search of Protection

From Disembeddedness to Populist Persuasions

> But to turn against regulation means to turn against reform. With the liberal the idea of freedom thus degenerates into a mere advocacy of free enterprise—which is today reduced to a fiction by the hard reality of giant trusts and princely monopolies.
>
> —Karl Polanyi, *The Great Transformation*

Takeaways

The 2007–2010 financial crisis laid bare the vulnerabilities of the American economy, and challenged the naïve, if not vulgar, view of the 1990s as a time of unparalleled growth and prosperity. While the immediate concerns in the aftermath of the crisis revolved around dwindling growth, skyrocketing unemployment, and plunging stock prices, it's crucial to understand that such crises are not just short-term bottlenecks that governments can throw money at. They often unmask and invite a rethinking about the deep-seated assumptions and structural mechanisms that govern economic procedures. As such, our focus must be on those underlying assumptions and structures. With that in mind, in this book I have explored the ideas and policies that sculpted the regulatory milieu within which the American economy financialized and the roots of the financial crisis took hold. Drawing on Polanyi's work, I have characterized it as "disembedded financialization"— the expansion and transformation of the financial sector in an environment characterized by deficiencies in the structures of risk protection. In this concluding chapter, I intend to weave together the threads of regulation, financialization, and democracy, and broaden the discussion to the political ramifications of disembedded economic systems. Before I do that, however, let me first revisit the main takeaways and contributions of this study, of which there are six.

Disembedded. Basak Kus, Oxford University Press. © Oxford University Press 2024.
DOI: 10.1093/oso/9780197764862.003.0007

A New Regulatory Creed

The new creed on regulation originated in the field of economics. It was founded on two primary pillars: firstly, a multifaceted critique of direct and specific government regulation; and secondly, a conviction that market discipline and actor rationality could inherently assure safety and stability as effective risk regulation mechanisms. This shift occurred during a period of rapid growth in financial markets, and it was further reinforced by the rising dominance of financial economics within the larger academic sphere.

As noted earlier, when the ideas that changed the course of the state–economy relationship in the last quarter of the twentieth century are discussed—referred to as the neoliberal turn—it is often Hayek, Friedman, and the Mont Pelerin Society and its fraternal think tanks that get mentioned as the intellectual source of ideas. While their contributions are undeniably significant, focusing almost exclusively on these figures risks overshadowing the contributions of other, very powerful economists—powerful in the sense that it was in the image of their ideas that policy was made, and some of them personally served in key government positions and sat at the helm of policymaking themselves. In Chapters 2 and 3, I discussed the transformative role economists played in shaping the contours of the American regulatory state from the regulatory capture theories of the early 1970s, to the prominence of modern finance theory later in the 1990s. I hope that these chapters provide readers with a more detailed perspective on what we refer to when discussing neoliberalism as an ideational shift.

The Political Reception of the New Creed

One of the key takeaways here, articulated in Chapter 3, is that the political shift toward the new regulatory creed began not with the Reagan administration, as it is often thought, but earlier. As early as the early 1970s, those sitting at the helm of regulatory policy had already turned to economics, a field ablaze with anti-statist ideas of regulation. Furthermore, it was not only Republican politicians and policymakers but Democrats as well, who embraced the new creed and weaved its premises into the fabric of American governance and statecraft.[1] The combination of inflationary pressures and concerns about America's international competitiveness turned the

124 DISEMBEDDED

perceived excesses of the regulatory state into a convenient target, uniting both sides of the political aisle in criticism.

Initially, the critique was practical, suggesting that while regulation was beneficial for the public, it needed adjustments if the economic costs exceeded the public benefits. The goal of regulatory reform was to control inflation and promote growth by reducing regulations or introducing market incentives based on cost–benefit analysis. However, by the 1980s, the perspective shifted, viewing government regulation not as a solution but as the core problem. Policy elites in successive administrations no longer merely talked about cutting costs and government waste; they also began to explore the regulation of risk through incentives risk outside of government control. At this point, financial markets had started expanding and changing, largely due to a set of deregulatory policies that had been adopted in the early 1980s. Faced with an increasingly complex and financialized economy, policymakers were eager to use non-governmental tools. Financial economics and its hallmark ideas—particularly the idea of "efficient markets"—were instrumental in the turn to the notion of market discipline as a form of regulatory governance.

The Translation of the New Creed into Policy

How did the espousal of limited government, actor rationality, and market discipline translate into specific policies and tools in terms of risk regulation at a time of substantial financialization? This is one of the main questions this book addressed. I argued that while discussions about neoliberal policy effects typically center on deregulation, the actual policy landscape is more intricate. Yes, there were key deregulatory measures, especially in the 1980s, such as the DIDMCA in 1980 and AMPTA in 1982 (as detailed in Chapter 3), which profoundly reshaped financial markets. However, when it came to risk management and protection, other aspects of the neoliberal shift were even more influential.

Firstly, despite the sweeping changes in the financial sector, the government did not recalibrate its regulations or tools to address the emerging risks (a phenomenon referred to as regulatory drift). Secondly, regulatory strategy shifted toward ensuring the safety and soundness of individual institutions (known as micro-prudential regulation and principles-based regulation). This strategy operated on the belief that these institutions would inherently prioritize their well-being. Lastly, the government began leaning heavily into information dissemination, whether through disclosures, credit ratings, or financial literacy programs. This approach, termed information-based regulation, was adopted as the government gradually moved away from direct, substantial risk mitigation and protection efforts.

American Financialization: The Regulatory Dimension

We have learned so much about the financialization of the American economy during the past two decades. Scholars like Greta Krippner and Gerald Davis analyzed why the turn to finance has taken place, and what constituted it; Ken-Hou Lin and Donald Tomaskovic-Devey investigated its distributional consequences; Bruce Carruthers examined its institutional foundations, and Neil Fligstein has focused on the development of financial markets, in particular mortgage securitization, and the role banks played in this process.[2]

Here, I sought to enhance our understanding of American financialization and the ensuing crisis by examining the evolution of the state's regulatory relationship with the financial industry. I explored the driving ideas and policies that molded the regulatory backdrop in the course of the American economy's financialization. I delved into the state's actions, or lack thereof, in addressing the myriad risks associated with the evolving and burgeoning financial markets, pinpointing areas of oversight and shortfall. Understanding these dynamics not only deepens our insight into the American political economy but also provides crucial historical context to the 2007–2010 financial crisis and the resulting political changes.

Disembeddedness and "Risk Society" in Financial Times

Financialization of the American economy took place within a regulatory environment lacking in risk mitigation and protection. The prevailing risk regulation framework shifted responsibility away from the government, viewing consumers as rational adults capable of making responsible decisions if given adequate information. Instead of restricting what could be bought and sold, which policymakers argued would limit consumer choice and shift the burden of regulation onto consumers through higher prices, the focus turned toward empowering consumers with information. Increased disclosure regulations, the heightened role of credit rating agencies, and enthusiastic government promotion (and public acceptance) of financial literacy programs were the key ingredients of the new regulatory approach to risk protection. Similarly, over the course of the 2000s, systemic risk and the probability of financial crisis increased substantially as the government shied away from employing direct and substantive tools and policies in the face of expanding and transforming financial markets.

Although not a core part of my analysis in this book, the socio-economic risk protection deficit also needs to be mentioned, as it has embodied parallel trends. There is much work now that has established wage stagnation and increasing income inequality as a correlate of America's financializing economy. What is more, as Jacob Hacker, Arne Kalleberg, and others have shown, economic instability of American families has increased, even faster than economic inequality, and jobs have become more precarious.[3] These trends have not been effectively countered by direct and substantive distributive and redistributive policies on the part of the government. Instead, it was with access to credit that the gap between shrinking incomes and consumption needs was bridged. Rather than embeddedness, it was indebtedness that characterized the structures of work and consumption in the financializing economy. Throughout the 2000s, as systemic risk and the probability of crisis increased, as I discuss in Chapter 5, there was no direct action on the part of the government to address increasing household indebtedness. In fact, as I briefly discussed earlier, credit-fueled consumer welfare emerged as a substitute, a market solution to the problem of low earnings and income inequality.[4] The financial crisis made these redistributive and social protection deficiencies both conspicuous and more pronounced as millions of Americans lost their jobs, savings, and homes, and found the government to be of little recourse to their woes.

The heightened exposure to risks and fluctuations emanating from financialization of the economy broadly, and financialization of everyday life more pervasively, should also be understood in relation to discussions about the risk society—"A phase of development of modern society in which the social, political, ecological and individual risks created by the momentum of innovation increasingly allude the control and protective institutions of industrial society."[5]

The increasing size and complexity of financial markets and households' increased reliance on them, from using credit cards for everyday shopping and getting home loans to investing in 401K plans, were facilitated by global and technological forces; that is, major structural shifts that remained outside the direct control of individuals at a time when formal and collective structures of risk protection had been weakening, and a "personal responsibility crusade" had been launched.[6] In this sense, disembedded financialization was characterized by the twin processes of what Ulrich Beck calls "*organized irresponsibility*" and "*tragic individualization.*"[7] On the one hand, the increasingly complex nature of the financialized economy made it particularly difficult to identify who and what may be responsible for creating risk, which in turn was a factor in empowering economists as experts. On the other hand, people were "thrown back onto themselves."[8] In an environment where collective structures of risk protection were on a retreat, it was the "responsible consumers" who had to fend for themselves—a process Beck describes as "disembedding without embedding."[9]

The Crisis and the Limitations of Reform

Finally, I emphasized that the 2007–2010 financial crisis should not be narrowly viewed in terms of declining growth rates or stock market dips. At its core, it should be understood as a crisis of disembeddedness in a Polanyian sense. Likewise, when evaluating the government's response to the crisis, the measure should not be just the speed of recovery but, more importantly, whether and how adequately the protective deficiencies underpinning this disembeddedness were addressed.

Given the extent of deficiency in systemic risk protection, consumer financial protection, and socio-economic risk protection prevailing in America's financialized economy, the government's response for the most part embraced an incrementalistic and technocratic vision.[10] This is not to say that the steps taken were not significant; they were. A consumer financial protection agency was founded; the FSOC was established to monitor systemic risk, with its oversight extending to non-bank financial institutions; banks' capital and liquidity buffers have increased; and the government put in place an orderly resolution procedure for large financial companies and brought the derivatives markets under regulatory oversight.

Despite all these measures, which were not insignificant by any means, it is still hard to say that a fundamental transformation happened in the structures of risk mitigation and protection, and it is even harder to say that

128   DISEMBEDDED

there was much moral reckoning about this lack. As K. Sabeel Rahman states, Dodd–Frank was reform with technocratic spirit, "expanding the resources, insulation, and powers of neutral expert regulators to manage systemic risks and financial markets rather than radically restructuring the balance of economic and political power."[11]

Comparisons have been made in this respect with the reforms following the Great Depression. One striking difference in terms of the context of reform process is the public mobilization that emerged in the aftermath of the Great Depression with clear policy demands on the part of the workers, in particular. Contrary to the image depicted in popular accounts, the Roosevelt administration was not always eager listen to the demands of the public. Mass mobilization, however, seems to have played a significant role in prompting the government to incorporate some critical demands, leading to some truly transformational consequences for workers and consumers.[12] The aftermath of the recent financial crisis has not seen a comparable mobilization.[13] One instance of mobilization that did occur, however, was in relation to the consumer financial protection bureau. As discussed in Chapter 5, "more than 200 civil rights, consumer, labor, business, investor, faith-based, and civic and community groups" came together for the reform attempt to reflect the interests of consumers—individuals and households who have consumer credit and mortgages. Still, the consumer mobilization that led to the successful incorporation of CFPB, a David-and-Goliath moment according to some, can also be seen as saying something about not the strength but the weakness of the civic landscape, especially in terms of helping to bring about structural transformations. As Theda Skocpol and others have shown, the past few decades have seen a decline in direct membership in national, decentralized, grassroots organizations, and a rise in professionally run advocacy groups located in Washington, DC.[14] These organizations, which focus their efforts on lobbying legislators, signify an important change in the civic character of American democracy. It is technocratic expertise that they rely on rather than grassroots mobilization. They represent ordinary citizens, but ordinary citizens cannot easily find their way into involvement with them.[15] Such was exactly the nature of the post-crisis civic mobilization around consumer protection. As a note of clarity, the mobilization of consumer groups was immensely instrumental for the inclusion of CFPB in the Act. That is not being disputed here. After all, Lizabeth Cohen, one of the most important historians of American consumerism and consumer movements, did not say for no reason that the consumer mobilization that took place at the wake of the financial crisis can be seen as "a fourth wave of the twentieth-century consumer movement."[16] At the same time, using Cohen's own historical examples of the previous waves of consumer movements and taking to heart Skocpol's critique regarding what is lost when civic participation becomes a matter of centralized, professional advocacy, one could perhaps posit that this was not a case of the public asserting its will on policy, but advocacy groups effectively making a seat for themselves at the table where regulatory reform was being negotiated in an incrementalistic and technocratic vision.

Perhaps it is partly for those very reasons that attempts to undermine the components of said reform began as soon as an administration whose ideological position did not quite align with the foundational premises of the new consumer agency entered office. From the start of his administration, Donald J. Trump made the focal point of his policy platform rolling back the regulatory measures put in place in response to the crisis and, more broadly speaking, limiting the regulatory powers of the government. He advocated for getting rid of Dodd–Frank, arguing that regulators had started running the banks and the banks weren't able to lend money to those who need it because of the restrictions in place.[17] In 2017, Republicans in the House, under the leadership of Jeb Hensarling (R-TX), the chair of the House Financial Services Committee, introduced the Financial CHOICE Act to roll back the regulations that Dodd–Frank put in place in relation to stress testing, capital, and liquidity requirements. The CHOICE Act aimed to repeal the FDIC's orderly liquidation authority, the FSOC's authority to designate non-bank financial institutions as "systemically important," and the Federal Reserve Board's authority to "supervise and take enforcement action against non-bank financial companies."[18] Moreover, it aimed to convert the Consumer Financial Protection Bureau (CFPB) into a consumer law enforcement agency subject to the congressional appropriations process. Although it passed the Republican-led House along party lines, it did not find support in the Senate, where another bill was in the making under the leadership of Mike Crapo. The Crapo bill found bipartisan support and was signed into law on May 24, 2018, as The Economic Growth, Regulatory Relief and Consumer Protection Act. While it did not quite dismantle Dodd–Frank, as some have argued, it rolled back some of its key features and loosened the regulatory oversight over financial institutions in several ways. Dodd–Frank had designated banks with more than $50 billion in assets as systemically important financial institutions and subjected them to higher prudential regulation and capital requirements. The Economic Growth, Regulatory Relief and

130   DISEMBEDDED

Consumer Protection Act raised that "systemically risky" threshold to $250 billion, exempted banks and credit unions with less than $10 billion in assets from the Volcker Rule, and decreased the regulatory reach of the FSOC. Under Trump's leadership, the CFPB also weakened, as discussed in the previous chapter. According to a report prepared by the Consumer Federation of America, law enforcement activity at the CFPB has dropped significantly since 2017 (see Table 5.4 in Chapter 5). The administration went so far as to challenge the constitutionality of the agency.

The limitations of Dodd–Frank as a reform attempt, and the persistent attempts to undermine it in the years after its establishment, necessitate that we think about regulatory politics in a broader framework that does not confine it to the workings of the government. It has now been almost thirty years since Peter Evans wrote that "Sterile debates about 'how much' states intervene have to be replaced with arguments about different kinds of involvement and their effects."[19] Along these lines, economists like Raghuram Rajan and Luigi Zingales have moved away from anti-statist arguments that became popular in the 1970s and recognized, as Robert Shiller articulates, both "the need for appropriate regulation in many places" and the necessity for the public to "exert oversight over regulators to help prevent their capture by private interests."[20] How can that be achieved? The answer lies in recognizing that regulatory processes must be a part of and subject to the democratically grounded, civil society based processes. As Rahman argues:

> If our current economic pathologies are rooted in disparities of economic and political power, then we must find solutions not just in economic policy changes, but also through building a more equitable, inclusive, and responsive democratic system. This democratic commitment to agency also suggests the value of rebuilding our civil society associations outside of party politics, expanding the voice and political participation of ordinary people. Taken together, these reforms can help create a more "distributed" approach to governance: Instead of placing all our hopes for progress on a small handful of powerful elected and appointed experts, we should multiply the ways in which regular people, social movements, and civil society groups can share in the actual challenge of policymaking.[21]

The role played by AFR surely attests to the role and power civil society can play in influencing policy change. In short, the regulatory process should be open to oversight and influence by civil society groups. Creating "entry points for the public voice" through deliberative polling, mini-publics, or citizen assemblies might be a step in that direction.[22]

So now we come to the concluding point: matters of regulation—to the extent that they affect the workings of the economy, its risk formations, and thus, essentially, the livelihoods and wellbeing of millions of people who participate in it as workers, homeowners, borrowers, savers, and investors—are not some esoteric matters of policy or technocratic governance but are inherently related to and consequential for popular democracy. The regulatory environment deficient of risk regulation within which the financializing economy developed is among the factors we need to consider if we want to understand the rise of populism in the early twenty-first century.

From Regulation of Finance to the Crisis of Democracy

The thesis that risks and precarities rooted in economic structures are among the chief causes of the rise of various forms anti-system politics has found ample discussion in both scholarly accounts and popular press in the past decade.[23] Several scholars have pointed to the financial crisis, specifically, as a turning point in that regard—as a period when anti-establishment currents took hold due to heightened economic anxieties. Various studies have provided historical data showing how the aftermath of financial crises, characterized by uncertainty and precarity, has typically remained a breeding ground not only for voices critical of the political and economic establishment, but also for extremist and fanatical political currents. Sebastian Doerr et al. showed, for instance, that the German banking crisis "was crucial to boosting the Nazi movement's electoral fortunes."[24] In a 2015 paper, Manuel Funke et al., based on their analysis of "more than 800 elections from 1870 to 2014," as well as existing historical data on financial crises, demonstrations, riots, and strikes, showed that in the uncertainty-ridden environment of financial crises "voters seem to be systematically lured by the political rhetoric of the far right, with its frequently nationalistic or xenophobic tendencies."[25] Alan de Bromhead et al., meanwhile, demonstrated a link between hard times and political extremism looking at data from elections in the 1920s and 1930s.[26]

The financial crisis, beginning in 2007, was a period of uncertainty and precarity and has clearly exacerbated the public's discontent with Washington. As Jonathan Hopkin puts it, "when the wheels came off" what

132 DISEMBEDDED

the public found was that "conventional democratic politics was unable to provide adequate solutions to the acute economic distress this caused."[27] According to the various polls available, trust in government declined during the crisis (see Figure 6.1). Trump knew, of course, that he was channeling everyday Americans' confusion with the financial markets when he said in the summer of 2015 on *Face the Nation*, "The hedge fund guys are getting away with murder.... They're paying nothing, and it's ridiculous." In his 2016 campaign speech in Iowa, he once again directly took aim at Wall Street: "I know Wall Street. I know the people on Wall Street . . . . I'm not going to let Wall Street get away with murder. Wall Street has caused tremendous problems for us."[28] He blasted Hillary Clinton in a tweet a few months later: "Hillary will never reform Wall Street. She is owned by Wall Street!" He repeated the same critique at another campaign event in Florida the same year: "It's a global power structure that is responsible for the economic decisions that have robbed our working class, stripped our country of its wealth, and put that money into the pockets of a handful of large corporations and political entities." These words have clearly found resonance with the American public.[29]

None of this is to say that economic factors, or the fallout from the financial crisis, can on their own explain the rise of anti-establishment politics or various forms of extremist mobilization that have gained steam during the past decade; they cannot. In the case of the US, it is clear that racial and ethnic resentments, as well as a variety of cultural factors, constitute an important part of the explanation given the prominence of anti-immigration messages, references to the plight of *white* workers, and the popularity of the critiques of elite and urban cultural capital.[30]

To clarify then, the argument is not that the rise of populism comes down to the economy, but that it is important to think about the role economic structures within which Americans operate—as workers, consumers, savers, and borrowers—play in shaping their opinions about their government and political future. At the same time, in our thinking about the role of such structures, I argue, we must take a more historical, Polanyian approach. While the immediate circumstances of the crises—both in terms of the distressing objective indicators that constitute them, such as rising unemployment or inequality, and the bleak zeitgeist that they embody—may be pivotal in mobilizing various political currents against the status quo, the kind of protective deficit that I find so detrimental to the way the public relates to and feels about democratic governance is a much deeper structural phenomenon.

For Polanyi, the systematic shifts in the political landscape in the 1930s were not an immediate result of the Great Depression but of a greater, longer transformation that had started much earlier. It was the disembeddedness of industrial capitalism, according to Polanyi, that was at the heart of the challenges to popular democracy. "In order to comprehend German fascism," he argued, "we must revert to Ricardian England."[31] Following Polanyi's historical insights, I argue that it is at the intersection of the rise of neoliberal creed and financialization—in *disembedded financialization*—that we should look for the seeds of contemporary populism,[32] and realize that modest stimulus checks or various forms of technocratic tweaking around the edges cannot address the challenges to democracy in the absence of meaningful structural change.

For those who saw the Trump presidency as a time when a populist politician was using that highest office in a way that undermined the formal and institutionalized channels of democratic governance, the 2020 presidential election was a matter of life and death for America's constitutional democracy. Joe Biden entered in the office with 51.3 percent of the popular vote. It is important to remember that he became president at a time when the trust in government was historically very low.

If Polanyi's analysis is any indication, the threat to democracy is by no means at bay. The current moment is precisely reminiscent of the twin economic and political crises of the early twentieth century in this very sense. "In the period 1924–29, when the restoration of the market system seemed ensured, fascism faded out as a political force altogether. After 1930 market economy was in a general crisis. Within a few years fascism was a world power," Polanyi reminds us.[33]

To be sure, comparisons such as these conjure the danger of presentism, which may present itself in both directions—in terms of "the tendency to interpret the past in presentist terms,"[34] which is less of a concern in this case, but also in terms of the "assumption that fundamental elements of the past and the present are substantially alike,"[35] which is to some extent what I am arguing here. While I acknowledge that there are drawbacks to drawing historical analogies between economic and political transformations that are a century apart, as this involves overlooking contingencies and peculiarities and inevitably involves some decontextualization, there surely is something to be gained from this comparative enterprise.

Notes

Chapter 1

1. William J. Clinton, "Remarks on Achieving a Budget Surplus, September 30, 1998," in *Public Papers of the Presidents of the United States: William J. Clinton (1998, Book II)* (Washington, DC: US Government Publishing Office), 1707–1710.
2. For an overview of Clinton–Gore administration "record of progress," see "The Clinton Presidency: A Historic Era of Progress and Prosperity," https://clintonwhitehouse5.archives.gov/WH/Accomplishments/eightyears-01.html. For historical data on S&P 500 and the Dow Jones Industrial Average, see Yahoo Finance (S&P tripled its value between 1990 and 2000, while DIJA more than doubled).
3. For data and discussion on the impact of the crisis on the labor market, see David B. Grusky, Bruce Western, and Christopher Wimer, eds., *The Great Recession* (New York: Russell Sage Foundation, 2011). For data and discussion on bank failures, see FDIC, "Bank Failures in Brief—Summary 2001 Through 2020," https://www.fdic.gov/bank/historical/bank/. For data and discussion on home foreclosures, see Isaac Martin and Christopher Niedt, *Foreclosed America* (Stanford: Stanford University Press, 2015).
4. Edward N. Wolff, "The Asset Price Meltdown and the Welfare of the Middle Class," NBER Working Paper No. 18559 (2012).
5. It also creates a view of deregulation as something that is necessarily prone to producing a crisis. This is not always the case. Some regulations that are outdated in the face of technological change undermine the institutions and the constituents they serve, and their elimination might lead to improved outcomes. See a discussion of some of the benefits of the removal of branching restrictions, for instance, in Raghuram Rajan and Luigi Zingales, *Saving Capitalism from the Capitalists* (New York: Crown [Kindle edition], 2004).
6. For Polanyi's discussion of the embeddedness of the economy, see Karl Polanyi, "The Economy as Instituted Process" in *Trade and Market in the Early Empires. Economies in History and Theory*, ed. K. Polanyi, C. M. Arensberg, and H. W. Pearson (New York: Free Press, 1957), 243–270; Karl Polanyi, "The Economistic Fallacy," in *The Livelihood of Man*, ed. Karl Polanyi and Harry Pearson (New York: Academic Press, 1977), 5–17; Karl Polanyi, *The Great Transformation: The Political and Economic Origins of Our Time* (Boston: Beacon Press, 2001 [1944]). While the notion of disembeddedness is implicitly discussed in all these texts, for explicit references to it, see Karl Polanyi, "Aristotle Discovers the Economy," in *Trade and Market in the Early Empires*, ed. Karl Polanyi, Conrad Arensberg, and Harry Pearson (Chicago: Henry Regnery, 1957), 64–94.
7. Polanyi, *The Great Transformation*, 3.

136 NOTES

8. Ibid., 248.
9. Ibid., 35.
10. Karl Polanyi, "The Economistic Fallacy," *Review (Fernand Braudel Center)* 1, no. 4 (1977): 9–18.
11. "For all practical purposes, the economy *did* now consist of markets, and the market *did* envelop society," Polanyi argues in "The Economistic Fallacy," 12.
12. He remarks: "Our purpose in thus evoking the plight of the people brought about by enclosures and conversions will be on the one hand to demonstrate the parallel between the devastations caused by the ultimately beneficial enclosures and those resulting from the Industrial Revolution, and on the other hand—and more broadly—to clarify the alternatives facing a community which is in the throes of unregulated economic improvement." *The Great Transformation*, 36.
13. Ibid., 36
14. He remarks: "it was not the statesmen of Tudor England who misunderstood economic realities; rather, it was modern economists who erroneously applied contemporary market principles to historical settings where such a framework did not exist." *The Great Transformation*, 40.
15. Christopher Ansell, *The Protective State* (Cambridge: Cambridge University Press, 2019), 1. While the origins of the state's protective efforts predate modernity, over time, particularly in the twentieth century, the scope of state protection expanded, and its toolkit got more sophisticated, reflecting the state's growing "infrastructural power," as articulated in Michael Mann, "The Autonomous Power of the State: Its Origins, Mechanisms and Results," *European Journal of Sociology* 25, no. 2 (1984): 185–213.
16. David A. Moss, *When All Else Fails: Government as the Ultimate Risk Manager* (Cambridge: Harvard University Press, 2004), 2.
17. Polanyi, *The Great Transformation*, 252.
18. As Marx noted, adding "first time as tragedy, second time as farce" in *The Eighteenth Brumaire of Louis Napoleon* (1852).
19. See, on this topic, Jonathan Hopkin, *Anti-System Politics: The Crisis of Market Liberalism in Rich Democracies* (New York: Oxford University Press, 2020).
20. See Francis Fox-Piven and R. A. Cloward, *Poor People's Movements: Why They Succeed, How They Fail* (New York: Pantheon Books, 1977).
21. John Gerard Ruggie, "International Regimes, Transactions, and Change: Embedded Liberalism in the Postwar Economic Order," *International Organization* 36, no. 2 (1982): 379–415.
22. Mary O. Furner, "From 'State Interference' to the 'Return to the Market': The Rhetoric of Economic Regulation from the Old Gilded Age to the New," in *Government and Markets: Toward a New Theory of Regulation*, ed. Edward J. Balleisen and David A. Moss (New York: Cambridge University Press, 2009), 110.
23. Marc A. Eisner, *Regulatory Politics in Transition*, 2nd ed. (Baltimore: Johns Hopkins University Press, 2000 [1993]), 73.
24. Franklin D. Roosevelt, "Presidential Statement Signing the Social Security Act" (August 14, 1935).

25. Ibid.

26. For a good discussion of welfare expansion on this period, see Michael B. Katz, "The American Welfare State and Social Contract in Hard Times," *Journal of Policy History* 22, no. 4 (2010): 508–529.

27. Lizabeth Cohen, *A Consumers' Republic: The Politics of Mass Consumption in Postwar America* (New York: Knopf Doubleday Publishing Group [Kindle edition], 2003), 41.

28. David Vogel, *The Politics of Precaution: Regulating Health, Safety, and Environmental Risks in Europe and the United States* (Princeton: Princeton University Press, 2012).

29. K. Sabeel Rahman, *Democracy Against Domination*, 1st ed. (Oxford: Oxford University Press, 2016), 34.

30. As Prasad notes, this was one of the justifications for the deregulatory policies undertaken during the Clinton administration in the 1990s (see Monica Prasad, *The Land of Too Much: American Abundance and the Paradox of Poverty* (Cambridge, MA: Harvard University Press, 2012), 175.

31. Along these lines, Konings recently argued, for instance, that "the New Deal, while very much a response to popular discontent, enjoyed considerable support by sections of the business community." See M. Konings, "The Construction of US Financial Power," *Review of International Studies* 35, no. 1 (2009): 82. This line of critique is prominent in the scholarship of left-wing historians, as well. For instance, Gabriel Kolko argued in his 1963 book that what has passed as progressive reform in American history in the first half of the twentieth century "was invariably controlled by the leaders of the regulated industry and directed toward ends they deemed acceptable or desirable." See Gabriel Kolko, *Triumph of Conservatism: A Reinterpretation of American History 1900–1916* (New York: The Free Press, 1963), 3.

32. Cybelle Fox's *Three Worlds of Relief: Race, Immigration, and the American Welfare State from the Progressive Era to the New Deal* (Princeton: Princeton University Press, 2012) provides a brilliant analysis along these lines, examining the racial and ethnic boundaries of the developing welfare state.

33. Furner, "From 'State Interference' to the 'Return to the Market,' " 132.

34. Greta R. Krippner, *Capitalizing on Crisis: The Political Origins of the Rise of Finance* (Cambridge: Harvard University Press, 2012), 16.

35. Ibid., 16–17.

36. This is not surprising. As Hay elaborated, crisis periods are oriented to building a new institutional equilibrium around a new paradigm as "the very parameters that previously circumscribed policy options are cast asunder and replaced, and the realm of politically possible, feasible and desirable is correspondingly reconfigured." Colin Hay, "The Crisis of Keynesianism and the Rise of Neoliberalism in Britain: An Ideational Institutionalist Approach," in *The Rise of Neoliberalism and Institutional Analysis*, ed. John L. Campbell and Ove K. Pedersen (Princeton: Princeton University Press, 2001), 197.

37. Krippner, *Capitalizing on Crisis*, 22. The author notes that fostering financialization was not an intentional policy objective, but an unintended consequence of the government's attempts to address economic troubles.

138 NOTES

38. Basak Kus, "Financialisation and Income Inequality in OECD Nations: 1995–2007," *Economic and Social Review* 43, no. 4 (2012): 477–495.

39. Greta R. Krippner, "The Financialization of the American Economy," *Socio-Economic Review* 3, no. 2 (2005): 173–208.

40. Neil Fligstein, *The Architecture of Markets: An Economic Sociology of Twenty-First Century Capitalist Societies* (Princeton: Princeton University Press, 2001); Neil Fligstein and Taekjin Shin, "Shareholder Value and the Transformation of the U.S. Economy, 1984–2000," *Sociological Forum* 22, no. 4 (2007): 399–424.

41. Tim Smart, "Jack Welch's Encore," *BusinessWeek*, October 28, 1996, https://www.bloomberg.com/news/articles/1996-10-27/jack-welchs-encore.

42. Basak Kus, "GE's Return to Its Industrial Roots Offers Hope US Economy May Do the Same," *The Conversation*, July 24, 2015, https://theconversation.com/ges-return-to-its-industrial-roots-offers-hope-us-economy-may-do-the-same-45140.

43. Krippner, *Capitalizing on Crisis*, 186.

44. Ken-Hou Lin and Megan Tobias Neely, *Divested: Inequality in the Age of Finance* (Oxford: Oxford University Press [Kindle edition], 2020), 14.

45. Lisa A. Keister, *Getting Rich: America's New Rich and How They Got That Way* (New York: Cambridge University Press, 2005).

46. Basak Kus, "Income Inequality, Credit and Public Support for Redistribution," *Intereconomics* 50, no. 4 (2015): 198–205.

47. See Elizabeth Kimberly Pernell, "The Causes of the Divergent Development of Banking Regulation in the U.S., Canada, and Spain," PhD diss., Harvard University, Graduate School of Arts & Sciences, 2016.

48. Forbes, "The World's 2,000 Largest Public Companies", March 29, 2007, https://www.forbes.com/2007/03/29/forbes-global-2000-biz-07forbes2000-cz_sd_0329global_l and.html?sh=3b49e30814ac.

49. Xavier Freixas, Luc Laeven, and Jose-Luis Peydro, *Systemic Risk, Crises, and Macroprudential Regulation* (Cambridge, MA: The MIT Press, 2015), 37–38.

50. See Monica Billio et al., "Economic Measures of Connectedness and Systemic Risk in the Finance and Insurance Sectors," *Journal of Financial Economics* 104, no. 3 (2012): 535–559.

51. US Financial Crisis Inquiry Commission, *The Financial Crisis Inquiry Report: Final Report of the National Commission on the Causes of the Financial and Economic Crisis in the United States* (Washington, DC: US Government Publishing Office, 2011), 67.

52. Martin Neil Baily et al., "The Origins of the Financial Crisis," in *Fixing Finance Series* (Washington, DC: Initiative on Business and Public Policy at Brookings, 2008), 7.

53. On this issue, see *The Financial Crisis Inquiry Report* and Souphala Chomsisengphet and Anthony Pennington-Cross, "The Evolution of the Subprime Mortgage Market," *Federal Reserve Bank of St. Louis Review* 88, no. 1 (2006): 31–56.

54. Elizabeth Warren, "Product Safety Regulation as a Model for Financial Series Regulation," *Journal of Consumer Affairs* 42, no. 3 (2008): 457.

55. See Solomon Deku and Alper Kara, *Securitization: Past, Present and Future* (London: Palgrave Macmillan, 2017), 9.

NOTES 139

56. Baily et al., "The Origins of the Financial Crisis," 27. As the authors note, these products "in good times generated large profits, but have been the source of some of the biggest losses since the crisis unfolded in 2007."

57. Board of Governors of the Federal Reserve System, Federal Deposit Insurance Corporation, Office of the Comptroller of the Currency, and National Credit Union Administration, *Joint Report: Report to the Congress on the Effect of Capital Rules on Mortgage Servicing Assets* (2016), https://www.federalreserve.gov/publications/other-reports/files/effect-capital-rules-mortgage-servicing-assets-201606.pdf.

58. Chomsisengphet and Pennington-Cross, "The Evolution of the Subprime Mortgage Market."

59. Pernell, "The Causes of the Divergent Development of Banking Regulation," 250.

60. Quoted in *Financial Times*, February 8, 2008.

61. Iñaki Aldasoro and Torsten Ehlers, "The Credit Default Swap Market: What a Difference a Decade Makes," *BIS Quarterly Review* (June 2018).

62. Wendy Brown, *Undoing the Demos: Neoliberalism's Stealth Revolution* (Princeton: Princeton University Press, 2015), 17.

63. Ibid., 17.

64. See Quinn Slobodan, "Against the Neoliberalism Taboo," https://www.focaalblog.com/2018/01/12/quinn-slobodian-against-the-neoliberalism-taboo/.

65. Nancy Fraser, "Can Society Be Commodities All the Way Down?," *Economy and Society* 43, no. 4 (2014): 543.

66. Elizabeth Warren, "Redesigning Regulation: A Case Study from the Consumer Credit Market," in *Government and Markets: Toward a New Theory of Regulation*, ed. Edward J. Balleisen and David A. Moss (Cambridge: Cambridge University Press, 2010), 408.

67. Federal Reserve Board, *The Federal Reserve System: Purposes & Functions*, 10th ed. (2016), https://www.federalreserve.gov/aboutthefed/files/the-fed-explained.pdf.

68. European Central Bank, "The Concept of Systemic Risk," special feature in the *ECB Financial Stability Review* (2009), https://www.ecb.europa.eu/pub/pdf/fsr/financialstabilityreview200912en.pdf.

69. Onur Ozgode, "Governing the Economy at the Limits of Neoliberalism: The Genealogy of Systemic Risk Regulation in the United States, 1922–2012," PhD diss., Columbia University, 2015.

70. Adam J. Levitin, "Hydraulic Regulation: Regulating Credit Markets Upstream," *Yale Journal on Regulation* 26, no. 2 (2009): 143–227.

71. Wendy Brown, "Neoliberalism and the End of Liberal Democracy," in *Edgework: Critical Essays on Knowledge and Politics*, ed. Wendy Brown (Princeton: Princeton University Press, 2005), 42.

72. Norah MacKendrick, "The Individualization of Risk as Responsibility and Citizenship: A Case Study of Chemical Body Burdens," PhD diss., University of Toronto, 2012, 81.

73. Ibid., 81.

74. Ibid., 81.

140 NOTES

75. *The Clinton–Gore Plan for Financial Privacy and Consumer Protection in the 21st Century* (Washington, DC: Securities and Exchange Commission Historical Society, May 4, 1999).

76. See Donald Tomaskovic-Devey and Ken-Hou Lin, "Income Dynamics, Economic Rents, and the Financialization of the US Economy," *American Sociological Review* 76, no. 4 (2011): 538–559; Ken-Hou Lin and Donald Tomaskovic-Devey, "Financialization and US Income Inequality, 1970–2008," *American Sociological Review* 118, no. 5 (2013): 1284–1329; Colin Crouch, "Privatised Keynesianism: An Unacknowledged Policy Regime," *British Journal of Politics and International Relations* 11, no. 3 (2009): 382–399; Kus, "Financialisation and Income Inequality in OECD Countries"; Kus, "Sociology of Debt: States, Credit Markets, and Indebted Citizens," *Sociology Compass* 9, no. 3 (2015): 212–223; Kevin T. Leicht and Scott T. Fitzgerald, *Middle Class Meltdown in America: Causes, Consequences, and Remedies* (New York: Routledge, 2013).

77. Arne L. Kalleberg, "The Social Contract in an Era of Precarious Work," *Pathways* (Fall 2012): 3–6.

78. Jacob S. Hacker, *The Great Risk Shift: The Assault on American Jobs, Families, Health Care, and Retirement and How You Can Fight Back* (Oxford: Oxford University Press, 2006).

79. For a discussion on this, see Basak Kus, "Consumption and Redistributive Politics: The Effect of Credit and China," *International Journal of Comparative Sociology* 54, no. 3 (2012): 187–204; Kus, "Sociology of Debt"; Leicht and Fitzgerald, Middle Class Meltdown in America.

80. Kus, "Consumption and Redistributive Politics"; Kus, "Sociology of Debt"; Leicht and Fitzgerald, *Middle Class Meltdown in America*.

81. T. H. Marshall, "Citizenship and Social Class," in *Citizenship and Social Class*, ed. T. H. Marshall and Tom Bottomore (London: Pluto Press, 1992), 8.

82. For a discussion of "financial citizenship," see Basak Kus, "Financial Citizenship and the Hidden Crisis of the Working Class in the 'New Turkey,'" *Middle East Report* (2016); Kus, "Consumption and Redistributive Politics."

83. Kus, "Consumption and Redistributive Politics."

84. For a discussion on this issue, see Kus, "Consumption and Redistributive Politics."

85. Gerald F. Seib, "In Crisis, Opportunity for Obama," *Wall Street Journal*, November 21, 2008.

86. For a discussion of "the rise of the xenophobic Right and the anti-capitalist Left as part of a common global trend," see Jonathan Hopkin, *Anti-System Politics: The Crisis of Market Liberalism in Rich Democracies* (New York: Oxford University Press, 2020), 3.

87. To be sure, there are many variables at play behind the contemporary rise of populism in the US. Scholarship on the prevalence of populist sentiments among the white working-class has revealed the resentment against racial and ethnic minorities to be a key variable. See, for instance, Michael Tesler, "Trump Is the First Modern Republican to Win the Nomination Based on Racial Prejudice," *Washington Post*, August 1, 2016, or Arlie R. Hochscild, *Strangers in their Own Land: Anger and Mourning on the American Right* (New York: The New Press, 2016). Hochscild argues that the resentment among working-class whites is rooted in having to share the material and social purviews of the American dream with racial and ethnic minorities.

NOTES 141

88. Hat tip to Michael Kazin for the term "Populist Persuasion." See Kazin, *Populist Persuasion: An American History* (Ithaca: Cornell University Press, 1995).

Chapter 2

1. The literature on neoliberalism is vast. Scholars have examined it comparatively and historically, as a set of ideas, as a style of reasoning, as a bundle of policies, and as a form of politics. My take here is focused on the US context and tackles it in terms of its relationship to regulation and financialization. For purposes of parsimony, I will not provide a review of the larger literature on neoliberalism. The following works are some of the major anchors of the now long-going conversation: John L. Campbell and Ove K. Pedersen, *The Rise of Neoliberalism and Institutional Analysis* (Princeton, NJ: Princeton University Press, 2001); Marion Fourcade and Sarah Babb, "The Rebirth of the Liberal Creed: Paths to Neoliberalism in Four Countries," *American Journal of Sociology* 108, no. 3 (2002): 533–579; Mark Blyth, *Great Transformations: Economic Ideas and Institutional Change in the Twentieth Century* (New York: Cambridge University Press, 2002); Monica Prasad, *The Politics of Free Markets: The Rise of Neoliberal Economic Policies in Britain, France, Germany, and the United States* (Chicago, IL: University of Chicago Press, 2006); Stephanie Mudge, "What is Neoliberalism," Socio-Economic Review 6, no. 4 (2008): 703–731; Jamie Peck, *Constructions of Neoliberal Reason* (New York: Oxford University Press, 2010); Angus Burgin, *The Great Persuasion: Reinventing Free Markets since the Depression* (Cambridge, MA: Harvard University Press, 2015); Quinn Slobodian, *Globalists: The End of Empire and the Birth of Neoliberalism* (Cambridge, MA: Harvard University Press [Kindle edition], 2018); Wendy Brown, *Undoing the Demos* (New York: Zone Books, 2015).

2. Mudge, "What is Neoliberalism?".

3. Slobodian, *Globalists*, 20.

4. Certainly, "the turn to the market" whether it is the nineteenth century, or the late twentieth century that is in question, is grounded in certain concepts that remain consistent regardless of the time or place. However, it is crucial that we don't take this shift as an instance of "what goes without saying." Instead, we should delve into the unique historical context of each "turn" to the market. This includes understanding who championed it, the specific policies that defined it, and the nature of the market economy during that period, in reference to which the turn to "market" can meaningfully be discussed.

5. Jodi L. Short, "The Paranoid Style in Regulatory Reform," *Hastings Law Journal* 63, no. 3 (2012): 648.

6. Ibid., 650.

7. On this, see:Marion Fourcade, Etienne Ollion, and Yann Algan, "The Superiority of Economists," *Journal of Economic Perspectives* 29, no. 1 (2015): 89–114.

8. On this point, see Elizabeth Popp Berman, *Thinking Like an Economist: How Efficiency Replaced Equality in U.S. Public Policy* (Princeton: Princeton University Press [Kindle edition], 2022).

142 NOTES

9. Fourcade et al., "The Superiority of Economists," 105.
10. Berman, *Thinking Like an Economist*, 19.
11. Ibid., 19.
12. Ibid., 4.
13. George J. Stigler, "The Theory of Economic Regulation," *Bell Journal of Economics* 2, no. 1 (1971): 3–21.
14. Sam Peltzman, "Toward a More General Theory of Regulation," *The Journal of Law and Economics* 19, no. 2 (August 1976): 211–240.
15. Gary Becker, "Theory of Competition among Pressure Groups," *Quarterly Journal of Economics* 98, no. 3 (1983): 371–400.
16. It must be noted, however, that Friedman was not a capture theorist himself in a scholarly sense.
17. Milton Friedman and Rose Friedman, *Free to Choose: A Personal Statement* (New York: Harcourt, 1990 [1980]), 118.
18. For a thorough review of this literature, see William J. Novak, "A Revisionist History of Regulatory Capture," in *Preventing Regulatory Capture: Special Interest Influence and How to Limit It*, ed. Daniel Carpenter and David Moss, The Tobin Project (Cambridge: Cambridge University Press, 2013).
19. Samuel P. Huntington, "The Marasmus of the ICC: The Commission, The Railroads, and the Public Interest," *Yale Law Journal* 61 (1952): 467.
20. "Extensive" in the sense that the book discussed seven different agencies.
21. Marver H. Bernstein, *Regulating Business by Independent Commission* (Princeton: Princeton University Press, 1955).
22. Gabriel Golko, *The Triumph of Conservatism: A Reinterpretation of American History, 1900–1916* (New York: Free Press, 1963), 3
23. James Weinstein, *The Corporate Ideal in the Liberal State, 1900–1918* (Boston: Beacon Press, 1968).
24. Paul W. MacAvoy, *The Economic Effects of Regulation: The Trunk-Line Railroad Cartels and the Interstate Commerce Commission Before 1900* (Cambridge, MA: MIT Press, 1965).
25. Sam Peltzman, "The Economic Theory of Regulation after a Decade of Deregulation," in *A Reader on Regulation*, ed. Robert Baldwin, Colin Scott, and Christopher Hood (Oxford: Oxford University Press, 1998), 94.
26. Now called the George J. Stigler Center for the Study of the Economy and the State.
27. Buchanan and Tullock's seminal work, "The Calculus of Consent," released in 1962, is recognized as a cornerstone text in public choice theory. Here, they applied economic analysis to political decision making, and argued that politicians and government officials, like everyone else, act in their own self-interest, and this affects the policy decisions they make. See J. M. Buchanan and G. Tullock, *The Calculus of Consent: Logical Foundations of Constitutional Democracy* (Ann Arbor: University of Michigan Press, 1962).
28. "James C. Buchanan: National Humanities Medal," The National Endowment for the Humanities (2006), https://www.neh.gov/about/awards/national-humanities-med als/james-m-buchanan.
29. Ibid.

NOTES 143

30. James M. Buchanan, "Rent Seeking and Profit Seeking," in *Toward a Theory of the Rent-Seeking Society*, ed. James Buchanan, Robert Tollison, and George Tullock (College Station: Texas A&M University Press, 1980), 7.

31. G. Tullock, "Rents and Rent-Seeking," in *The Political Economy of Rent-Seeking: Topics in Regulatory Economics and Policy, Vol. 1*, ed. C. K. Rowley, R. D. Tollison, and G. Tullock (Boston, MA: Springer, 1988), 51: "Rents are a perfectly good economic category and there is absolutely nothing in general against seeking them. If I were to invent and patent a cure for cancer and then became extremely wealthy by claiming rents on the patent, most people would regard me as a public benefactor. Nevertheless, 'rent-seeking' is regarded as an unadulterated evil. The reason of course is the type of rent. The rents that attract rent-seeking waste resources in static models. In dynamic settings, their injury to society is even greater. The purpose of this essay is to clearly distinguish between what we may call 'good rents' and 'bad rent-seeking.' "

32. Ibid., 59.

33. Anne O. Krueger, "The Political Economy of the Rent-Seeking Society," *American Economic Review* 64, no. 3 (June 1974): 291–303. According to Krueger's estimations, rent from import licenses amounted to 15 percent of Turkey's GNP in 1968, and 7.3 percent of India's national income in 1964.

34. Ludwig von Mises, *Bureaucracy* (Indianapolis: Liberty Fund, 2007), https://oll.libertyfund.org/title/greaves-bureaucracy?html=true.

35. William A. Niskanen, "Bureaucrats and Politicians," *Journal of Law & Economics* 18, no. 3 (1975): 618.

36. On this point, see Peter Aucoin, "Administrative Reform in Public Management: Paradigms, Principles, Paradoxes and Pendulums," *Governance: An International Journal of Policy and Administration* 3, no. 2 (April 1990): 115–137.

37. David T. Osborne, "Reinventing Government," *League for Innovation in the Community College* 6, no. 1 (January 1993): 2–3, https://files.eric.ed.gov/fulltext/ED367424.pdf.

38. Ibid.

39. Mark Bevir, "Democratic Governance: A Genealogy," *L'Observatoire de la société britannique* 16 (2014): 19–36, https://journals.openedition.org/osb/1695.

40. Osborne, "Reinventing Government."

41. Osborne and Gaebler were not scholars of policymaking. Osborne was a journalist, and Gabler was a city manager. They found themselves under spotlight after the publication of their 1992 book, which became an inspiration for the Clinton era government reforms.

42. See Franck Jovanovic, "The Construction of the Canonical History of Financial Economics," *History of Political Economy* 40, no. 2 (2008): 213–242. Jovanovic explains that "Before the 1960s, works in financial economics were very marginal in the scientific field" (216). Friedman's reaction to then PhD student Harry Markowitz, a financial economist and winner of the 1990 Nobel Prize in economics, is often recollected as an illustration of this. As quoted in Jovanovic: "Harry, I don't see anything wrong with the math here, but I have a problem. This isn't a dissertation in economics, and we can't give you a Ph.D. in economics for a dissertation that's not economics. It's not math, it's not economics, it's not even business administration."

144 NOTES

43. On this issue, see Donald MacKenzie, *An Engine Not a Camera: How Financial Models Shape Markets* (Cambridge, MA: MIT Press, 2008), 5.

44. Franco Modigliani and Merton Miller, "The Cost of Capital, Corporate Finance and the Theory of Investment," *American Economic Review* 48, no. 3 (1958): 261–297; Harry M. Markowitz, Portfolio Selection: Efficient Diversification of Investments (New York: John Wiley and Sons, 1959); Michael C. Jensen, "Takeovers: Folklore and Science," *Harvard Business Review*, November 1984; Michael C. Jensen, "CEO Incentives: It's Not How Much You Pay, But How," *Harvard Business Review*, May– June 1990: 138–153; Michael C. Jensen and William H. Meckling, "Theory of the Firm: Managerial Behavior, Agency Costs, and Ownership Structure," *Journal of Financial Economics* 3, no. 4(1976): 305–360; Eugene F. Fama, "Random Walks in Stock Market Prices," *Financial Analysts Journal* 21, no. 5 (1965): 55–59; Eugene F. Fama, "Efficient Capital Markets: A Review of Theory and Empirical Work," *Journal of Finance* 25 (1970): 383–417; Fischer Black and Myron Scholes, "The Pricing of Options and Corporate Liabilities," *Journal of Political Economy* 81, no. 3 (1973): 637– 654; Robert C. Merton, "Theory of Rational Option Pricing," *The Bell Journal of Economics and Management Science* 4, no. 1 (1973): 141–183.

45. On this issue, see Marion Fourcade and Rakesh Khurana, "From Social Control to Financial Economics: The Linked Ecologies of Economics and Business in Twentieth-Century America," *Theory and Society* 42 (2013): 121–159, and Richard A. Bettis, "Modern Financial Theory, Corporate Strategy and Public Policy: Three Conundrums," *Academy of Management* 8, no. 3 (July 1983): 406–415.

46. MacKenzie, *An Engine Not a Camera*, 5: "Five of the finance theorists discussed in this book—Harry Markowitz, Merton Miller, William Sharpe, Robert C. Merton, and Myron Scholes—became Nobel laureates as a result of their work in finance theory, and other economists who won Nobel Prizes for their wider research also contributed to finance theory."

47. Fourcade and Khurana talk about the linked ecologies of economics and business in the US, addressing how the ascendancy of financial economics in the discipline played a role in shaping the curricula of the business schools, popularizing a narrow financial understanding of the firm and providing a fuel for deregulatory policies. I am making a parallel argument here. I think we should also think about the linked ecologies of economics—the rise of financial economics being a key development— and policymaking. Where I differ from Fourcade and Khurana is that describing the developments in the latter as "deregulatory policies" is both narrow and misleading.

48. Oliviero Roggi and Edward I. Altman, "An Evolutionary Perspective on the Concept of Risk, Uncertainty and Risk Management," in *Managing and Measuring of Risk: Emerging Global Standards and Regulations after the Financial Crisis*, ed. Oliviero Roggi and Edward I. Altman (World Scientific Publishing Company, 2013), 3–37.

49. Fama, "Efficient Capital Markets," 383.

50. Peter L. Bernstein, *Capital Ideas: The Improbably Origins of Modern Wall Street* (Hoboken, NJ: John Wiley & Son [Kindle edition], 2005).

51. Ibid.

NOTES 145

52. Binyamin Appelbaum, *The Economists' Hour* (Little, Brown and Company [Kindle edition], 2019), 289.

53. Ronald J. Gilson and Reinier Kraakman, "Market Efficiency after the Financial Crisis: It's Still a Matter of Information Costs," *Virginia Law Review* 100, no. 2 (2014): 315.

54. Ibid.

55. Appelbaum, *The Economists' Hour*, 289.

56. Ibid., 288.

57. Robert R. Bliss and Mark J. Flannery, "Market Discipline in the Governance of US," *Federal Bank of Chicago Working Paper* (2000): 1. See also David Min, "Understanding the Failures of Market Discipline," *Washington University Law Review* 92, no. 6 (2015): 1421–1501. Min notes that by the 1990s "the theory of market discipline had come to dominate the banking literature, both in economics and law" and MD as a mode of risk regulation must be understood as a corollary of EMH (1434).

58. Min, "Understanding the Failures of Market Discipline," 1425.

59. Ibid.

60. Bliss and Flannery, "Market Discipline in the Governance of US," 2.

61. One needs to look no further than Alan Greenspan's testimony to Congress in 2008 when he said that, all along, he had believed—mistakenly, he would admit—that "the self-interests of organizations, specifically banks and others, were such that they were best capable of protecting their own shareholders and their equity in the firm." Testimony of Alan Greenspan, former Chairman of the US Federal Reserve, The Financial Crisis and the Role of Federal Regulators: Hearing Before the House Comm. on Oversight and Government Reform, *110th Congress*, October 23, 2008, https://www.govinfo.gov/content/pkg/CHRG-110hhrg55764/html/CHRG-110hh rg55764.htm.

62. Testimony of Alan Greenspan, former Chairman of the US Federal Reserve, The Financial Crisis and the Role of Federal Regulators: Hearing Before the House Comm. on Oversight and Government Reform, *110th Congress*, October 23, 2008, https://www.govinfo.gov/content/pkg/CHRG-110hhrg55764/html/CHRG-110hh rg55764.htm.

63. Children, for instance, according to Friedman. See Milton Friedman, *Capitalism and Freedom* (Chicago: University of Chicago Press, 2002 [1962]), 34.

64. On this point, see Norah MacKendrick, *Better Safe Than Sorry: How Consumers Navigate Exposure to Everyday Toxics*, 1st ed. (Oakland: University of California Press, 2018).

65. Yascha Mounk, *The Age of Responsibility: Luck, Choice, and the Welfare State* (Cambridge, MA: Harvard University Press, 2017), 70.

Chapter 3

1. Robert Britt Horwitz, *The Irony of Regulatory Reform: The Deregulation of American Telecommunications* (New York: Oxford University Press, 1989), 265.

146 NOTES

2. On this, see George Eads and Michael Fix, *Relief or Reform? Reagan's Regulatory Dilemma (The Changing Domestic Priorities Series)* (Washington, DC: Urban Institute Press, 1984), 46. Also see George Charles Halvorson, "Valuing the Air: The Politics of Environmental Governance from the Clean Air Act to Carbon Trading," PhD diss., Columbia University, 2017.

3. The White House Office of Management and Budget, "Chapter I. The Role of Economic Analysis in Regulatory Reform: Report to Congress on the Costs and Benefits of Federal Regulations," https://obamawhitehouse.archives.gov/omb/infore g_chap1#tnfrp.

4. Gerald R. Ford, "Address to a Joint Session of Congress on the Economy," Speech, Washington, DC, October 8, 1974, Gerald R. Ford Presidential Library & Museum, https://www.fordlibrarymuseum.gov/library/speeches/740121.asp.

5. Murray Weidenbaum, "Regulatory Process Reform: From Ford to Clinton," *Regulation* 20 (1997): 20.

6. Even before directing policy research for Richard Nixon's presidential campaign in 1968, Greenspan had penned various articles criticizing government regulation, and his views became increasingly significant to financial markets in subsequent decades. Greenspan went on to serve as chair of the Federal Reserve for two decades, under four successive presidents beginning with Reagan.

7. Gerald R. Ford, "Address Before a Joint Session of the Congress Reporting on the State of the Union," Speech, Washington, DC, January 19, 1976, Gerald R. Ford Presidential Library & Museum, https://www.fordlibrarymuseum.gov/library/speeches/760019. asp. As a point of comparison, in his State of the Union addresses, Richard Nixon had mentioned regulation only once, suggesting that comprehensive new regulations were needed to deal with pollution and environmental degradation. During the Ford administration, rhetoric regarding limited government emerged more systematically.

8. Gerald R. Ford, "Address Before a Conference of the National Federation of Independent Business," Speech, Washington, DC, June 17, 1975, *American Presidency Project*, https://www.presidency.ucsb.edu/documents/address-before-conference-the-national-federation-independent-business.

9. Ibid.

10. James L. Pierce, "The FINE Study," *Journal of Money, Credit and Banking* 9, no. 4 (November 1977): 606.

11. Statement of Fernand J. St Germain, "Financial Institutions and the Nation's Economy (FINE): 'Discussion Principles,' Hearings Before the Subcommittee on Financial Institutions Supervision, Regulation and Insurance of the Comm. on Banking, Currency, and Housing," *94th Congress* (December 1975 and January 1976).

12. Statement of Thomas Kauper, FINE.

13. Statement of James L. Pierce, FINE.

14. Statement of Milton Friedman, FINE.

15. Halvorson, "Valuing the Air," 214.

16. Binyamin Appelbaum, *The Economists' Hour* (Boston: Little, Brown and Company [Kindle edition], 2019), 173.

17. Ibid. On this, see also Berman, *Thinking Like an Economist*.

NOTES   147

18. James E. Anderson, "The Carter Administration and Regulatory Reform: Searching for the Right Way," *Congress & the Presidency* 18, no. 2 (1991): 121.

19. Charles L. Shultze, *The Public Use of Private Interest* (Washington, DC: Brookings Institution Press, 1977), 5–6. This book is a revision of Shultze's Godkin lectures.

20. "Alfred E. Kahn Interview," *The First Measured Century: Host/Essayist Ben Wattenberg*, PBS: Public Broadcasting Service, https://www.pbs.org/fmc/interviews/kahn.htm.

21. Jimmy Carter, "State of the Union Address," Speech, Washington, DC, January 19, 1978, https://millercenter.org/the-presidency/presidential-speeches/january-19-1978-state-union-address.

22. Jimmy Carter, "Anti-Inflation Program," Speech, Washington, DC, October 24, 1978, https://www.pbs.org/wgbh/americanexperience/features/carter-anti-inflation/.

23. Arthur Andersen and Co., "Cost of Government Regulation Study for the Business Roundtable: A Study of the Direct Incremental Costs Incurred by 48 Companies in Complying with the Regulations of Six Federal Agencies in 1977" (New York, 1979).

24. Michael E. Simon, "The Business Roundtable Study: What We Did," *American Enterprise Institute*, August 6, 1979, https://www.aei.org/articles/the-business-roundtable-study-what-we-did/.

25. See the discussion on this in Halvorson, "Valuing the Air," 269.

26. On this topic, see Prasad, *The Politics of Free Markets*. Prasad notes that by the time Reagan was in office, there was a left–right convergence on the question of extensive government regulation. She argues that deregulation was a pro-consumer issue when it first moved onto the political stage, and rather than right-wing politicians or big business leaders, the protagonists of the deregulation movement were people like Ralph Nader, Edward Kennedy, and Stephen Breyer.

27. Horwitz, *The Irony of Regulatory Reform*, 209. Also see Prasad, *The Politics of Free Markets* for a revealing exchange between Nader and Reagan.

28. Prasad, *The Politics of Free Market*, 69. The quote from Ted Kennedy that Prasad included in her discussion is exemplary of this view: "Regulators all too often encourage or approve unreasonably high prices, inadequate service, and anticompetitive behavior. The cost of this regulation is always passed on to the consumer" (70).

29. Ibid.

30. Jimmy Carter, "Financial Reform Legislation Message to the Congress Proposing the Legislation," Speech, Washington, DC, May 22, 1979, *American Presidency Project*, https://www.presidency.ucsb.edu/documents/financial-reform-legislation-message-the-congress-proposing-the-legislation.

31. Robert F. Himmelberg, *Regulatory Issues Since 1964: The Rise of the Deregulation Movement* (New York: Routledge, 1994), 297.

32. Ronald Reagan, "America's New Beginning: A Program for Economic Recovery" (February 18, 1981), https://fraser.stlouisfed.org/title/1221.

33. Michael Fix and George C. Eads, "The Prospects for Regulatory Reform: The Legacy of Reagan's First Term," *Yale Journal on Regulation* 2, no. 2 (1985): 298.

34. Ronald Ragan, "Remarks Announcing the Establishment of the Presidential Task Force on Regulatory Relief," Speech, January 22, 1981.

148 NOTES

35. Ibid.

36. *Economic Report of the President: Transmitted to the Congress* (Washington, DC: GPO, 1982), 4, https://fraser.stlouisfed.org/files/docs/publications/ERP/1982/ERP_1982.pdf.

37. Ibid.

38. Ibid., 43.

39. Ibid., 43.

40. Ibid., 42.

41. "Remarks on Signing the Garn–St Germain Depository Institutions Act of 1982," Ronald Reagan Presidential Library and Museum, October 15, 1982, https://www. reaganlibrary.gov/archives/speech/remarks-signing-garn-st-germain-depository-institutions-act-1982.

42. William M. Isaac, "Disciplining the Financial Marketplace," *Christian Science Monitor*, September 13, 1983, https://www.csmonitor.com/1983/0913/091347.html. Later, in 1985, Isaac reiterated his point: "Our role as insurer of bank deposits in a deregulated banking environment presents a threshold question: how, in this environment, do we control destructive competition and abusive practices without adding a new layer of laws and regulations and hiring thousands of additional examiners to monitor and enforce them. There is but one option: increase marketplace discipline as an efficient and reliable supplement to our supervisory programs." See William M. Isaac, "FDIC: Stability and Change," Speech, April 2, 1984, https://fraser.stlouis fed.org/files/docs/historical/fdic/speeches/isaac_19840402.pdf.

43. James C. Treadway Jr., "A Regulatory Conflict That Must Eventually Be Resolved; Banks Will Either Be Totally Regulated for 'Safety' or Will Come under Market Discipline," *American Banker*, November 30, 1983.

44. Robert L. Bevan, "Market Discipline," *United States Banker*, August 1985, National Edition.

45. See "Federal Deposit Insurance Corporation Improvement Act of 1991," Federal Reserve History, December 19, 1991, https://www.federalreservehistory.org/ess ays/fdicia: "After the establishment of the Federal Deposit Insurance Corporation (FDIC) in 1934 the number of bank failures in the United States averaged roughly fifteen per year until 1981, when the number of bank failures began to rise and reached roughly 200 per year by the late 1980s . . . . From roughly the beginning of 1980 until the end of 1991, nearly 1,300 commercial banks either failed or required failing bank assistance from the FDIC." Moreover, "From 1983 to 1990, nearly 25 percent of S&Ls were closed, merged, or placed in conservatorship by the Federal Savings and Loan Insurance Corporation (FSLIC). This collapse drove the FSLIC into insolvency, leading to its abolishment by the Financial Institutions Reform, Recovery, and Enactment Act (FIRREA) in 1989."

46. Statement of Paul A. Volcker, Chairman, Board of Governors of the Federal Reserve System before the Committee on Banking, Housing, and Urban Affairs, US Senate, September 11, 1985.

47. Nina Easton, "Bank Regulators: Taking Lessons from the Thrift Industry?" *American Banker*, December 23, 1985.

NOTES   149

48. Nina Easton, "In 1985, US Bank Regulators Tried to Emulate That Dutch Boy with His Finger in the Dike," *American Banker*, January 2, 1986. The article quoted Richard Whiting, regulatory counsel to the Association of Bank Holding Companies.

49. Appelbaum, *The Economists' Hour*, 293.

50. Ibid. After stepping down from her leadership of CFTC and joining Enron's board of directors, Gramm would continue advocating against proposals for new rules to regulate derivatives, cautioning not "to over-regulate what we just do not understand," as she put it in a 1993 *Wall Street Journal* piece, quoted in Appelbaum, *The Economists' Hour*, 293.

51. Executive Order 12631, Working Group on Financial Markets, National Archives, https://www.archives.gov/federal-register/codification/executive-order/12631.html. Going forward, the President's Working Group on Financial Markets remained an important policymaking platform and played a direct and critical role in shaping financial regulation under President Bill Clinton.

52. *Economic Report of the President*, January 1989, https://fraser.stlouisfed.org/files/docs/publications/ERP/1989/ERP_1989.pdf.

53. Ronald Reagan, "Message to the Congress Transmitting the Annual Economic Report of the President," February 5, 1985, https://www.presidency.ucsb.edu/documents/message-the-congress-transmitting-the-annual-economic-report-the-president-1.

54. Murray Weidenbaum, "Regulatory Process Reform: From Ford to Clinton," *Heartland Institute* (Winter 1997), https://www.heartland.org/publications-resources/publications/regulatory-process-reform-from-ford-to-clinton.

55. Reagan's regulatory politics were similar to those concerning welfare, in the way Pierson articulated. See Paul Pierson, *Dismantling the Welfare State? Reagan, Thatcher and the Politics of Retrenchment* (Cambridge: Cambridge University Press, 1994).

56. "Bush Orders Study of Reducing Scope of Deposit Insurance," *Associated Press*, February 9, 1989.

57. Ibid.

58. George J. Benston and George G. Kaufman, "FDICIA After Five Years," *Journal of Economic Perspectives* 11, no. 3 (1997): 139.

59. Ibid.

60. Ibid. Benston and Kaufman argue that FDICIA "is the most important banking legislation in the United States since the Banking (Glass–Steagall) Act of 1933, which, among other things, created deposit insurance and the FDIC, prohibited interest payments on demand deposits, imposed Regulation Q interest rate ceilings on time deposits, and separated commercial and investment banking for private securities."

61. "Reinventing Regulation," National Partnership for Reinventing Government, April 2000, https://govinfo.library.unt.edu/npr/initiati/common/index.html.

62. "Phase II of the Performance Review: Creating a Common Sense Government," National Partnership for Reinventing Government, 1995, https://govinfo.library.unt.edu/npr/whoweare/historypart3.html.

63. William J. Clinton, "Address Before a Joint Session of the Congress on the State of the Union," Speech, Washington, DC, January 23, 1996, *American Presidency Project*,

150 NOTES

https://www.presidency.ucsb.edu/documents/address-before-joint-session-the-congress-the-state-the-union-10.

64. On this topic, see Prasad, *The Land of Too Much*.

65. A decade later, the Financial Crisis Inquiry Commission report noted that "deference to the self-correcting property of markets inhibited supervisors from imposing prescriptive views." See Financial Crisis Inquiry Commission, *The Financial Crisis Inquiry Report: Final Report of the National Commission on the Causes of the Financial and Economic Crisis in the United States* (Washington, DC: GPO, January 27, 2011), 171, https://fcic-static.law.stanford.edu/cdn_media/fcic-reports/fcic_final_report_full.pdf.

66. Arthur Levitt, Chairman of the SEC; Robert Rubin, Secretary of the Treasury; William Rainer, Chairman of the Commodity Futures Trading Commission; and Alan Greenspan, Chairman of the Board of Federal Reserve System had all established careers in the financial sector before taking a role in public service. Later Larry Summers would a part of the Group when he assumed the role of Secretary of the Treasury. When Robert Rubin was the co-chair of Goldman's trading and arbitrage division in the mid-1980s, he had hired a team of finance professors known for their contributions to the efficient-market hypothesis. See Michael Rogers, "Professors Who Work on Wall Street: Goldman Sachs has Recruited Five Prominent Finance Theorists to Help Solve Real-world Problems and Design New Products," *CNN Money*, November 25, 1985, https://money.cnn.com/magazines/fortune/fortune_archive/1985/11/25/66655/index.htm. Summers, while he recommended a hands-off approach to markets where "sophisticated" parties participated, in his academic economist capacity in the 1980s had published work criticizing various assumptions and implications of EMH (see Summers, "Does the Stock Market Rationally Reflect Fundamental Values?," *Journal of Finance* 41, no. 3 (1985): 591–601).

67. Alan Greenspan, "Government Regulation and Derivative Contracts," Speech, Financial Markets Conference of the Federal Reserve Bank of Atlanta, Coral Gables, FL, February 21, 1997), Federal Reserve Board, https://www.federalreserve.gov/boarddocs/speeches/1997/19970221.htm.

68. Financial Crisis Inquiry Commission, *The Financial Crisis Inquiry Report*, 171.

69. Basel Committee on Banking Supervision, *Consultative Document: Pillar 3 (Market Discipline)* (2001), 1, https://www.bis.org/publ/bcbsca10.pdf.

70. Alan Greenspan, "Remarks at the 2003 Conference on Bank Structure and Competition," Speech, Chicago, May 8, 2003, https://www.federalreserve.gov/boarddocs/speeches/2003/20030508/default.htm.

71. "A New Capital Adequacy Framework: Consultative Paper Issued by the Basel Committee on Banking Supervision," June 1999, 17, https://www.bis.org/publ/bcbs50.pdf.

72. Remarks by Mr. Ben S. Bernanke, Chairman of the Board of Governors of the US Federal Reserve System, at the Federal Reserve Bank of Atlanta's 2006 Financial Markets Conference, Sea Island, Georgia, May 16, 2006.

73. Ibid.

NOTES 151

74. Henry Paulson, "Closing Remarks at 'Day 1: Responding to the Global Financial Crisis' Event," *Brookings Institute*, September 11, 2018, https://www.brookings.edu/events/day-1-responding-to-the-global-financial-crisis/. Speaking of capitalization levels specifically, Paulson: "One of the things that struck me when I arrived in Washington was the extent to which regulators felt financial institutions, banks, were adequately capitalized, or more than adequately capitalized, when people coming from Wall Street knew that they weren't."

75. Tim Clarke, Panelist, "'Day 1: Responding to the Global Financial Crisis' Event," *Brookings Institute*, September 11, 2018, https://www.brookings.edu/events/day-1-responding-to-the-global-financial-crisis/.

76. Chairman Ben S. Bernanke Federal Reserve Bank of Boston 54th Economic Conference, Chatham, MA, https://www.federalreserve.gov/newsevents/speech/bernanke20091023a.htm.

Chapter 4

1. Scott Alvarez, quoted in Sheila Bair, *Bull by the Horns: Fighting to Save Main Street from Wall Street and Wall Street from Itself* (New York: Simon & Schuster, 2012), 48. Please note that Alvarez is referring to the 1990s and the early 2000s, specifically.

2. Taking a cue from Lessig, consider how the government might regulate cigarette sales for health protection: it could either ban the sales outright, impose age restrictions, limit the number of licensed sellers, or control nicotine levels in the cigarettes— these are direct, substantive measures. Alternatively, it might indirectly influence the market by imposing a high tax, thereby making cigarettes more expensive and presumably reducing sales. The government may also adopt a *laissez-faire* approach, merely mandating companies to disclose harmful cigarette content, allowing individuals to make informed decisions. This analogy is easily transferable to financial products. For instance, in directly regulating subprime mortgage markets, the government could limit who originates such loans or define the terms of their sale. Alternatively, it might adopt a non-substantive approach, merely requiring lenders to disclose mortgage terms without dictating the terms themselves, thereby enabling consumers to make informed decisions. See Lawrence Lessig, "The New Chicago School," *Journal of Legal Studies* 27, no. 2 (1998).

3. Elizabeth Warren, "Redesigning Regulation: A Case Study from the Consumer Credit Market," in *Government and Markets: Toward a New Theory of Regulation*, ed. Edward J. Balleisen and David A. Moss (Cambridge: Cambridge University Press, 2010), 408.

4. Steven K. Vogel, *Freer Markets, More Rules: Regulatory Reform in Advanced Industrial Countries* (Ithaca: Cornell University Press, 1996), 5.

5. Jacint Jordana and David Levi-Faur, "The Politics of Regulation in the Age of Governance," in *The Politics of Regulation* (2004), 1.

6. John Braithwaite, *Regulatory Capitalism: How It Works, Ideas for Making It Work Better* (Cheltenham: Edward Elgar, 2008), 10.

7. Ibid., 34.

8. Ibid., 8.

152 NOTES

9. Martijn Konings, "Rethinking Neoliberalism and the Subprime Crisis: Beyond the Re-Regulation Agenda," *Competition & Change* 13, no. 2 (2009): 110.

10. Ibid.

11. Jacob Hacker, Paul Pierson, and Kathleen Thelen, "Drift and Conversion: Hidden Faces of Institutional Change," Paper presented at the Annual Meeting of the American Political Science Association, Chicago, 2013, 8, https://papers.ssrn.com/sol3/papers.cfm?abstract_id=2303593.

12. Marc Allen Eisner, *Regulatory Politics in an Age of Polarization and Drift: Beyond Deregulation* (New York: Routledge, 2017), 15–17.

13. Ibid., 33.

14. See Robert Britt Horwitz, *The Irony of Regulatory Reform: The Deregulation of American Telecommunications* (Oxford: Oxford University Press, 1991); Halvorson, "Valuing the Air."

15. Prasad, The Politics of Free Markets.

16. Thomas Philippon and Ariell Reshef, "Wages and Human Capital in the U.S. Financial Industry: 1909–2006," NBER Working Paper no. 14644 (2009): 9, https://www.nber.org/system/files/working_papers/w14644/w14644.pdf.

17. Monica Prasad, *The Land of Too Much: American Abundance and the Paradox of Poverty* (Cambridge, MA: Harvard University Press, 2012): 175.

18. Patrick McLaughlin and Oliver Sherouse, "Did Deregulation Cause the Financial Crisis?" Mercatus Center, August 31, 2017, https://www.mercatus.org/publications/regulation/did-deregulation-cause-financial-crisis. Their analysis is based on the number of restrictive words and phrases in the Code of Federal Regulations, such as "may not," "must," "shall," "prohibited," and "required."

19. Norbert Michel, "The Popular Narrative About Financial Deregulation Is Wrong," *The Daily Signal*, July 29, 2016, https://www.dailysignal.com/2016/07/29/the-popular-narrative-about-financial-deregulation-is-wrong/.

20. See Paul G. Mahoney, "Deregulation and the Subprime Crisis," *Virginia Law Review* 104, no. 2 (2018): 235–300.

21. For a thorough discussion on the inadequacy of relying on regulation counts, see Jodi Short, "The Trouble with Counting: Cutting through the Rhetoric of Red Tape Cutting," *Minnesota Law Review* 103 (2018): 93–149.

22. Gosta Esping-Andersen, *The Three Worlds of Welfare Capitalism* (Cambridge: Polity Press, 1990), 19.

23. Alan Greenspan, "Remarks at the Annual Convention of the American Bankers Association," Speech, Boston, MA, October 5, 1997, The Federal Reserve Board.

24. Ibid.

25. *Marquette Nat. Bank v. First of Omaha Svc. Corp.*, 439 US 299 (1978).

26. Matthew Sherman, "A Short History of Financial Deregulation in the United States," Center for Economic and Policy Research (2009), 1

27. "Garn–St Germain Depository Institutions Act of 1982," *Federal Reserve History*, October 1982, https://www.federalreservehistory.org/essays/garn-st-germain-act.

28. Sherman, "A Short History of Financial Deregulation in the United States," 7.

NOTES **153**

29. Patricia A. McCoy, Andrey D. Pavlov, and Susan M. Wachter, "Securitization and Systemic Risk Amid Deregulation and Regulatory Failure," *Connecticut Law Review* 41, no. 4 (2009): 1333.

30. Ibid. It did so, as McCoy et al. note, "by allowing borrowers to exchange lower initial monthly payments for higher payments on the back end."

31. See Sherman, "A Short History of Financial Deregulation in the United States," 8.

32. David J. Bleckner, "Section 106 of the Secondary Mortgage Enhancement Act of 1984 and the Need for Overriding State Legislation," *Fordham Urban Law Journal* 13, no. 3 (1985): 681.

33. Christopher Lewis Peterson, "Predatory Structured Finance," *Cardozo Law Review* 28, no. 5 (2007): 2201.

34. See Simon Kwan, "Cracking the Glass–Steagall Barriers," *FRBSF Economic Letter*, March 21, 1997, https://www.frbsf.org/economic-research/publications/econo mic-letter/1997/march/cracking-the-glass-steagall-barriers/: "The provisions of the Glass–Steagall Act that separated commercial banking from investment banking are in Sections 16, 20, 21, and 32 of the Act. Section 16 bars national banks from investing in shares of stocks, limits them to buying and selling securities as an agent, and prohibits them from underwriting and dealing in securities. Section 20 prohibits Federal Reserve member banks from being affiliated with any organization that is 'engaged principally' in underwriting or dealing in securities. Section 21 makes it unlawful for securities firms to accept deposits. Section 32 prohibits officer, director, or employee interlocks between a Federal Reserve member bank and any organization 'primarily engaged' in underwriting or dealing in securities."

35. Sandra L. Suarez and Robin Kolodny, "Paving the Road to 'Too Big to Fail'–Business Interests and the Politics of Financial Deregulation in the U.S.," *Politics & Society* 39, no. 1 (2010): 86.

36. Arthur E. Wilmarth, Jr., "The Road to Repeal of the Glass–Steagall Act," *Wake Forest Journal of Business & Intellectual Property Law* 17, no. 4 (Summer 2017): 492.

37. Suarez and Kolodny, "Paving the Road," 78.

38. "Times: Treasury Now Favors Creating Huge Banks," *Associated Press*, June 6, 1987, https://apnews.com/article/f0578e3bf1ea78378f786eb922b870fd.

39. Arthur E. Wilmarth, Jr., "The Transformation of the US Financial Services Industry, 1975–2000: Competition, Consolidation, and Increased Risks," *University of Illinois Law Review* 215 (2002): 223.

40. Sherman, "A Short History of Financial Deregulation," 9.

41. "Remarks of Senator Sarbanes at the signing of the Financial Modernization Bill," US Department of the Treasury Press Release, November 12, 1999, https://www.treasury. gov/press-center/press-releases/Pages/ls241.aspx.

42. "Financial Services Modernization Act of 1999, commonly called Gramm–Leach–Bliley," *Federal Reserve History*, November 12, 1999, https://www.federalreservehist ory.org/essays/gramm-leach-bliley-act.

43. Ibid.

44. Ellen Harshman, Fred C. Yeager, and Timothy J. Yeager, "The Door Is Open, But Banks Are Slow to Enter Insurance and Investment Arenas," *Federal Reserve Bank of St. Louis*, October 1, 2005, https://www.stlouisfed.org/publications/regional-economist/octo

154 NOTES

ber-2005/the-door-is-open-but-banks-are-slow-to-enter-insurance-and-investment-arenas.

45. Wilmarth, Jr., "The Transformation of the US Financial Services Industry," 305.

46. Hacker et al., "Drift and Conversion," 1.

47. Ibid., 10.

48. Ibid., 1, 10–11.

49. Appelbaum, *The Economists' Hour*, 288.

50. Quoted in Simon Johnson and James Kwak, *13 Bankers: The Wall Street Takeover and the Next Financial Meltdown* (New York: Knopf Doubleday Publishing Group, 2010), 101.

51. McCoy et al., "Securitization and Systemic Risk," 500.

52. Sherman, "A Short History of Financial Deregulation in the United States," 8.

53. McCoy et al., "Securitization and Systemic Risk," 500.

54. Bair, *Bull by the Horns*, 49–50.

55. Ibid., 48.

56. Financial Crisis Inquiry Commission, *The Financial Crisis Inquiry Report* (Washington, DC: Government Printing Office, 2011), xvii, https://www.govinfo.gov/content/pkg/GPO-FCIC/pdf/GPO-FCIC.pdf.

57. Wilmarth, Jr., "The Transformation of the US Financial Services Industry," 223.

58. Harshman et al., "The Door Is Open."

59. Wilmarth, Jr., "The Transformation of the US Financial Services Industry," 224.

60. Alan Greenspan, "Financial Derivatives," Speech at a Meeting of the Futures Industry Association, Boca Raton, FL, March 19, 1999, The Federal Reserve Board, https://www.federalreserve.gov/boarddocs/speeches/1999/19990319.htm.

61. Richard Schmitt, "The Born Prophecy," *ABA Journal*, May 2, 2009, https://www.abajournal.com/magazine/article/the_born_prophecy.

62. Brooksley Born, Interview for "The Warning," *Frontline*, PBS, October 20, 2009.

63. Ibid.

64. Schmitt, "The Born Prophecy."

65. Manuel Roig-Franzia, "Brooksley Born, the Cassandra of the Derivatives Crisis," *Washington Post*, May 26, 2009, https://www.washingtonpost.com/wp-dyn/content/article/2009/05/25/AR2009052502108.html.

66. Commodity Futures Trading Commission, "Over-the-Counter Derivatives," Washington, DC, May 6, 1998, https://www.cftc.gov/sites/default/files/opa/press98/opamntn.htm.

67. "Joint Statement by Treasury Secretary Robert E. Rubin, Federal Reserve Board Chairman Alan Greenspan and Securities and Exchange Commission Chairman Author Levitt," US Treasury Department Press Release, May 7, 1998, https://www.treasury.gov/press-center/press-releases/Pages/rr2426.aspx.

68. Testimony of Alan Greenspan, Chairman of the Federal Reserve Board, "The Regulation of OTC Derivatives: Hearing before the House Committee on Banking and Financial Services," *105th Congress*, July 24, 1998.

NOTES 155

69. Testimony of Brooksley Born, Chairman of the Commodity Futures Trading Commission, "Hedge Fund Operations: Hearing before the House Committee on Banking and Financial Services," *105th Congress*, October 1, 1998.

70. *Over-the-Counter Derivatives Market and the Commodity Exchange Act: Report of The President's Working Group on Financial Markets* (1999), https://home.treasury.gov/system/files/236/Over-the-Counter-Derivatives-Market-Commodity-Exchange-Act.pdf.

71. *The Financial Crisis Inquiry Report*, 49.

72. Kadija Yilla and Nellie Liang, "What Are Macroprudential Tools?" *Brookings Institute*, February 11, 2020, https://www.brookings.edu/blog/up-front/2020/02/11/what-are-macroprudential-tools/.

73. Ibid. The authors note: "A bank that needs to increase its capital ratio (measured as a percentage of its asset) can either raise new capital or decrease assets (loans). When bank losses are increasing because the economy is weak and bank capital ratios are falling, the difference between the two approaches is consequential. If every firm were to decrease assets instead of raise capital, that action would lead to a substantive contraction of credit and cause the economy to weaken further."

74. Ibid.

75. Remarks of Chairman Ben S. Bernanke, "Financial Regulation and Supervision after the Crisis: The Role of the Federal Reserve," Speech, Federal Reserve Bank of Boston 54th Economic Conference, Chatham, Massachusetts, 1999.

76. Brigitte Burgemeestre, Joris Hulstijn, and Yao-hua Tan, "Rule-based versus Principle-based Regulatory Compliance," in *Legal Knowledge and Information Systems* ed. G. Governatori (Amsterdam: IOS Press, 2009), 37.

77. Bair, *Bull by the Horns*, 27.

78. Meg Fletcher, "Dinallo Lays Out New Approach to Regulation," *Business Insurance*, November 11, 2007, https://www.businessinsurance.com/article/20071111/STORY/100023398?template=printart.

79. Sheila Bair discusses this issue in her book *Bull by the Horns*. Also see her remarks in the Senate Hearing, "An Update on the New Basel Capital Accord: Hearing before the Senate Committee on Banking, Housing, and Urban Affairs," *109th Congress*, September 26, 2006, https://www.govinfo.gov/content/pkg/CHRG-109shrg50306/html/CHRG-109shrg50306.htm.

80. Bair, *Bull by the Horns*, 27.

81. The idea that switching to principles-based regulation was necessary "for New York to remain the financial capital of the world," as Dinallo put it, was prevalent as late as 2007. See "N.Y. Insurance Department Advances First Principles-Based Regulation," *Insurance Journal*, November 5, 2007, https://www.insurancejournal.com/news/east/2007/11/05/84761.htm.

82. Stephen Breyer, *Regulation and Its Reform* (Cambridge, MA: Harvard University Press, 1984), 161.

83. Mary Graham, *Democracy by Disclosure: The Rise of Technopopulism* (Washington, DC: Brookings Institution Press, 2002), 3.

84. Franklin D. Roosevelt, "Address Accepting the Presidential Nomination at the Democratic National Convention in Chicago," Speech, Chicago, July 2, 1932, https://www.presidency.ucsb.edu/documents/address-accepting-the-presidential-nomination-the-democratic-national-convention-chicago-1.

85. Ibid.

86. Graham, *Democracy by Disclosure*, 13.

87. On this point, see Anne Fleming, "The Long History of Truth in Lending," *Journal of Policy History* 30, no. 2 (2018): 236–271.

88. Congressional Findings and Declaration Purpose, 15 U.S. Code § 1601, Legal Information Institute, https://www.law.cornell.edu/uscode/text/15/1601.

89. Fleming, "The Long History," 250.

90. Ibid.

91. Paula J. Dalley, "The Use and Misuse of Disclosure as a Regulatory System," *Florida State University Law Review* 34, no. 4 (Summer 2007): 1092.

92. Graham, *Democracy by Disclosure*, 4.

93. Lauren E. Willis, "Against Financial-Literacy Education," *Iowa Law Review* 94, no. 1 (2008): 197.

94. Dalley, "The Use and Misuse of Disclosure," 1093.

95. Dee Pridgen, "Putting Some Teeth in TILA: From Disclosure to Substantive Regulation in the Mortgage Reform and Anti-Predatory Lending Act of 2010," *Loyola Consumer Law Review* 34, no. 4 (Summer 2007): 615.

96. Ibid.

97. Ibid.

98. On this topic, see Graham, *Democracy by Disclosure*; Suzanne Mettler, *The Submerged State: How Invisible Government Policies Undermine American Democracy* (Chicago: University of Chicago Press, 2011).

99. Graham, *Democracy by Disclosure*, 11.

100. Mettler, *The Submerged State*, 16.

101. Ibid., 8.

102. Pierre Pénet, "Calculating and Governing Risk in Times of Crisis: The Role of Credit Ratings in Regulatory Reasoning and Legal Change (1930s–2010s)," PhD diss., Northwestern University, 2014, 35.

103. Ibid., 379.

104. Ibid., 213.

105. Ibid., 218.

106. Pénet, "Calculating and Governing Risk," 87.

107. Ibid., 224.

108. Richard Cantor and Frank Packer, "The Credit Rating Industry," *Journal of Fixed Income* 5, no. 3 (Winter 1995): 15.

109. White, "Markets: The Credit Rating Agencies," 214.

110. Willis, "Against Financial-Literacy Education," 197.

111. Ibid., 197.

112. Robert T. Kiyosaki and Sharon L. Lechter, *Rich Dad, Poor Dad: What the Rich Teach Their Kids About Money That the Poor and Middle Class Do Not!* (Paradise Valley, AZ: Techpress Inc., 1998).

NOTES 157

113. "The State of Financial Literacy and Education in America: Hearings Before the Senate Committee on Banking, Housing, and Urban Affairs," *107th Congress*, 2nd session, February 5 and 6, 2002.

114. Statement of Alan Greenspan, Chairman of the Federal Reserve Board, "The State of Financial Literacy and Education in America: Hearings Before the Senate Committee on Banking, Housing, and Urban Affairs," *107th Congress*, 2nd session, February 5 and 6, 2002.

115. Statement of Harvey L. Pitt, "The State of Financial Literacy and Education in America: Hearings Before the Senate Committee on Banking, Housing, and Urban Affairs," *107th Congress*, 2nd session, February 5 and 6, 2002.

116. Statement of Paul O'Neill, "The State of Financial Literacy and Education in America: Hearings Before the Senate Committee on Banking, Housing, and Urban Affairs," *107th Congress*, 2nd session, February 5 and 6, 2002.

117. Those testifying included Susan Molinari, national chairperson, Americans for Consumer Education and Competition; Steven Brobeck, executive director, Consumer Federation of America; Don M. Blandin, president, American Savings Education Council; Esther "Tess" Canja, president, AARP; and Raul Yzaguirre, president and CEO, National Council of La Raza.

118. Statement of Steven Brobeck, "The State of Financial Literacy and Education in America: Hearings Before the Senate Committee on Banking, Housing, and Urban Affairs," *107th Congress*, 2nd session, February 5 and 6, 2002.

119. Establishment of Financial Literacy and Education Commission, 20 U.S.C. 9702 (2009).

120. "Improving Financial Literacy in the United States: Hearing before the Committee on Banking, Housing, and Urban Affairs," *109th Congress*, 2nd session, May 23, 2006.

121. Statement of Ben S. Bernanke, Chairman, Board of Governors of the Federal Reserve System, "Improving Financial Literacy in the United States: Hearing before the Committee on Banking, Housing, and Urban Affairs," *109th Congress*, 2nd session, May 23, 2006.

122. Ibid.

Chapter 5

1. Joseph Stiglitz, "The Roaring Nineties," *The Atlantic*, October 2002, https://www.theatlantic.com/magazine/archive/2002/10/the-roaring-nineties/302604/.

2. Ibid.

3. Karl Marx, *Capital*, vol. 1, part 1: "Commodities and Money." Accessed December 15, 2023. https://www.d.umn.edu/cla/faculty/jhamlin/4111/MarxReadings/1867%20Capital%20I%20--%20Ch_%201.htm: "vulgar economy, which deals with appearances only, ruminates without ceasing on the materials long since provided by scientific economy, and there seeks plausible explanations of the most obtrusive phenomena, for bourgeois daily use, but for the rest, confines itself to systematizing

158 NOTES

in a pedantic way, and proclaiming for everlasting truths, the trite ideas held by the self-complacent bourgeoisie with regard to their own world, to them the best of all possible worlds."

4. Kadija Yilla and Nellie Liang, "What Are Macroprudential Tools?" Brookings Institution, February 11, 2020, https://www.brookings.edu/blog/up-front/2020/02/11/what-are-macroprudential-tools/.

5. See Adam J. Levitin, "The Consumer Financial Protection Bureau: An Introduction," *Review of Banking & Financial Law* 32 (2013): 330.

6. Ibid., 331.

7. On this, see Cristie L. Ford, "Principles-Based Securities Regulation in the Wake of the Global Financial Crisis," *McGill Law Journal* 55 (2010): 257–307.

8. Statement of Sheila Bair before the Subcommittee on Financial Institutions and Consumer Credit of the Committee on Financial Services, US House of Representatives, September 14, 2006.

9. Ibid.

10. Testimony of Diana Taylor, Superintendent of New York State Banking Department on behalf of state bank supervisors, before the Committee on Banking, Housing and Urban Affairs, US Senate, September 26, 2006.

11. Testimony of Travis B. Plunkett before the Committee on Financial Services of the US House of Representatives, July 25, 2007.

12. Omri Ben-Shahar et al., *More Than You Wanted to Know: The Failure of Mandated Disclosure* (Princeton: Princeton University Press, 2014), 5.

13. Mary Graham, *Democracy by Disclosure: The Rise of Technopopulism* (Washington, DC: Brookings Institution, 2002), 5.

14. G. Mattarocci, *The Independence of Credit Rating Agencies: How Business Models and Regulators Interact* (Amsterdam: Elsevier Academic Press, 2014), 72.

15. Lauren E. Willis, "Decision Making and the Limits of Disclosure: The Problem of Predatory Lending: Price," *Maryland Law Review* 65, no. 3 (2006): 749.

16. Ibid.

17. Ben-Shahar et al., *More Than You Wanted to Know*, 34.

18. Ibid., 8.

19. Elizabeth Warren, "Redesigning Regulation: A Case Study from the Consumer Credit Market," in *Government and Markets: Toward a New Theory of Regulation*, ed. Edward J. Balleisen and David Moss (Cambridge: Cambridge University Press, 2010), 401.

20. David A. Moss, *When All Else Fails: Government as the Ultimate Risk Manager* (Cambridge, MA: Harvard University Press, 2004), 305.

21. Volcker Alliance Report, *Reshaping the Financial Regulatory System* (2015).

22. Elizabeth Kimberly Pernell, "The Causes of the Divergent Development of Banking Regulation in the U.S., Canada, and Spain," PhD diss., Harvard University, Graduate School of Arts & Sciences, 2016, 48.

23. Ibid., 49.

24. Henry M. Paulson Jr., quoted in Volcker Alliance Report, *Reshaping the Financial Regulatory System*, 12.

NOTES 159

25. Warren, "Redesigning Regulation," 405.
26. On this issue, see Levitin, "The Consumer Financial Protection Bureau."
27. A similar orientation also characterized the way the state understood and approached the mitigation of socio-economic risks. Socio-economic risks were increasingly understood as something to be tackled at the individual level (the rise of personal responsibility discourse) and by market mechanisms.
28. Xavier Freixas et al., *Systemic Risk, Crises, and Macroprudential Regulation* (Boston, MA: MIT Press, 2015), 43.
29. G. Kaufman and K. E. Scott, "What Is Systemic Risk, and Do Bank Regulators Retard or Contribute to It?" *The Independent Review* 7, no. 3 (2003): 371–91.
30. ECB, "The Concept of Systemic Risk," *ECB Financial Stability Review* (2009), 134, https://www.ecb.europa.eu/pub/pdf/fsr/financialstabilityreview200912en.pdf.
31. Governor Daniel K. Tarullo, "Regulatory Restructuring" before the Committee on Banking, Housing, and Urban Affairs, US Senate, Washington, DC, July 23, 2009, https://www.federalreserve.gov/newsevents/testimony/tarullo20090723a.htm.
32. Christian Brownlees and Robert F. Engle, "SRISK: A Conditional Capital Shortfall Measure of Systemic Risk," *The Review of Financial Studies* 30, no. 1 (2017): 49.
33. See V-Lab, Systemic Risk Analysis, https://vlab.stern.nyu.edu/docs/srisk.
34. Ibid.
35. Viral V. Acharya, Lasse H. Pedersen, Thomas Philippon, and Matthew Richardson, "Measuring Systemic Risk," *Federal Reserve Bank of Cleveland, Working Papers* no. 10-02 (2010): 2.
36. Ibid., 3.
37. Onur Ozgode, "Governing the Economy at the Limits of Neoliberalism: The Genealogy of Systemic Risk Regulation in the United States, 1922–2012," PhD diss., Columbia University, 2015, 31.
38. See Moritz Kuhn, Moritz Schularick, and Ulrike I. Steins, The Great American Debt Boom, 1949–2013 (2017), http://conference.nber.org/conf_papers/f96641.pdf.
39. Data is from the American Bankruptcy Institute, https://www.abi.org/newsroom/chart-of-the-day/household-mortgage-debt-as-percentage-of-gdp-since-1952.
40. On this issue, see Elizabeth Warren and Amelia Warren Tyagi, *The Two-Income Trap: Why Middle-Class Parents Are Going Broke* (New York: Basic Books, 2004); Aldo Barba and Massimo Pivetti, "Rising Household Debt: Its Causes and Macroeconomic Implications: A Long-Period Analysis," *Cambridge Journal of Economics* 33, no. 1 (2009): 113–137; Raghuram Rajan, *Fault Lines: How Hidden Fractures Still Threaten the World Economy* (New York: HarperCollins, 2010); Kus, "Consumption and Redistributive Politics"; K. T. Leicht and S. T. Fitzgerald, "The Real Reason 60 Is the New 30: Consumer Debt and Income Insecurity in Late Middle Age," *The Sociological Quarterly* 55, no. 2 (2014): 236–260.
41. Data is from https://www.sec.gov/news/speech/speech-clayton-2018-05-02.
42. Cohen, *Consumers' Republic*, 29.
43. Ibid.
44. Edwards, "Article 2 of the Uniform Commercial Code and Consumer Protection," 702.

160 NOTES

45. Anne Fleming, "Consumer Rights Are Worthless without Enforcement," *The Conversation*, March 15, 2019, https://theconversation.com/consumer-rights-are-worthless-without-enforcement-113244.

46. Lizabeth Cohen, "Colston E. Warne Lecture: Is It Time for Another Round of Consumer Protection? The Lessons of Twentieth Century U.S. History," *The Journal of Consumer Affairs* 44, no. 1 (2010): 5.

47. Edwards, "Article 2 of the Uniform Commercial Code," 701.

48. Homer Kripke, "Gesture and Reality in Consumer Credit Reform," cited in Edwards, "Article 2 of the Uniform Commercial Code," 701.

49. Edwards, "Article 2 of the Uniform Commercial Code," 690.

50. On this issue, see Anne Fleming, "The Rise and Fall of Unconscionability as the 'Law of the Poor,'" *The Georgetown Law Journal* 102, no. 5 (2014): 1383–1441.

51. Edwards, "Article 2 of the Uniform Commercial Code," 672.

52. Fleming, "The Rise and Fall of Unconscionability."

53. On this issue, see Lauren E. Willis, "Decision Making and the Limits of Disclosure: The Problem of Predatory Lending: Price," *Maryland Law Review* 65, no. 3 (2006): 707, http://digitalcommons.law.umaryland.edu/mlr/vol65/iss3/3.

54. Testimony of Elizabeth Warren before House Financial Services Committee, "Regulatory Restructuring: Enhancing Consumer Financial Products Regulation," Wednesday, June 24, 2009.

55. Ellen Schloemer, Wei Li, Keith Ernst, and Kathleen Keest, *Losing Ground: Foreclosures in the Subprime Market and Their Cost to Homeowners* (Durham, NC: Center for Responsible Lending, 2006), https://www.responsiblelending.org/sites/default/files/nodes/files/research-publication/foreclosure-paper-report-2-17.pdf.

56. Debbie Gruenstein Bocian, Wei Li, Carolina Reid, and Roberto G. Quercia, *Lost Ground, 2011: Disparities in Mortgage Lending and Foreclosures* (Durham, NC: Center for Responsible Lending, 2011), https://www.responsiblelending.org/mortgage-lending/research-analysis/Lost-Ground-2011.pdf.

57. Schloemer et al., *Losing Ground*, 8.

58. Martin Isaac and Christopher Niedt, *Foreclosed America* (Stanford, 2015), 6.

59. Ibid., 8.

60. Ibid., 25.

61. Ibid., 25.

62. See Kuhn et al., *The Great American Debt Boom*.

63. Center for Responsible Lending, *The Plastic Safety Net* (Durham, NC: Center for Responsible Lending, 2005), 4–5, https://www.responsiblelending.org/credit-cards/research-analysis/DEMOS-101205.pdf.

64. Center for Responsible Lending, *Congress Should Cap Interest Rates*, Research Brief (Durham, NC: Center for Responsible Lending, 2009) https://www.responsiblelending.org/sites/default/files/nodes/files/research-publication/interest-rate-survey.pdf.

65. Wei Li, Leslie Parrish, Keith Ernst, and Delvin Davis, *Predatory Profiling: The Role of Race and Ethnicity in the Location of Payday Lenders in California* (Durham, NC: Center for Responsible Lending, 2009), 2, https://www.responsiblelending.org/sites/default/files/nodes/files/research-publication/predatory-profiling.pdf.

NOTES   161

66. See Tomaskovic-Devy and Lin "Income Dynamics." See also Kus "Financialisation and Income Inequality."
67. Colin Crouch, *The Strange Non-Death of Neoliberalism* (Cambridge, MA: Polity Press, 2011), 116.
68. See Kus, "Financial Citizenship and the Hidden Crisis of the Working" and Kus, "Consumption and Redistributive Politics."

Chapter 6

1. Several important books were published in the past decade or so on the financial crisis, including Johnson and Kwak, 13 Bankers; B. McLean, and J. Nocera, *All the Devils Are Here: The Hidden History of the Financial Crisis* (New York: Portfolio, 2011); Craig Calhoun and Georgi Derlugguian, *Business as Usual: The Roots of the Global Financial Meltdown* (New York: New York University Press, 2011); Robert G. Kaiser, *The Act of Congress: How America's Essential Institution Works, and How It Doesn't* (New York: Vintage Books, 2013); Barry Eichengreen, *Hall of Mirrors: The Great Depression, the Great Recession, and the Uses-and Misuses-of History* (New York: Oxford University Press, 2014); Manuel Castells, Joao Caraca, and Gustavo Cardoso, *Aftermath: The Cultures of the Economic Crisis* (New York: Oxford University Press, 2014); K. Sabeel Rahman, *Democracy Against Domination* (New York: Oxford University Press, 2016). All these books shed light on the roots of the financial crisis in the US, and the government's response to the crisis. As a political sociologist, I view economic crises not only as economic bottlenecks, but as politically generative phenomena that showcase the limits and potentiality of statecraft and democratic citizenship. In that sense, I share the political sensibilities of K. Sabeel Rahman's work, although my book addresses a different set of questions.
2. Ben Bernanke, closed-door session with FCIC, November 17, 2009, quoted in Financial Crisis Inquiry Commission, *Final Report* (2011), 354, https://fcic-static.law. stanford.edu/cdn_media/fcic-reports/fcic_final_report_full.pdf.
3. William Dudley in Brookings Institution, "Responding to the Global Financial Crisis" (Conference Proceedings, Day 1, September 11, 2018), https://www.brookings.edu/ wp-content/uploads/2018/09/es_20180911_financial_crisis_day1_transcript.pdf.
4. Patricia Mosser in Brookings Institution, "Responding to the Global Financial Crisis" (Conference Proceedings, Day 1, September 11, 2018), https://www.brookings.edu/ wp-content/uploads/2018/09/es_20180911_financial_crisis_day1_transcript.pdf.
5. For section 13, Powers of Federal Reserve Banks, see https://www.federalreserve.gov/ aboutthefed/section13.htm.
6. Dennis Jacobe, "Six in 10 Oppose Wall Street Bailouts," *Gallup*, April 3, 2008, https:// news.gallup.com/poll/106114/six-oppose-wall-street-bailouts.aspx.
7. Pew Research Center, "Small Plurality Backs Bailout Plan," *Pew Research Center*, September 30, 2008, https://www.pewresearch.org/politics/2008/09/30/small-plural ity-backs-bailout-plan/.
8. Johnson and Kwak, 13 Bankers, 165.

162 NOTES

9. Johnson and Kwak, *13 Bankers*, 166.
10. "Treasury Announces TARP Capital Purchase Program Description," https://www.treasury.gov/press-center/press-releases/Pages/hp1207.aspx.
11. Quoted in Nina Easton, "How the Bailout Bashed the Banks," *CNN Money Special Report*, June 22, 2009, https://money.cnn.com/2009/06/19/news/economy/trouble_with_tarp_bailout.fortune/index.htm?postversion=2009062206.
12. See US Department of Housing and Urban Development, "Neighborhood Stabilization Program Data," https://www.huduser.gov/portal/datasets/NSP.html.
13. One of the critical voices was Sheila Bair. Early on in February 2009, Bair shared her reservations about the limited relief that was planned for homeowners in distress under the Home Affordable Modification Program with Larry Summers, but her views were dismissed. See Reed Hunt, *A Crisis Wasted* (New York: Rosetta Books [Kindle edition], 2019), 78.
14. Isaac William Martin and Christopher Niedt, *Foreclosed America* (Redwood City, CA: Stanford University Press, 2015).
15. Notes from Brookings Institution, "Responding to the Global Financial Crisis," September 12, 2018. Aaron Sorkin asks: "I know one of the issues that you think about a lot is Fannie and Freddie and how that you think ultimately did help homeowners." Secretary Paulson responds: "I don't think it, it did. Imagine how far housing prices would have fallen if we didn't have mortgage funding during the financial crisis, and Fannie and Freddie were the only source of mortgage financing, so that made a very significant difference. So, I just can't imagine what would have happened if they hadn't gone into conservatorship." See https://www. brookings.edu/wp-content/uploads/2018/09/es_20180912_financial_crisis_day2_transcript.pdf.
16. Neel Kashkari, Brookings Institution, "Responding to the Global Financial Crisis," Day 1.
17. Polanyi, *The Great Transformation*, 162.
18. Jones, "Preserving Homeownership," 10.
19. Ibid.
20. Quoted in Hunt, *A Crisis Wasted*, 210.
21. John Maynard Keynes, "From Keynes to Roosevelt: Our Recovery Plan. Assayed," *New York Times*, December 31, 1933, https://www.nytimes.com/1933/12/31/archives/from-keynes-to-roosevelt-our-recovery-plan-assayed-the-british.html.
22. Allstate/National Journal, *Heartland Monitor Poll*, conducted September 28 to October 2, 2011, https://www.allstate.com/resources/allstate/attachments/heartland-monitor/heartland_x_topline_data.pdf.
23. Ibid.
24. C. Romer, "Economic Policy in the First Year of the Obama Administration," 2010, https://obamawhitehouse.archives.gov/blog/2010/01/15/economic-policy-first-year-obama-administration.
25. See Peter Hall, "Policy Paradigms, Social Learning, and the State: The Case of Economic Policymaking in Britain," *Comparative Politics* 25 (1993): 275–296; Peter Gourevitch, *Politics in Hard Times: Comparative Responses to International Economic Crises* (Ithaca, NY: Cornell University Press, 1986); Colin Hay, "The 'Crisis' of

NOTES 163

Keynesianism and the Rise of Neoliberalism in Britain: An Ideational Institutionalist Approach," in *The Rise of Neoliberalism and Institutional Analysis*, ed. J. Campbell and O. Pedersen (Princeton, NJ: Princeton University Press, 2001); Mark Blyth, *Great Transformations: Economic Ideas and Institutional Change in the Twentieth Century* (Cambridge: Cambridge University Press, 2002).

26. United States Department of the Treasury, "Financial Regulatory Reform: A New Foundation: Rebuilding Financial Supervision and Regulation," 2009, 5, 6, 13, 19, 44, https://fraser.stlouisfed.org/title/financial-regulatory-reform-5123.

27. Ibid., 4.

28. Ibid., 3.

29. Prepared Statement of Edward L. Yingling, President and Chief Executive Officer, American Bankers Association, Hearing before the Committee on Banking, Housing, and Urban Affairs, July 14, 2009.

30. Statement of Michael S. Menzies, Sr., President and Chief Executive Officer, Easton Bank and Trust Company, on behalf of the Independent Community Bankers Association, House of Representatives Committee on Financial Services Hearing on "Banking Industry Perspectives," July 15, 2009.

31. Statement of Steve Bartlett, President and Chief Executive Officer, The Financial Services Roundtable, House of Representatives Committee on Financial Services Hearing on "Banking Industry Perspectives," July 15, 2009.

32. Statement of Edward L. Yingling, House of Representatives Committee on Financial Services Hearing on "Banking Industry Perspectives," July 15, 2009.

33. Elizabeth Warren, "Unsafe at Any Rate," *Democracy* 5 (Summer 2007), https://democracyjournal.org/magazine/5/unsafe-at-any-rate/.

34. Statement of Steve Bartlett, Hearing on "Banking Industry Perspectives," July 15, 2009.

35. See the AFSA website at https://afsaonline.org/about-afsa/afsa-membership/.

36. Statement of Chris Stinebert, President and Chief Executive Officer, The American Financial Services Association, House of Representatives Committee on Financial Services Hearing on "Banking Industry Perspectives," July 15, 2009.

37. Statement of John A. Courson, President and Chief Executive Officer, Mortgage Bankers Association, House of Representatives Committee on Financial Services Hearing on "Banking Industry Perspectives," July 15, 2009.

38. Michael S. Menzies, Sr., President and Chief Executive Officer, Easton Bank and Trust Company, on behalf of the Independent Community Bankers Association, House of Representatives Committee on Financial Services Hearing on "Banking Industry Perspectives," July 15, 2009.

39. Ibid.

40. Statement of Steven I. Zeisel, Vice President and Senior Counsel, The Consumer Bankers Association, House of Representatives Committee on Financial Services Hearing on "Banking Industry Perspectives," July 15, 2009.

41. Statement of Edward L. Yingling, House of Representatives Committee on Financial Services Hearing on "Banking Industry Perspectives," July 15, 2009.

164 NOTES

42. Statement of John Taylor, President and Chief Executive Officer, National Community Reinvestment Coalition (NCRC), "Community and Consumer Advocates' Perspectives on the Obama Administration's Financial Regulatory Reform Proposals," *Hearing Before the Committee on Financial Services,* US House of Representatives, July 16, 2009, https://www.govinfo.gov/content/pkg/CHRG-111hh rg53241/html/CHRG-111hhrg53241.htm.

43. Statement of Travis B. Plunkett, Legislative Director, Consumer Federation of America, "Community and Consumer Advocates' Perspectives on the Obama Administration's Financial Regulatory Reform Proposals," Hearing Before the Committee on Financial Services, US House of Representatives, July 16, 2009, https://www.govinfo.gov/content/pkg/CHRG-111hhrg53241/html/CHRG-111hhrg53 241.htm.

44. Ibid.

45. Adam Levitin, "The Consumer Financial Protection Agency," *Pew Financial Reform Project Briefing Papers* 2 (2009).

46. Ibid.

47. Statement of Edmund Mierzwinski, the Consumer Program Director of US Public Research Interest Group, "Community and Consumer Advocates' Perspectives on the Obama Administration's Financial Regulatory Reform Proposals," Hearing Before the Committee on Financial Services, US House of Representatives, July 16, 2009, https://www.govinfo.gov/content/pkg/CHRG-111hhrg53241/html/CHRG-111hh rg53241.htm.

48. Statement of Nancy Zirkin, Executive Vice President of the Leadership Conference on Civil Rights (LCRR), "Community and Consumer Advocates' Perspectives on the Obama Administration's Financial Regulatory Reform Proposals," Hearing Before the Committee on Financial Services, US House of Representatives, July 16, 2009, https://www.govinfo.gov/content/pkg/CHRG-111hhrg53241/html/CHRG-111hh rg53241.htm.

49. Ibid.

50. See Plunkett and Zirkin's testimonies on this issue.

51. Statement of Edmund Mierzwinski, Consumer Program Director, US Public Interest Research Group (US PIRG), "Community and Consumer Advocates' Perspectives on the Obama Administration's Financial Regulatory Reform Proposals," Hearing Before the Committee on Financial Services, US House of Representatives, July 16, 2009, https://www.govinfo.gov/content/pkg/CHRG-111hhrg53241/html/CHRG-111hhrg53241.htm.

52. Statement of Travis B. Plunkett, "Community and Consumer Advocates' Perspectives on the Obama Administration's Financial Regulatory Reform Proposals," Hearing Before the Committee on Financial Services, US House of Representatives, July 16, 2009.

53. See Ellen M. Immergut, "Institutions, Veto Points, and Policy Results," *Journal of Public Policy* 10, no. 4 (2008): 391–416.

54. Sven Steinmo, "Why Is Government So Small in America?" *Governance: An International Journal of Policy and Administration* 8, no. 3 (1995): 303–334.

NOTES   165

55. On this point, see Kaiser, *Act of Congress*.

56. Ibid., 103.

57. Ibid., 103.

58. Gary Rivlin, "How Wall Street Defanged Dodd–Frank," *The Nation Magazine*, May 20, 2013, https://www.thenation.com/article/archive/how-wall-street-defanged-dodd-frank/.

59. On this, see D. Vogel, *The Politics of Precaution: Regulating Health, Safety, and Environmental Risks in Europe and the United States* (Princeton, NJ: Princeton University Press, 2012).

60. Kaiser, *Act of Congress*, 75.

61. Heather Booth, Director of Americans for Financial Reform, quoted in Brady Dennis, "A 'David and Goliath' Fight over Financial Reform," *Los Angeles Times*, August 24, 2009, https://www.latimes.com/archives/la-xpm-2009-aug-24-fi-boot h24-story.html.

62. See Mark Mizruchi, *The Fracturing of the American Corporate Elite* (Cambridge, MA: Harvard University Press, 2013).

63. Cornelia Woll, "Politics in the Interest of Capital: A Not-So-Organized Combat," *MaxPo Discussion Papers* 2 (2015): 17.

64. Congressman Barney Frank quoted in Kaiser, *Act of Congress*, 140–141.

65. Jim MacPhee, Mike Menzies, and Sal Marranca, "The Good Is Oft Interred with Their Bones," *ICBA Commentary, United States Congress, Congressional Record: Proceedings and Debates of the 111th Congress* 156, no. 104, July 14, 2010.

66. Ibid.

67. Ibid.

68. See https://ourfinancialsecurity.org/about/. As of 2009, these organizations were the members and partners of AFFR: A New Way Forward; AARP; ACORN; Adler and Colvin; AFL-CIO; AFSCME; Alliance For Justice; Americans for Democratic Action, Inc; American Income Life Insurance; Americans for Fairness in Lending; Americans United for Change; Calvert Asset Management Company, Inc.; Campaign for America's Future; Campaign Money; Center for Digital Democracy; Center for Economic and Policy Research; Center for Economic Progress; Center for Responsible Lending; Center for Justice and Democracy; Center of Concern; Change to Win; Clean Yield Asset Management; Coastal Enterprises Inc.; Color of Change; and Common Cause. Communications Workers of America; Community Development Transportation Lending Services; Consumer Action; Consumer Association Council; Consumers for Auto Safety and Reliability; Consumer Federation of America; Consumer Watchdog; Consumers Union; Corporation for Enterprise Development; CREDO Mobile; CTW Investment Group; Demos; Economic Policy Institute; Essential Action; Greenlining Institute; Good Business International; HNMA Funding Company; Home Actions; Housing Counseling Services; Information Press; Institute for Global Communications; Institute for Policy Studies: Global Economy Project; International Brotherhood of Teamsters; Institute of Women's Policy Research; and Krull & Company. Laborers' International Union of North America; Lake Research Partners; Lawyers' Committee for Civil Rights Under Law; Leadership

166   NOTES

Conference on Civil Rights; Move On; NASCAT; National Association of Consumer Advocates; National Association of Neighborhoods; National Coalition for Asian Pacific American Community Development; National Community Reinvestment Coalition; National Consumer Law Center (on behalf of its low-income clients); National Consumers League; National Council of La Raza; National Fair Housing Alliance; National Federation of Community Development Credit Unions; National Housing Institute; National Housing Trust; National Housing Trust Community Development Fund; National NeighborWorks Association; National Training and Information Center/National People's Action; National Council of Women's Organizations; Next Step; OMB Watch; Opportunity Finance Network; and Partners for the Common Good. PICO; Progress Now Action; Progressive States Network; Poverty and Race Research Action Council; Public Citizen; Sargent Shriver Center on Poverty Law; SEIU; State Voices; Taxpayer's for Common Sense; The Association for Housing and Neighborhood Development; The Fuel Savers Club; The Seminal; US Public Interest Research Group; Union Plus; United Food and Commercial Workers; United States Student Association; USAction; Veris Wealth Partners; Veterans Chamber of Commerce; Western States Center; We the People Now; Woodstock Institute; World Privacy Forum; UNET; Union Plus; and Unitarian Universalist for a Just Economic Community.

69. Cohen, "Is It Time for Another Round of Consumer Protection?," 235.
70. Heather Booth, Director of Americans for Financial Reform, quoted in Dennis, "A 'David and Goliath' Fight."
71. Lisa Kastner, *Civil Society and Financial Regulation: Consumer Finance Protection and Taxation After the Financial Crisis* (London: Routledge, 2017).
72. Ibid.
73. Wall Street Journal Opinion, "The Uncertainty Principle," *Wall Street Journal*, July 14, 2010, https://www.wsj.com/articles/SB100014240527487042882045753631626 64835780.
74. Ibid.
75. Eichengreen, *Hall of Mirrors*.
76. On this issue, see Rahman, *Democracy against Domination*.
77. Johnson and Kwak, *13 Bankers*.
78. Sheila Bair, quoted in Hunt, *A Crisis Wasted*.
79. Johnson and Kwak, *13 Bankers*, 222.
80. US Department of the Treasury, "Designations," https://home.treasury.gov/policy-iss ues/financial-markets-financial-institutions-and-fiscal-service/fsoc/designations.
81. Ibid.
82. The Trump administration went so far as to challenge the CFPB's constitutionality and asked the Supreme Court to limit its independence.
83. In fact, as of now, they are above the 2008 level.
84. Johnson and Kwak, *13 Bankers*, 222.
85. Rahman, *Democracy against Domination*.
86. Ibid., 169.

NOTES 167

Chapter 7

1. Other scholars have explored this aspect in far more detail than I have here. See Horwitz, *The Irony of Regulatory Reform*; Prasad, *The Politics of Free Markets*; Halvorson, "Valuing the Air."

2. Gerald Davis, *Managed by the Markets: How Finance Re-Shaped America* (New York: Oxford University Press, 2009); Krippner, *Capitalizing on Crisis*; Lin and Tomaskovic-Devey, "Financialization and US Income Inequality, 1970–2008"; Bruce Carruthers, "Financialization and the Institutional Foundations of New Capitalism" *Socio-Economic Review* 13, no. 2 (2015): 379–398; Neil Fligstein, *The Banks Did It: An Anatomy of the Financial Crisis* (Cambridge, MA: Harvard University Press, 2021).

3. Hacker, *The Great Risk Shift*; Kalleberg, "The Social Contract in an Era of Precarious Work."

4. On this, see my 2012 article, Kus, "Consumption and Redistributive Politics."

5. Ulrich Beck, A. Giddens, and S. Lash, *Reflexive Modernization: Politics, Tradition, and Aesthetics in Modern Social Order* (Cambridge: Polity, 1994), 27.

6. Hacker, *The Great Risk Shift*, 8.

7. Ulrich Beck, "Living in the World Risk Society," *Economy and Society* 35, no. 3 (2006): 336.

8. Ibid.

9. Beck, "Living in the World Risk Society," 336.

10. In reading Obama's memoir, *A Promised Land*, published in 2020 by Random House, it is clear that Obama himself was aware that his administration's response to the crisis was limited and conservative; although by his own account, he thought he would have time for structural reform later on.

11. Rahman, *Democracy Against Domination*, 78–79.

12. Frances Fox Piven and Richard A. Cloward, *Poor People's Movements: Why They Succeed, How They Fail* (New York: Pantheon Books, 1977).

13. Surely, Occupy Wall Street cannot be overlooked, but the Occupy movement had not even started until late 2011, more than a year after Dodd–Frank was signed. Moreover, as some have argued, the Occupy movement was in some critical ways not a movement with a leadership structure and specific policy demands, which are often seen as prerequisites of successful mobilization, but more of a "moment."

14. Theda Skocpol, "Associations without Members," *American Prospect* 45 (1999): 66–73.

15. Dana Fisher, *Activism, Inc.: How the Outsourcing of Grassroots Campaigns Is Strangling Progressive Politics in America* (Stanford: Stanford University Press, 2006).

16. Lizabeth Cohen, "Colston E. Warne Lecture: Is it Time for Another Round of Consumer Protection? The Lessons of Twentieth-century U.S. history," *The Journal of Consumer Affairs* 44, no. 1 (2010): 234–246, 2.

17. Kevin Cirilli and Bob Cusack, "Trump: Economic Bubble About to Burst," *The Hill*, October 14, 2015, https://thehill.com/homenews/campaign/256851-trump-econo mic-bubble-about-to-burst.

18. Financial Choice Act of 2017, https://www.congress.gov/bill/115th-congress/house-bill/10.

168 NOTES

19. Peter Evans, *Embedded Autonomy: States and Industrial Transformation* (Princeton, NJ: Princeton University Press, 1995).

20. Robert Shiller, *Finance and the Good Society* (Princeton, Princeton University Press, 2012).

21. Rahman, *Democracy against Domination*, 3.

22. James Fishkin, "Deliberation by the People Themselves: Entry Points for the Public Voice," *Election Law Journal: Rules, Politics, and Policy* 12, no. 4 (2013): 490–507.

23. See Jonathan Hopkin, *Anti-System Politics: The Crisis of Market Liberalism in Rich Democracies* (New York: Oxford University Press [Kindle edition], 2020) for a thorough exploration of this topic.

24. Sebastian Doerr, José-Luis Peydró, and Hans-Joachim Voth, "How Failing Banks Paved Hitler's Path to Power: Financial Crisis and Right-Wing Extremism in Germany, 1931–33," *VoxEU*, March 15, 2019, https://cepr.org/voxeu/columns/how-failing-banks-paved-hitlers-path-power-financial-crisis-and-right-wing-extremism.

25. Manuel Funke, Moritz Schularick, and Christoph Trebesch, "Going to Extremes: Politics after Financial Crises, 1870–2014," *CESifo Working Paper Series* no. 5553 (2015): 2.

26. Alan de Bromhead, Barry Eichengreen, and Kevin H. O'Rourke, "Right Wing Political Extremism in the Great Depression," *Discussion Papers in Economic and Social History* no. 95 (2012).

27. Hopkin, *Anti-System Politics*, 5.

28. January 9, 2016, Campaign Speech in Ottumwa, Iowa.

29. Once in power, however, Trump did not exactly work to curb the power of Wall Street. In fact, as I described in earlier pages, his administration weakened and repealed various regulatory measures that had been put in place after the crisis by the Obama administration.

30. For an analysis of the multitude of factors—economic, racial, ideological and institutional—see John L. Campbell, *American Discontent: The Rise of Donald Trump and the Decline of the Golden Age* (New York: Oxford University Press, 2018).

31. Polanyi, *The Great Transformation*, 32.

32. This structural understanding of contemporary American populism I advocate for here is in line with Michael Kazin's analysis of the development of American populism in the late nineteenth century, and there are indeed important comparisons to be drawn between two cases. As Kazin explains, in the US, when a populist movement developed in the late nineteenth century, it attracted to its ranks those who were being adversely affected by the march of industrialization—small farmers who "wanted, above all, equal treatment in a marketplace increasingly dominated by industrial corporations and large landowners" and workers who "wanted to stop the process of proletarianization." American historians' discussions of this late-nineteenth-century movement were characterized by a dualistic debate, reminiscent of the contemporary debates on populism, with one side speaking of the role of legitimate economic grievances in fueling the populist movement, and the other emphasizing the role of antisemitism, racism, and conspiratorial thinking. See Michael Kazin, "Democracy

NOTES   169

Betrayed and Redeemed: Populist Traditions in the United States," *Constellations* 5, no. 1 (1998): 75–84.

33. Polanyi, *The Great Transformation*, 251.
34. David Armitage, "In Defense of Presentism," in *History and Human Flourishing*, ed. Darrin M. McMahon (Oxford: Oxford University Press, 2022), 7.
35. Ibid., 13.

Index

For the benefit of digital users, indexed terms that span two pages (e.g., 52–53) may, on occasion, appear on only one of those pages.

401K 90, 126–27

Acharya, Viral 87
Alternative Mortgage Transaction Parity Act (AMTPA) 62–63, 66–67
Alvarez, Scott 56–57
American Banker, The 47, 48
American Bankers Association (ABA) 61, 63–65, 108, 110, 115–16
American Enterprise Institute 44
American Financial Services Association 109–10
American International Group (AIG) 1–2, 101, 118
American Recovery and Reinvestment Act (2009) 105–6
Americans for Financial Reform (AFR) 116, 130–31
Ansell, Christopher 4
Appelbaum, Binyamin 34–35, 43, 65–66
arbitrage 86
Arthur Andersen 44
auto industry 101

Bair, Sheila 66–68, 72, 82–83, 118
bank failures 40, 47, 48, 50–51
bank holding companies 7–8, 63–65, 68
Bank Holding Company Act (Glass–Steagall Act, 1933) 63–65
Bank Holding Company Act (1956) 7–8
Bank of America 1–2, 63–65, 101
Bank of New York Mellon 101
Banking Act (1933) 7–8, 62
banking assets 10–11
banking regulators 14–15, 47
banking sector 10–11, 54, 101
concentration in 119–20
Bartlett, Steve 109–10

Basel Committee on Banking Supervision 52, 82–83
"New Basel Capital Accord" 52
Quantitative Impact Study 82–83
Basel II Accord 53, 72
Basel II Advanced Approaches 82–83
Beck, Ulrich 126–27
Becker, Gary 24, 28–29
Ben-Shahar, Omri 83, 84
Benston, George 50–51
Berman, Elizabeth 28, 39
Bernanke, Ben 53, 54, 70–71, 78, 98
Bernstein, Marver 29–30
Bernstein, Peter 34–35
Bevir, Mark 32–34
Biden, Joe 133
"Black Monday" 49
"Black Tuesday" x–xi
Bliss, Robert 35–36
Booth, Heather 116
Born, Brooksley 68–69
Bowles, Erskine 1
Braithwaite, John 58
Brandeis, Louis D. 73–74
Bretton Woods system 75–76
Breyer, Stephen 73
Brobeck, Steven 78
brokers 12–13
mortgage 13–14, 67, 113
Brookings Institute 43–44, 53
Brown, Wendy 16, 20–21
Brownlees, Christian 87
Buchanan, James M. 24, 31
bureaucracy 16–17, 27, 31–34, 37, 51–52
Burgemeestre, Brigitte 72
Bush, George 46, 50, 51
Bush, George W. 1–2, 53, 54, 101, 104–5
Business Roundtable 44
Business Week 9–10

172 INDEX

CAMELS 81–82
Cantor, Richard 76
capital 42–43, 48, 52–53, 70, 72, 81–83,
   87, 100–1, 113, 129–30
   accumulation 80
   cultural 132
   markets 9, 76
Capital Purchase Program 101
capitalism 4–5, 8
   industrial 3, 6, 132–33
   US CPP12, 80
Carruthers, Bruce 125
Carter, Jimmy 39–40, 43–45, 62
   Executive Order 12044 44
   Regulatory Analysis Review Group
      (RARG) 44
Center for Responsible Lending 93–94, 95
Chase Manhattan 44
Chicago School of Economics 28–29,
   31–32, 58
Churchill, Winston 22–23
Citicorp 63–65
Citigroup 1–2, 65, 101
citizen assemblies 130–31
citizenship 121
   financial 22, 96
   social 22, 96
civil society 130–31
civil rights movement 111–12
Clarke, Tim 53
Clayton Antitrust Act 91
Clinton, Bill ix, 1–2, 32–34, 40, 51–52, 54,
   63–65, 69, 96, 98
   State of the Union Address
      (1996) 51–52
Clinton, Hillary 131–32
Clinton–Gore Plan for Financial Privacy
      and Consumer Financial
      Protection in the 21st Century
      (1999) 20–21
Code of Federal Regulations 60–61
Cohen, Lizabeth 7, 91–92, 116, 128–29
Cold War 27–28
Committee on Banking and Financial
      Services 69
Commodity Exchanges Act (CEA) 69
Commodity Futures Modernization Act
      (CFMA, 2000) 60, 69–70

Commodity Futures Trading Commission
      (CFTC) 48–49, 68–70
competitiveness (US economic) 50, 72,
      123–24
consumer activism 116
Consumer Bankers Association 110
Consumer Bill of Rights 91–92
consumer education 77
Consumer Federation of America 78,
      82–83, 111, 112, 116, 121,
      129–30
Consumer Financial Protection
      Agency 108, 109–10
Consumer Financial Protection Bureau
      (CFPB) 113–16, 119–21,
      128–30
Consumer Product Safety Act
      (1970) 91–92
consumer protection agencies 109–10,
      115, 116
consumer reporting agencies 7–8
consumers 7–8, 22, 28–29, 31–32, 36, 44,
      77, 78, 82–83, 84, 86, 91–92,
      110–11
   low-income 92
   mobilization of 116
   as rational actors 20–21, 92–93, 125–26
consumption 22, 96, 126
cost-benefit analysis 39, 41, 44, 46, 54,
      124
Council of Economic Advisors
      (CEA) 28–29, 30, 31–32, 40–41,
      43–44, 49–50, 105–6
Council on Competitiveness (1989) 50
Courson, John 109–10
CNBC 77
   CNBC Business News 103
   Suze Orman Show 77
Crapo, Mike 129–30
credit xi, 13–14, 20, 42–43, 63–65, 73–74,
      81, 92, 102
   access to x, 96, 126
   cards 62–63, 84, 93, 95, 113, 119–20,
      126–27
   markets x, 10, 22, 89–90, 95, 109–10
   as redistributive tool 126
   reliance on 22, 89–90, 96
credit default swaps (CDS) 15, 68–69

INDEX   173

credit rating agencies 18–19, 57–58, 72–73, 76, 84–85, 106, 125–26
credit unions 129–30
crisis 16, 24–25, 78–79, 102–3, 127, 133
  economic 8–9, 22–24, 85–86, 111, 117–18
  energy 8–9
  financial (2007–2010) 2–3, 4–5, 10–15, 18, 20–21, 34–36, 54, 56–57, 60, 70–71, 83, 87–90, 93–95, 98, 106, 110, 122, 125–26, 127, 128–29, 131–32
    government responses to
      "blank check option" 100–1
      "takeover option" 100–1
    legitimation 8–9
Crouch, Colin 96

Dalley, Paula 74
Davis, Gerald 125
Davis Polk & Wardwell LLP 117
de Bromhead, Alan 131
debt 10, 93, 95, 104–5
  household 10, 89–90, 119–20
  private 53
  public ix
  see also indebtedness
debt-to-income ratio 70
Democrats 39, 48, 59, 75, 113, 114, 123–24
deposit accounts 10, 42–43
Depository Institutions Deregulation and Monetary Control Act (DIDMCA, 1980) 62, 66–67, 124
derivatives 15, 66, 68, 70
  markets 13–14, 17–18, 48, 68–69, 113, 119–20, 127
  "OTC" (over-the-counter) 68–69, 106
Dinallo, Eric 72
disability benefits 6–7
disclosure regulations 7–8, 18–19, 49, 50–51, 52, 57–58, 73–75, 76, 77, 83–85, 92–93, 125–26
Dodd, Chris 114, 115–16
Dodd–Frank Wall Street Reform and Consumer Protection Act 112–16, 117–21, 127–28, 130

Doerr, Sebastian 131
Douglas, Paul H. 73–74
Dow Jones Industrial Average 1–2
Dudley, William 98–99

Economic Growth and Regulatory Paperwork Reduction Act (1996) 63–65
Economic Growth, Regulatory Relief and Consumer Protection Act (2018) 129–30
Economic Stimulus Act (2008) 104–5
economics 27–28, 30–32, 34, 123–24
  financial 16–17, 24, 27, 32–34, 37, 40, 123, 124
  macro 9–10, 20, 87–89
  micro 18, 28, 34, 36–37, 39, 43, 70, 87
  Nobel prizes in 34
Edwards, Caroline 91–92
efficient-market hypothesis (EMH) 34–36
Eisner, Marc 6–7, 59
Emanuel, Rahm 22–23
Emergency Economic Stabilization Act (2008) 101
  Troubled Asset Relief Program (TARP) 101–2, 109
  Congressional Oversight Panel 109
Engels, Friedrich 80
England 132–33
  Tudor era 3–4, 80
Engle, Robert 87
Environmental Protection Agency (EPA) 39
escrow accounts 94
Esping-Andersen, Gosta 60–61
Equal Credit Opportunity Act (1974) 91–92
Evans, Peter 130
extremism 131, 132

Face the Nation 131–32
Fair Credit Reporting Act (1970) 7–8
Fair and Accurate Credit Transactions Act (2003) 78
Fair Packaging and Labeling Act (1966) 91–92
Fama, Eugene 34–35
Fannie Mae and Freddie Mac 1–2, 101–2

174 INDEX

fascism 4, 132–33
Federal Deposit Insurance Corporation
(FDIC) 1–2, 7–8, 46–47, 49–51,
72, 114, 129–30
Improvement Act (FDICIA,
1991) 50–51
Federal Food, Drug, and Cosmetic Act 91
Federal Housing Administration
(FHA) 94, 101–2
Federal Register 58–59
Federal Reserve 1–2, 7–8, 19–20, 42–43,
48, 49, 52, 53, 54, 63–65, 66–69,
70–71, 77, 78, 98–99, 114, 121
Act 98–99
Bank of New York 98–99
Bankers Council 110–11
Board 48, 53, 56–57, 67, 109, 129–30
Division for Supervision and
Regulation
Consumer Advisory Council 110–11
St. Louis 89–90
Federal Savings and Loan Insurance
Corporation (FSLIC) 49, 50–51
Federal Trade Commission (FTC) 114
Act 91
finance companies 13–14
financial assets 10, 17–18
Financial CHOICE Act (2017) 129–30
Financial Crisis Inquiry Commission 68
financial holding companies (FHCs) 65,
68
financial instruments 9–10, 13–14, 17, 22,
75–76
financial literacy 13–14, 20–21, 22, 57–58,
75, 77–78, 84–85, 92–93, 109–
10, 124–26
Financial Literacy and Education
Commission 78
Financial Markets Conference of the
Federal Reserve Bank of Atlanta
(1997) 52
Financial Reform Act (FRA, 1976) 42–43
financial sector 2–3, 9–10, 12–13, 15,
23–24, 34, 43, 47, 52, 56–57,
63–65, 70, 81, 87–89, 108–9,
115, 119–20, 124–25
concentration in 10–11, 65–66, 119–20
Financial Services Oversight Council 108

Financial Services Roundtable 109–10
Financial Stability Oversight Council
(FSOC) 113, 119–21, 127, 129–30
"Volcker Rule" 113, 129–30
firms 2–3, 18, 36, 46, 73–74, 86
as economic actors 36–37, 82–83
Fitch 76, 83
Flannery, Mark 35–36
Fleming, Anne 73–74, 91–92
Fligstein, Neil 125
Food and Drug Administration (FDA) 91
Forbes 11
Ford, Gerald 30, 39–41, 45
Council on Wage and Price Stability
(CWPS) 40–41
Domestic Council Review Group
on Regulatory Reform
(DCRG) 40–41
Executive Order 11821 40–41
Task Force on Regulatory Reform 30
foreclosure 1–2, 22–23, 93–94, 101–3, 104
Fourcade, Marion 27–28
Frank, Barney 115
Fraser, Nancy 16
free markets 5, 83
theories of 3–4
Freixas, Xavier 86–87
Friedman, Milton 26–27, 28–29, 31–32,
42–43, 123
Friedman, Rose 28–29
Funke, Manuel 131
Furner, Mary O. 8

Gaebler, Ted 32–34
Gallup surveys 100
Garn–St Germain Depository Institutions
Act
see Alternative Mortgage Transaction
Parity Act (AMTPA)
General Electric (GE) 9–10
George Mason University 31
Germany 63–65, 85–86
Nazi movement 131
Gilson, Ronald 35–36
Goldman Sachs Group 101
Golko, Gabriel 29–30
Gore, Al 32–34, 51–52
National Performance Review 32–34

INDEX

government spending 45–46, 104–5
government-sponsored enterprises
(GSEs) 1–2, 14–15
Graham, Mary 73–75, 83
Gramlich, Edward 67
Gramm, Wendy 48
Gramm–Leach–Bliley Act (GLBA,
1999) 60
Great Depression x–xi, 6–7, 8, 17, 42–43,
45, 56–57, 73–74, 75, 98–99,
116, 117–18, 128–29, 132–33
Great Recession xi, 98, 106
Great Society 6–7
Greenspan, Alan 15, 36–37, 40–41, 48,
52, 53, 61–62, 63–65, 66, 67,
68–69, 77
Gross Domestic Product (GDP) 9–10,
89–90, 104–6, 117
growth
economic 6–7, 8–9, 19–20, 22–23, 43,
54, 63–65, 66, 70, 80
GDP 117
monetary 44

Hacker, Jacob 58–59, 65–66, 126
Halvorson, Charles 59
Harvard Business Review 110
Harvard Law School 93
Hayek, Friedrich 26–27, 37–38, 123
health insurance 6–7
hedge funds 12–13, 53, 69, 113, 131–32
Hensarling, Jeb 129–30
Heritage Foundation 59–60
Home Ownership and Equity Protection
Act (HOEPA, 1994) 67
homeownership 1, 62–63, 111–12
Hoover, Herbert x–xi
HOPE for Homeowners 101–2
Hopkin, Jonathan 131–32
Horwitz, Robert 59
House Committee on Banking, Currency,
and Housing 42–43
Financial Institutions in the Nation's
Economy Study (FINE) 42–43
households 10, 46, 92–93, 95, 96, 98–99,
126–27, 128–29
Housing and Economic Recovery Act
(HERA, 2008) 101–2

housing prices 13–14, 102
Huntington, Samuel 29–30

indebtedness 22, 96, 119–20, 126
Independent Bankers Association 43–44
Independent Community Bankers
Association (ICBA) 108–9, 110,
115–16
Industrial Revolution 3–4
inequality 21–22, 89–90, 95–96, 126,
132–33
inflation 8–9, 39, 40–42, 43–44, 54, 62,
80, 124
insecurity 21–22, 89–90
insolvency 36
insurance companies 12–13, 65, 76
interbank exposure 70
interest rates 13–14, 45, 66–67, 93–94
ceilings 61–62
International Monetary Fund (IMF) 58
Interstate Commerce Commission
(ICC) 29–30
Investment Company Act (1940) 7–8
investors 2, 10, 34–37, 49–50, 62, 63–65,
67, 106, 131
Isaac, William M. 46–47

JPMorgan Chase 101
Johnson, Lyndon B. 91–92
Johnson, Simon 100–1, 118, 121
Jordana, Jacint 58
Journal of Finance 34–35

Kahn, Alfred 43–44
Kaiser, Robert 113
Kalleberg, Arne 126
Kashkari, Neel 102
Kastner, Lisa 116
Kaufman, George 50–51
Kauper, Thomas 42–43
Kennedy, John F. 91–92
Kennedy, Ted 44
Keynes, John Maynard 104–5
Keynesianism 9, 104–5
Konings, Martijn 58
Kraakman, Reinier 35–36
Krippner, Greta 8–9, 125
Krueger, Alan 24

176 INDEX

Krueger, Anne 31
Kwak, James 100–1, 118, 121

"law of the poor" 92
Leadership Conference on Civil Rights
   (LCCR) 111–12
legislation 21–22, 40–41, 43–44, 65–66,
   91–92
  anti-trust 91
  minimum-wage 96
  equal-pay 96
Lehman Brothers x–xi, 1–2
lending standards 13–14, 67–68
Levi-Faur, David 58
Levitin, Adam 81–82, 111
Levitt, Arthur 52, 68–69
Liang, Nellie 81–82
liberalism (economic) 3–4, 29–30
  "embedded" 6–7, 8–9, 80, 96
  postwar 8
  see also neoliberalism
life insurance 10
Lin, Ken-Hou 10, 125
liquidity 14–15, 81–82, 106, 119–20, 127,
   129–30
Long-Term Capital Management 69

MacAvoy, Paul W. 30
MacKendrick, Norah 20–21
Mahoney, Paul 60
Making Home Affordable program
   (MHA, 2009) 101–2
  Home Affordable Modification
     Program 101–2
  Home Affordable Refinance
     Program 101–2
market discipline (MD) 17, 27, 37, 46–48,
   54, 57–58, 72–73, 76, 81, 91, 106,
   123, 124
  as regulatory framework 35–36, 49–51,
     52–53, 54, 56–57, 73, 124
market economy 2, 5, 133
market influence 36
market monitoring 36
Markowitz, Harry 34–35
Marquette vs. First of Omaha 62
Marx, Karl 80
McCain, John x–xi

McCoy, Patricia 62–63, 66–67
Meat Inspection Act 91
Medicaid 6–7
Medicare 6–7
Menzies, Michael 108–9, 110
Mercatus Center 59–60
Merrill Lynch 1–2, 101
Mettler, Suzanne 74–75
Mierzwinski, Edmund 111
Miller, James C. 44
Mills, C. W. 22
Mises, Ludwig von 31–32
Modern Portfolio Theory 34–35
Mont Pelerin Society 26–27, 123
Moody's 76, 83
Morgan Stanley 101
Mortgage Bankers Association 109–10
mortgage market 1–2, 13–14, 63, 66–67,
   93–94, 101–2
Moss, David A. 4, 84–85
Mosser, Patricia 98–99
Mudge, Stephanie 26–27
mutual funds 7–8, 10, 76

Nader, Ralph 44
National Community Reinvestment
   Coalition 110–11
National Credit Union
   Administration 114
National Federation of Independent
   Business 41
"National Financial Capability Month" 78
National Partnership for Reinventing
   Government (RG, 1993) 51–52
National Press Club 115–16
National Traffic and Motor Vehicle Safety
   Act (1966) 91–92
Nationally Recognized Statistical Rating
   Organization 76
Neely, Megan Tobias 10
Neighborhood Stabilization
   Program 101–2
neoliberalism 2–3, 6, 16, 20–21, 24, 26–27,
   37–38, 54–55, 58, 78–79, 96, 123
  see also liberalism
New Deal 4, 6–7, 8–9, 27–28, 42–43, 60, 91
New Public Management (NPM) 16–17,
   24, 27, 32–34, 40, 51–52

INDEX 177

New Right 58
New York State Banking
        Department 82–83
Niskanen, William A. 24, 31–32, 51–52
Nixon, Richard 28–29, 39, 45, 91–92
    Office of Management and Budget
        (OMB) 39
    Quality-of-Life Review 39
non-bank financial institutions
        (NBFIs) 10–14, 17–18, 98–99,
        117–18, 119–20, 127, 129–30

Obama, Barack 22–23, 78, 105–6, 108–9,
        118
Office of the Comptroller of the Currency
        (OCC) 114
Office of Thrift Supervision
        (OTS) 117–18
O'Neill, Paul H. 77
Organization for Economic Co-operation
        and Development (OECD) 10
Osborne, David 32–34
Ozgode, Onur 19–20

paternalism 37, 46, 77
Paulson, Henry 53, 86, 101, 102
pawnshops 95
payday loans 84, 95, 113
Pecker, Frank 76
Peltzman, Sam 24, 28–29
Pénet, Pierre 75–76
pension funds 9–63
pensions 6–7, 76, 90
Personal Responsibility and Work
        Opportunity Reconciliation Act
        (1996) 22
Pernell, Elizabeth Kimberly 15, 85–86
Pew Research Center 100
Pierce, James 42–43
Pierson, Paul 58–59
Pillippon, Thomas 59
Pitt, Harvey L. 77
Plunkett, Travis B. 82–83, 111
Polanyi, Karl 2–6, 8, 16, 22, 26, 102–3,
        122, 127, 132–33
polarization (political) 74–75, 112–13
political economy (US) 2–3, 80, 125
political science 29–30, 31

pollution 41–42, 51–52
populism 4–6, 23–25, 116, 131, 132–33
Prasad, Monica 44, 59
precarity 21–22, 126, 131–32
presidential veto 65–66
President's Working Group on Financial
        Markets 49, 52, 68–69
privacy notices 84
profitability 2–3, 18, 19–21, 35–36, 63–65,
        70, 81–82, 111
profits (corporate) 1, 9–10, 110
Progressive era 29–30, 91, 116
protectionism 4–5, 121
public choice theory 31, 32–34
public health 41–42
public interest theory 9, 73–74
public safety 41–42
public sector 27
Pure Food and Drug Act 91

Rahman, K. Sabeel 7–8, 121, 127–28, 130
Rainer, William 52
Rajan, Raghuram 130
rationality (actor) 16–17, 27, 37, 52, 54,
        57–58, 76, 123, 124
Reagan, Ronald 28–29, 32, 37–38, 39, 40,
        44, 45–47, 48–51, 54, 58–59,
        62–65, 96, 123–24
    Economic Policy Advisory
        Board 28–29
    Economic Report of the President
        (1982) 46
    Executive Order 12291 46
    Task Force on Regulatory Relief 46, 50
real estate markets 108–9
redistribution xi, 21–22, 89–90, 96
regulation
    information-based 17–19, 24, 57–58,
        72–73, 76, 77, 78–79, 81, 124–25
    micro-orientation in 57–58, 70, 72
    principles-based 18, 57–58, 72, 82–83,
        84
    rules-based 82–83
Regulation Q 42–43, 62
regulatory commissions 29–30, 40–41, 43
regulatory drift 17–18, 24, 56–57, 65–67,
        68–70, 78–79, 124–25
rent-seeking 16–17, 27, 31–32, 37

178　INDEX

Republicans 39, 59, 74–75, 102–3, 114,
　123–24, 129–30
　Tea Party 103–4
Reshef, Ariel 59
retirement planning 1–2, 20, 21–22, 77,
　90
Ricardo, David 132–33
Rich Dad, Poor Dad 77
Riegle–Neal Interstate Banking and
　Branching Efficiency Act
　(1994) 63–65
risk
　diversification of 2–3
　protection 2–3, 4, 6–7, 18, 19, 20–21,
　　24–25, 80–81, 85–86, 92–93,
　　96–97, 119–20, 122, 125–27
　systemic nature of 2–3, 19–21, 68, 79,
　　86–89, 109, 119–20, 127
risk society 126
Romer, Christina 105–6
Roosevelt, Franklin D. 6–7, 73–74, 104–5,
　128–29
Roosevelt, Theodore 115
royal monopoly privilege 31
Rubin, Robert 52, 68–69

Santelli, Rick 103–4
Sarbanes, Paul 63–65
savings and loans (S&Ls) 1–2, 47, 50–51,
　62–63
Savings are Vital to Everyone's Retirement
　Act (1997) 22
Schloemer, Ellen 94
Schultze, Charles 43–44
Secondary Mortgage Market
　Enhancement Act
　(SMMEA) 63, 66–67
Securities Act (1933) 73–74
Securities and Exchange Act
　(1934) 73–74
Securities Exchange Commission
　(SEC) 7–8, 47, 49, 68–70, 76, 77
securitization 13–15, 17–18, 63, 65–67,
　106, 125
Senate Committee on Banking, Housing,
　and Urban Affairs 48
Shiller, Robert 130
Short, Jodi 27–28

Skocpol, Theda 128–29
Slobodian, Quinn 26–27
social contract 4
social insurance 21–22, 89–90
social protection 24–25, 95–96, 126
Social Security Act (1935) 6–7
socialism 4
St Germain, Fernand J. 42–43
Standard and Poor's 76
State Street 101
"status quo bias" 65–66
Steinmo, Sven 112–13
Stigler, George 24, 28–30
Stiglitz, Joseph 80
stock markets 20, 49, 90, 127
　indices 1
stock prices 9–10, 122
stock shares 10
student loans 113, 119–20
subprime lending 13–15, 17–18, 20–21,
　60, 65–67, 93–94, 106, 110
Summers, Lawrence 68–70

taxes 46, 94
　tax cuts 45–46
Taylor, Diana 82–83
Taylor, John 110–11
technological change 17, 56–57, 66, 95–96
Thelen, Kathleen 58–59
think tanks 26–27, 123
Tomaskovic-Devey, Donald 125
Treadway Jr., James 47
Trump, Donald J. 129–30, 131–32, 133
Truth in Lending Act (1968) 7–8, 73–74
Tullock, Gordon 24, 31

unemployment 1, 8–9, 22–23, 94, 104–5,
　106, 117, 122, 132–33
Uniform Commercial Code (UCC) 92
United States
　budget surplus 1, 98
　deficit 104–5
　Congress 1–2, 39, 40–41, 45, 48, 50–51,
　　59–60, 61–65, 66–67, 69–70,
　　73–74, 77, 91–92, 101–2, 106,
　　111, 112–13
　Department of Justice Antitrust
　　Division 42–43

House of Representatives 1–2, 109, 113, 129–30
   Financial Services Committee 129–30
   New Democratic Coalition 113
   Senate 47, 48, 65–66, 77, 109, 129–30
   Supreme Court 62
   Treasury Department 1–2, 49, 50, 63–65, 67, 98–99, 101, 102, 106
United States Banker 47
University of Chicago 30
   Center for the Study of the Economy and the State 30
University of Virginia 31
US Public Interest Research Group 111, 112

Vogel, David 7
Vogel, Steven 58
Volcker, Paul 48

Wachovia 1–2
wages 21–22, 89–90, 95–96
Wall Street 100, 110, 131–32
Wall Street Journal 117
Warren, Elizabeth 13–14, 17–18, 56–57, 84, 86, 93, 109

Washington Mutual 1–2
Washington Post, The 44
Water Quality Act (1965) 91–92
Weidenbaum, Murray 44, 49–50
Weinstein, James 29–30
Welch, Jack 9–10
welfare 19–20, 22, 29–30, 87, 89–90
   states 60–61
Wells Fargo 101
Wheeler–Lea Act (1938) 91
White House 1–2, 40–41, 49, 78, 91–92, 98
Willis, Lauren 73–74, 77, 84, 92–93
Wilson, Woodrow 115
Wilmarth, Arthur 63–65, 68
Woll, Cornelia 115
World War II 68–69, 80

Yilla, Kadija 81–82
Yingling, Edward 110

Zeisel, Steven 110
Zingales, Luigi 130
Zirkin, Nancy 111–12